# THE DESPOT'S ACCOMPLICE

BRIAN KLAAS

# The Despot's Accomplice

*How the West is Aiding and
Abetting the Decline of Democracy*

HURST & COMPANY, LONDON

First published in the United Kingdom in 2016 by
C. Hurst & Co. (Publishers) Ltd.,
41 Great Russell Street, London, WC1B 3PL
© Brian Klaas, 2016
All rights reserved.
Printed and bound in Great Britain by Bell & Bain Ltd, Glasgow

The right of Brian Klaas to be identified as the author of
this publication is asserted by him in accordance with the
Copyright, Designs and Patents Act, 1988.

A Cataloguing-in-Publication data record for this book
is available from the British Library.

ISBN: 9781849046879

This book is printed using paper from registered sustainable
and managed sources.

**www.hurstpublishers.com**

# CONTENTS

# ACKNOWLEDGEMENTS AND APOLOGIES

Since 2012, I have conducted roughly 250 interviews trying to understand the battle for global democracy. The list includes former prime ministers and presidents, diplomats, MPs, journalists, ex-rebels, generals, coup plotters, democracy promoters, election observers, academics, political analysts, economists, and torture victims. Many of them spoke to me candidly at great personal risk to their safety and wellbeing. I admire some of them more than others, but to everyone who spoke to me during my research over the last four years, thank you for taking the time, opening your homes, and helping me understand your point of view. I didn't always agree with you, but I did earnestly try to understand you. To the committed democrats I spoke to, I hope that this book catalyzes more support for you in the West. To the despots I spoke to, I'm sorry.

This book is dedicated to my parents, Paul and Barbara Klaas. "Couldn't you study French history in Paris or something?" they often asked, as I set off for war-torn, destabilized countries around the world. But in spite of their (understandable) worries, they have been unwaveringly supportive and selfless. Long ago, they gave me the best and simplest advice I've ever received as I pondered career paths: "Do something interesting with your life." Mom and Dad, I can never thank you enough. Parenting books should be written about you. For all the stories in here that I've never told you in the hopes that you'd worry less, I'm sorry.

Ann, James, and Kelsey Klaas inspired me. When I returned home after witnessing the depressingly cynical ploys of despots, Ann taught me

# ACKNOWLEDGEMENTS AND APOLOGIES

the power of strength through adversity, and James, Kelsey, and particularly their young son Thomas, taught me that there is never reason to lose hope. I'm only sorry I don't get to see you as often as I'd like.

Marcel Dirsus and David Landry provided excellent feedback. They also promised to call the embassy if I took too long to respond to messages when I was looking over my shoulder in Belarus or was navigating other worrisome situations, and they made me laugh when I needed it. You guys are fantastic friends. Sorry I asked your opinion about a specific argument, anecdote, or idea every day for months and expected an immediate reply.

Roy Grow, who lost a battle with cancer in 2013, advised me as an undergraduate. With his wife Mary Lewis, Roy never stopped urging me to understand the world by exploring it myself, to take calculated risks, and to keep an open mind to alternative views. I'm sorry we didn't get nearly enough time together before you left us.

Nic Cheeseman, my DPhil adviser at Oxford, made this book possible by shaping me into a scholar and believing in me when I was a wide-eyed student. Sorry about all the insurance and health and safety forms you had to fill out.

Thanks are also due to many, many other people who helped me with writing, research, and support: to Gemma Clucas, John James, Oliver Clarke, Edward Grigg, Oz Jungic, Jason Pack, Andy Cunningham, Hanan Haber, Joseph Baines, Rory McCarthy, Michael Willis, Juvence Ramasy, Nika Wegosky, Verapat Pariyawong, Jack Delehanty, Howard French, Sishuwa wa Sishuwa, Nancy Bermeo, Ben Ansell, Elliott Green, and literally hundreds of taxi drivers who shared their thoughts on local politics with me as we sat in traffic.

Finally, I couldn't have written this book without Ellie, my better half and my best friend. Ellie listened to every awful first draft of each chapter eagerly and patiently. She managed to always offer encouragement even as she (rightfully) told me when I was wrong. Ellie, I love you. Sorry in advance for the shock when you finally realize, as I've known all along, that you're clearly out of my league.

# INTRODUCTION

## ACCESSORY TO AUTHORITARIANISM

For the first time since the end of the Cold War, the world is losing faith in democracy. Between Donald Trump's rise in American politics and the predictable but self-inflicted "Brexit" economic shockwave, many are now openly asking what was previously an unthinkable question in the West: can people really be trusted with self-government? Is it time to ditch democracy and try something else?

After the Soviet Union fell, democracy expanded at an unprecedented rate. Today, global democracy has receded slightly every year since 2006; in other words, there has been no democratic forward progress for the last decade.[1]

At the other end of the spectrum, powerful authoritarian regimes are becoming more authoritarian.[2] Across multiple indexes and measures, democracy is stagnating at best and steadily declining at worst. Unless the trend is reversed, anyone born in 2016 will be, on average, less free than someone born during the 1990s. These declines are not an accident; they are the battle scars of a struggle between the rule of the people and the rule of despots and dictators. Right now, the people are losing.

However, the sky is not falling, democratically speaking. The world remains more democratic than it has been at almost any time in human history. Many countries that were bastions of authoritarian repression just a few decades ago are now democracies. Nonetheless, the recent retreat of democracy is serious cause for concern. This is not a theoreti-

1

cal philosophical debate. Billions of people remain trapped in unresponsive, unaccountable regimes where ruthless oppression is common.

As many despots have rolled back democracy or refused to embrace it, they have found an unlikely accomplice: the West. Western governments, in London, Paris, Brussels, and most of all Washington, have directly and indirectly aided and abetted the decline of democracy around the globe. This unfortunate truth comes despite the stated goals of all Western governments and despite the personal principles of almost everyone in those governments. Overwhelmingly, Western elites genuinely believe in democracy. They want democracy to spread. Moreover, Western governments have been, are, and will continue to be the biggest force backing democracy in the world. But their current approach is backfiring. This book explains why and gives a principled blueprint for how to reverse the trend and start defeating despots worldwide.

For the moment, though, the West is suffering an acute case of democracy promotion fatigue. Its leaders have less of a stomach for the short-term risks it presents than they used to. This feeling has only intensified in recent years as prolonged debacles in Ukraine, the Arab Spring, Libya, Afghanistan, and Iraq have replaced stable authoritarian regimes with violent chaos. As a result, democracy promotion has been knocked down several rungs on the priority list of Western governments as they set foreign policy agendas. It's perfectly understandable. After all, failed transitions to democracy in places like Libya after botched interventions are indeed tragedies. Yet it would be a greater tragedy still to doom the next generation to the rule of despots, dictators, and thugs, simply because this generation of political leaders is unwilling to make smart but difficult choices to support democracy consistently across the globe. Instead of running away from the challenge, Western governments need to learn from their mistakes and redouble their efforts. They need to stick to their principles and challenge despots, rather than aiding them in pursuit of nearsighted pragmatism. This will not be easy; there are few low-hanging authoritarian fruits just waiting to be plucked. Nor is there any guarantee that toppled despots will be replaced by genuine democrats. But the current approach needs to change, in order to give democracy a fighting chance.

I discovered a strange cast of characters on the frontlines of this battle for global democracy. Their voices are important but are rarely heard in the West. So, over the last five years, I have crisscrossed the world exploring local struggles for democracy to understand why the world is becoming less democratic and what can be done to reverse the trend.

I lived for months at a time in many different countries. Some seemed superficially democratic but were nonetheless home to toxic politics and broken societies. Dictators or juntas governed others. I had poetry read to me by a general in Madagascar who spoke of the glory days when he kidnapped politicians. I sipped mango juice with ex-rebels and was robbed at machete point in post-conflict Côte d'Ivoire. I was tailed by the KGB in Belarus as I spoke to presidential candidates bravely challenging Europe's last dictator. I had tea with a failed coup plotter's family in Zambia and coffee with generals in Thailand's junta café.

These were surreal experiences. But the crisis of democracy in the twenty-first century is all too real for the billions of people around the world who live either under the unforgiving yoke of a dictator or the illusion of freedom in what I call "counterfeit democracies"—countries that claim to be of the people, by the people, and for the people, but are really none of the above.[3]

A minority of the global population lives in true democracies, where people can meaningfully participate in decisions being made about their lives, where the laws matter more than the whims of strongmen, and where citizens have a real choice in electing leaders to represent them.

The true criminals in this heist against democracy are dictators and counterfeit democrats—the dictatorial wolves cloaked in democratic sheepskins. But the West is also an accessory to the crime, inadvertently robbing pro-democracy forces abroad of a path to power. Governments in Washington, London, and Brussels pick the side of the despot all too often, as they chase pyrrhic short-term economic and security victories. This approach undermines long-term Western interests, batters global democracy, and keeps billions oppressed with little hope for better governments.

If the West is doing so much damage, should Western governments even try to make the world more democratic? If so, how? After all, domestic factors are critical to democratization. Perhaps it's none of our business. Countries often democratize without a nudge from the outside. Moreover, many key barriers to democratization are difficult to remove or overcome: dynastic oil monarchies, poor countries with weak political institutions, and single-party states that manage strong economic performance are all less likely to democratize. But scholars have also shown that links to the West are a crucial aspect of democratization across all types of countries.[6]

How, then, can Western governments maximize the probability that a given country will become genuinely democratic?

There are three overarching camps that capture most thinking related to Western democracy promotion. First, do nothing. Don't worry about democracy elsewhere. Treat a country the same regardless of its political system. This is the approach that authoritarian China takes, but this amoral foreign policy has vocal backers in the West too. Proponents of this view tend to see the spread of democracy as a peripheral interest to the West, a distraction from what really matters—security, stability, and economic growth. Foreign policy, in this view, is about entrenching stability while serving ourselves—wrought by the cold, hard calculations of *realpolitik*. Out of necessity, those calculations often focus on short-term interests. Do whatever needs to be done; work with whoever will work with you; the ends justify the means.

The second camp has slightly more tolerance for democracy promotion. Try to promote democracy, but only when it is in the short-term geostrategic interest of Western governments. Push for democracy against unfriendly dictators who already hate the West, but leave friendly dictators alone—or at least don't press them aggressively. In this view, the dictatorial devil we know is much better than the democratic devil we don't. Encourage countries that are not strategically important to become democratic because it doesn't really matter anyway, but set an absurdly low bar so that most can at least hit the mostly meaningless target of claiming to be democracies and the West can cheer them along. This is the current approach. It is failing.

Third, promote democracy across the globe, as a long-term goal, even when it may not be in the immediate short-term interest of the United States and its Western allies. Think long-term. This does not mean pouring millions or billions into quixotic projects to rapidly democratize places unlikely to change, like North Korea. It also does not mean that the West should pursue any other foolish wars cloaked as adventures in democracy promotion, as Western governments have in Iraq, Afghanistan, and, most recently, Libya. But it does mean applying much more meaningful pressure to authoritarian regimes whether they are geostrategic friend or foe at any given political snapshot in time. It means respecting elections, even if the people of another country freely choose governments that are unfriendly to the West. It means making hard choices rather than easy ones now, in order to build a more prosperous and safer world for the future.

In this book, I argue for this third approach, while demonstrating how and why a combination of the first two strategies is shaping the world into a more volatile, less prosperous, and less democratic place.

In the last decade, most Western governments have simply tried to minimize risk in dealing with non-democratic governments. This is true even of terrible tyrants, so long as they are willing to work with the West. In the name of stability, security, and economic self-interest, the United States and its Western allies have repeatedly worked to forge an uneasy co-existence with dictators, despots, and counterfeit democrats, from powerful kingdoms like Saudi Arabia to the less menacing regimes stalled between dictatorship and democracy that are scattered across Sub-Saharan Africa, Southeast Asia, Central America, and elsewhere.[7] In most places, democracy promotion is done half-heartedly, aimed more at around-the-edges reforms of authoritarianism than at undermining authoritarianism itself.

The problem with this is simple: it's not working. We now have not only a less democratic world but also a more unstable one. Authoritarian regimes project a mirage of stability but then eventually tend to collapse catastrophically. Democracy can be risky and volatile too, but has built-in mechanisms to resolve domestic conflict, a safety valve that can help prevent violence and chaos. If nothing is done and the West remains an accomplice to despotism, we may have already hit "peak democracy". It's not too late. The trend can be reversed. If it is not, global democracy will remain at risk, economic growth will continue to underperform its potential, and Western security will be further imperiled.

The West helps despots in two main ways. The first involves a deliberately cozy relationship with an appalling undemocratic regime because of geostrategic expediency. I call this the "Saudi Arabia Effect." It's why Hillary Clinton has spoken highly of the brutal Saudi royal family, or, in Egypt, why she unflinchingly called the former authoritarian despot Hosni Mubarak and his wife "friends of my family."[8] It's why Tony Blair has called Rwandan despot Paul Kagame "a visionary leader," and why President Barack Obama hosted a dinner party for Equatorial Guinea's president Teodoro Obiang, who has ruled with an iron fist for thirty-seven years as "the country's god", claiming "all power over men and things."

The second way the West aids and abets despots arises from the laughably low standards set for counterfeit democracies, creating a counterproductive incentive for cynical leaders to do only the bare minimum—to simply appear democratic. This allows Western governments to accept deeply flawed counterfeit democracies so that they can work with them in seemingly good conscience. I call this the "Madagascar Effect," or the "curse of low expectations."

Three years ago, I was in Madagascar searching for signs of democracy. Most researchers come to the island to study its lovable lemurs; few come to explore the habitat of its predatory politicians. But I was drawn to this puzzling place for its strange struggle with democracy. In 2009, something exceptionally bizarre had happened in a country where politics is routinely stranger than fiction. Elected president Marc Ravalomanana—a powerful yogurt kingpin—was overthrown in a coup d'état by Andry Rajoelina, a 34-year-old radio disc jockey. Western governments did the right thing immediately after the coup by putting immense pressure on the new government to return to democracy. But that pressure wasn't enough, and it quickly became clear that the young coup president had more experience with spinning turntables than with governing an island home to 23 million people.

Madagascar was and is one of the world's poorest countries. After the coup, that poverty deepened, leaving nine out of ten islanders living on less than $2 per day.[9] For the poor in Madagascar, it seems that when tragedy rains, it also pours. Powerful Indian Ocean cyclones repeatedly destroyed already crumbling roads and swept away rickety bridges. Bubonic plague returned to the island, the only place on Earth where cases of the Medieval Black Death are commonplace in the twenty-first century. To add a sense of biblical doom to the post-coup years, locusts swarmed so thick while they devoured the island's crops that day sometimes turned to night, as literally billions of insects blocked out the sun.[10] Millions were left hungry and millions more remained at risk. If natural disasters weren't enough to spread misery, amidst the accompanying lawlessness heavily armed militias with rocket-propelled grenades turned to industrial-grade cattle rustling, exporting tens of thousands of humped cattle (known as zebus) for sale abroad while killing hundreds of villagers during their raids.[11]

Madagascar's disc jockey strongman failed to address any of these challenges, even as he claimed victory on all fronts. His failures would have been laughable if they weren't so tragic. I'll never forget watching the impromptu street celebrations that broke out in Antananarivo, one of the world's most forgotten capitals, when the president declared in June 2012 that the government had the upper hand in the fight against the cattle-rustling militias because it had finally captured the bandits' sorcerer. With much fanfare, the president destroyed the sorcerer's many "diabolical objects" on television for the nation to see. Smoldering talismans represented a rare victory for the government's failed policies.

Of course, I don't believe in the illusions of sorcerers or magic. But some illusions seem real in Western rhetoric, like the sort of sleight of hand that allows Madagascar to be seen as democratic when it certainly is not. Repeatedly, the West claims to believe that "reformers" are on the path to democracy, while those same "reformers" do everything in their power to subvert democracy whenever it clashes with their pursuit of power. When that happens, genuine democrats fall victim to the West's understandable but ultimately counterproductive efforts that end up entrenching despotism.

The Madagascar Effect became clear to me almost immediately. On my first of several visits to the island, I met with the head of one of Madagascar's political parties. He presented himself as the island's savior, a breath of Western-style fresh air who would blow away the smoke of smoldering talismans and replace it with more rational, effective, liberally minded governance.

"Unlike the other political parties," he told me, "we are a party of values."

"Okay," I responded, "which values?"

A look of panic crossed his face. After a moment, he recovered his composure.

"Someone go get the values for the American," he said. "I left the values in the car."

Presumably there was a dusty booklet full of pristine Western values just waiting to be read, left discarded in the backseat of a fancy car. I never could be sure, as he quickly moved on to other topics, hoping I'd forget about the case of the missing values.

It's hard to imagine that this amateurish posturing fools anybody. But the West's standards for democracy are so low in much of the world that flowery promises of democratic reforms coupled with superficial action are sufficient to lighten meaningful foreign policy pressure against a counterfeit democracy. Far too often the counterfeits manage to pass for the real thing, in the same way that a crude forgery of a $20 bill might fool a disinterested 15-year-old cashier at a gas station.

Madagascar benefited from the West's absurdly low expectations when it held its 2013 elections, the first since the 2009 coup d'état. The vote was touted by Western diplomats as an opportunity to return the island to the international fold of democratic nations. But Madagascar has never been more than an empty shell for democracy. These polls were no different. As an election observer, I saw the ugly array of electoral warts firsthand, and the word "democratic" was nowhere near the top of the list of adjectives I'd use to describe them. Illicit funding was funneled to the incumbent's favored successor. Several million people were left off the voter rolls. And all this took place in a toxic political environment that was characterized by one political analyst I spoke to as "a place where opposition politicians sometimes 'fall down the stairs', but somehow manage to lose all their fingernails on the way down."[12]

Yet, within hours of the polls closing, diplomats were falling over each other, each trying to outdo the next with words of praise for the vote. Only a few hundred ballots had been counted, but no matter. "Free and fair," said one; "free, transparent, and credible," added another; "free and transparent and reflected the will of the people," chimed in a third.[13] Even for those that knew all too well that this was not a democracy, it was easier to accept this step toward stability than to risk further volatility with a meaningful but much harder step toward true democracy.

Most, if not all, of these Western diplomats believe in democracy. Their staffs believe in democracy. These are well-intentioned people. But I'm also certain that every diplomatic cheerleader in this foreign policy crowd was aware of the election's failings. That didn't matter. Calling the country "democratic" while sweeping the undemocratic cobwebs under the rug was more politically convenient. Madagascar had cleared the West's low bar. It was allowed, yet again, to wear the badge of democracy with pride on the international stage. Somehow, Madagascar convinced us.

Yet since the election, Madagascar has become less, not more, democratic. Not even a year after the elected president was sworn in, a general was back in office, as had been the case so many times in Madagascar's history—this time as prime minister rather than president. This was hardly surprising. Given a free pass in its elections, Madagascar's political elites had little reason to embrace democracy any more than was necessary, basking in power rather than effective policy, greed over governance. Despotic criminals are allowed to hold Madagascar's people hostage, bound to economic misery and political powerlessness. Madagascar may be an island but it is not alone on this front. Across the globe, counterfeit democracies routinely pass for the real thing. When they do, democracy recedes and the world turns a little bit more toward authoritarian rule.

This is clearly a problem, but it is only part of the problem. The Saudi Arabia Effect is a more insidious form of Western support for dictatorships and counterfeit democracies around the world, where foreign policy that is knowingly complicit with despots' activities, intensifies into becoming an active accomplice to oppression. In those instances, the problem is less about the West applying low standards and more about a system that deliberately cozies up to dictators to advance other Western interests such as perceived stability or economic growth. Simply put, the West frequently turns a blind eye to ruthless authoritarianism in exchange for allegiance in strategically important regions. By helping despots shore up their grip on power, the West undermines nascent and fragile movements for democratic reform. This collateral damage is a major reason for democracy's recent decline.

This unfortunate reality does not match the rosy rhetoric from Western leaders. In June 2009, President Obama gave a landmark speech in Cairo, highlighting America's commitment to democracy in the Middle East. I couldn't agree more with much of the speech, particularly this excerpt:

But I do have an unyielding belief that all people yearn for certain things: the ability to speak your mind and have a say in how you are governed; confidence in the rule of law and the equal administration of justice; government that is transparent and doesn't steal from the people; the freedom to live as you choose. These are not just American ideas; they are human rights. And that is why we will support them everywhere.[14]

As the most powerful man in the most powerful government on Earth, President Obama had the opportunity to put those words into action. It was a missed opportunity, which soon became crystal clear when crowds gathered in Tahrir Square in 2011, just a few miles from where Obama spoke.

Less than two months before the Arab Spring germinated hope that democracy could take root in the stubbornly dictatorial Middle East, the United States—the world's self-proclaimed democratic City on a Hill—announced the largest weapons sale in history. The $60 billion deal shipped off 12,667 missiles, 18,350 bombs, 190 attack helicopters, and 84 F-15 fighter jets halfway across the world.[15] Those weapons of war were not destined for a democratic ally. They were not even heading to a country that pretended to be democratic or aspired toward democracy. Instead, they were gift-wrapped and delivered to ensure the survival of one of the world's few remaining absolute monarchies and one of the world's most ruthless states: the Kingdom of Saudi Arabia.

The deal was announced during the media storm just before the 2010 congressional midterm elections in the United States, a tactic likely used (in the world's most powerful democracy, no less) to avoid public debate—a cornerstone of democratic rule. Some in the Obama administration were eager to avoid discussing the wisdom of selling so much military might to a kingdom far away on the Arabian Peninsula. In spite of the sly timing, proponents in the foreign policy establishment found no cause for real concern. So long as the Kingdom remained stable and the royal family viewed the United States as friend rather than foe, what was the big deal? Giving them firepower was fine, so long as they used it against mutual enemies rather than against "us".

Unfortunately, Saudi Arabia mostly uses that firepower as a way to quash dissent and challenges from within. Saudi Arabia has one of the world's most oppressive governments, competing for that dubious label with countries like North Korea, Equatorial Guinea, Eritrea, Uzbekistan, and Turkmenistan—hardly good company. Many people are aware of the standard abuses in Saudi Arabia: thieves have their hands cut off; women can't drive; adultery can still be punished by death by stoning. But what is perhaps less well known is the extent to which the United States documents the scale of human rights atrocities and violence perpetrated against pro-democracy advocates—at the same time as it acts as the world's number one backer of the Saudi royal family. Western weapons and Western money for Saudi oil help the Kingdom stay a kingdom.

As a result of this assistance, the West—and the United States in particular—should at least have considerable leverage to force reform in this medieval regime. In fact, the US successfully used that leverage in the past. President John F. Kennedy insisted that the American-Saudi partnership could only remain close if Saudi Arabia abolished slavery (which the United States had done ninety-nine years earlier).[16] The king reluctantly obliged. This was in 1962—color TV, the Beatles, non-dairy creamer, and breast implants already existed. Of course, for the ultraconservative Saudi leadership in the 1960s, breast implants and the Beatles would have provoked far more outrage than slavery.

Since 1962, Western leverage has not been applied in any significant way to back democracy or scale back human rights abuses in Saudi Arabia. In fact, as one branch of the US government made final preparations for the biggest arms deal in world history, another—the State Department—was busily writing a report on that same government's beheadings, floggings, and abuse. Three weeks before the arms deal was announced, a report noted that two third-grade children in the ancient oasis town of Qatif on the Persian Gulf were sentenced to "six months in prison and 120 lashes for stealing examination papers."[17] At the same time, reports surfaced that a 17-year-old migrant working as a maid for the Saudi elite had been tortured, her lips cut off with scissors and her back burned repeatedly with a hot iron.[18] The government never punished the perpetrators. They paid a small fine.

This "leniency" in the Kingdom's criminal justice system does not extend to crimes that allegedly break the sacrosanct codes of puritanical Wahhabi Islam enforced at home (and exported around the world by Saudi foreign policy, to the delight of extremists and prospective terrorists). Breaking laws in the kingdom is dangerous. Dozens, and occasionally, hundreds of times per year, a macabre theatre of the absurd is performed publicly on Saudi streets. The protagonist is guilty of something different each time. Disavowing Islam. Homosexuality. Taking illegal drugs. Even practicing "witchcraft." No matter. Each protagonist in this medieval tale meets his or her end with predictable tragedy.

A man dressed in white approaches the condemned prisoner in the street, in full view of the public. The prisoner is lightly tranquilized, blindfolded, and placed on a plastic tarp to help contain the inevitable mess. Then, the executioner slashes at their neck with a long, curved sword, cleaving head from body. The epilogue to the beheading is often the same: the head is collected, bagged, and hung alongside the corpse.[19] The rest is nailed to a cross, a public reminder not to cross the kings and princes who rule Saudi Arabia with a proverbial iron fist—one that was largely smelted in the weapons factories of the West.

This is one of the West's closest allies.

Public beheadings were performed several times in November 2010, the same month that the young maid, Sumiati Binti Salan Mustapa, had her lips cut off with scissors. How did the West respond to such horrors? With risk-averse, status quo pragmatism. This is understandable but ultimately misguided. It's an example that showcases why democracy promotion is so difficult and fraught with peril. I'll be the first to admit that the prospect of a democratic Saudi Arabia is terrifying. The people are certainly more anti-West than the ruling family. Therefore, it's certainly true that a democratic Saudi Arabia could be a disaster for Western interests in the region. But the close-knit alliance is untenable over the longer term. If we keep supporting the ruthless kings in Riyadh, it'll be much, much worse for the West when Saudi Arabia's regime eventually collapses.

To ensure that collapse wouldn't happen any time soon, the United States sold 150 more Javelin anti-tank missiles to the Kingdom the same month as the slew of beheadings and the maid's horrific abuse, tacked on as an afterthought to its gangbuster October sale of bombs and helicopters and jets.[20] Business as usual.

But, a month later, something remarkable happened more than 2,000 miles away from the scorching hot streets of Riyadh. A humble young vegetable vendor in Tunisia, who could no longer stand living under a dictatorship, set himself on fire. That literal spark set the entire Middle East, a bastion of ruthless but stable authoritarian regimes, ablaze. One man set a chain of events in motion that exposed the uneasy hypocrisy of Western foreign relations in the region for what they were: loudly praising democracy while quietly petting dictatorships under the table, as kings, emirs, and despots purred with smug satisfaction about their seeming invincibility.

Soon, Tunisia's president, Zine El Abidine Ben Ali—a major despotic ally of the West in North Africa—was toppled, in January 2011. As he fell, the call for change spread to Cairo's Tahrir Square. Eventually, the protests grew too loud, too visible, too democratic for the West to ignore. For many elites in Western democracies, their hearts were with the democratic protesters, but their cynical, pragmatic minds sided with the dictators.

This is when things got interesting. The incipient buzz of democracy was an unprecedented challenge to Egypt's despot. Yet, for the play-it-safe West, the prospect of the democratic unknown was terrifying. Nonetheless, little by little, a seductive thought crept into foreign policy circles. Maybe, just maybe, the democrats could win, toppling Hosni Mubarak from his pharaoh's throne. Trapped between decades of lofty, hopeful democratic rhetoric and hard-nosed foreign policy reality, the Western establishment waited and watched in Egypt, hoping to determine the winner before backing them. In February 2011, it became clear that Mubarak was going to lose.

This revelation came, strangely enough, with a stampede of camels. In an era so advanced that images from the thronged Cairo square were beamed across the globe by satellites soaring thousands of miles above the Earth, viewers around the world watched on live television as regime supporters took a page from their long-dead Ottoman predecessors' playbook and unsuccessfully attempted to drive protesters off by galloping across the square on the humps of confused camels.[21] The thugs shook their sticks and clubs, a strikingly à propos metaphor for how outdated dictatorship in the Middle East was starting to seem in the twenty-first century. The protesters were undeterred. The thugs on camels eventually slunk away. The protesters' chants for change continued: *Ash-shab yurid isqat an-nizam!* (the people want to bring down the regime!)

They did bring Mubarak down. But the Tahrir Square protests were not about replacing one despot with another. They were about replacing a despot with a cadre of democrats. For the Middle East, that admirable goal was uncharted territory. In the eyes of the United States and its Western allies—the world's primary bastions of democracy—uncharted democratic territory was risky and dangerous. As a result, the West met Egypt's turn toward democracy with more of the reluctant acceptance reserved for an obnoxious but unavoidable in-law than the eager embrace reserved for a brother.

However, once President Obama and his Western allies realized that the democratic in-law was now in charge in Egypt, they began to do the right thing: actually try to support democracy. Soon after Mubarak exited the scene, the United States began disbursing $65 million in grants aimed at strengthening civil society and paving the way for Egypt's first modern free and fair elections.[22] There was even a sense of palpable albeit cautious optimism in the Western foreign policy establishment, where murmurs began that the long dormant forces for democracy might actually be able to pull it off and fulfill Egypt's peaceful, democratic aspirations. There were even hesitant whispers that Egypt's transformation could mark a new democratic dawn for the entire region.

Those aspirations soon fell flat with an astounding thud. Egypt's experiment with being led by a democratically elected president lasted for almost exactly one year, as the June 2012 election that propelled Mohammed Morsi into power was overshadowed by the July 2013 coup d'état that replaced him with generals in the presidential palace. President Obama now found himself in a bind. After reluctantly embracing the democratic transition, he found himself forced to grudgingly accept military rule. Egypt was deemed too strategically important to abandon, and it was even out of the question to pare down or withhold the $1.3 billion in foreign aid promised to Egypt annually since 1987 (given to reward willingness to work and cooperate with another US ally in the region: Israel).[23] Yet an obscure and rarely enforced 1961 law on the books explicitly forbade the US government from providing "any assistance to any country whose duly elected head of government is deposed by a military coup or decree."[24]

President Morsi had clearly been duly elected. His replacement came to power in an archetypal coup d'état. The new president was a general. So it was hard to dispute that Egypt's 2013 experience was precisely what the law was describing. Yet in acts of linguistic contortion that would have made Orwell's double-speaking Big Brother pay attention and take notes, the State Department and White House press secretaries searched the depths of their vocabularies for all phrases except "coup d'état" to describe the military takeover. They managed it, in spite of some cringeworthy press conferences. Everyone in the room knew that the poor press secretary had been instructed to tiptoe carefully around the rhetorically obvious word. But a coup is a coup, and dressing it up with linguistic legalese can't change that.

Nevertheless, the status quo pragmatism that dominates Western foreign policy remained in place, trading less risk now for more risk later. Billions continued to flow to the post-coup government, even though everyone knew it was a violation of the 1961 law. The US verbally reprimanded Egypt's military leaders, but $1.3 billion in military aid speaks louder than $65 million aimed at promoting democracy against that same regime.

The pro-democracy hearts and the pragmatic minds in the West were yet again at odds over General Sisi's post-coup Egypt. The United States sought ways to prod a return to democracy even while maintaining a friendly disposition (and waving a generous government checkbook) toward a group of generals that had overthrown a democratically elected leader. In the wake of the coup, the heartstrings still had some pull in Washington. Surely, the United States could count on its allies—allies like Saudi Arabia that sold their diplomatic loyalty for American weapons—to support a gradual pro-democracy reform agenda in Egypt if Washington asked them to.

When diplomatic push came to shove, however, the $60 billion Saudi arms deal wasn't worth much. Less than a week after the democratically elected President Morsi was overthrown, Saudi Arabia announced that it would provide a generous $5 billion aid package to Egypt. It coordinated with other regional despots to pump money into the military regime.[25] This move effectively ended the possibility that Egypt's Arab Spring would end in anything other than a desert Arab Winter for democracy.

The West may have had tepid support at best for Egyptian democracy in the first place, but the Saudis had undermined the West's last hope for a major Arab democratic regional power. Yet again, the West chose the seemingly safe path. That same day, rather than expressing anger at the Kingdom for undermining American foreign policy goals, the United States doubled down on its hypocritical relationships. The US government announced that it was selling $1.2 billion worth of special operations naval craft to Saudi Arabia.[26] Three weeks later, Raif Badawi, a Saudi pro-democracy blogger advocating for secular liberal reform, was sentenced to seven years in prison and 600 lashes. Six months after that, his sentence was increased to ten years in prison and 1,000 lashes.[27] He may still face the threat of beheading for "abandoning Islam", a punishment for speaking your mind that ends with severing your head. This is the Saudi Arabia Effect in action.

The West, unlike too many pro-democracy bloggers in the Kingdom, still has its head intact, but is clearly of two minds in this debate. Chasing democracy sometimes and stability other times often ends up creating neither. During the Arab Spring, and continuing today, the Western (and particularly American) governments allied themselves with two regimes that were not just undemocratic, but were actively opposing democracy. One autocratic outpost (Egypt) had just ousted a democratically elected president in favor of military rule and received billions from the West in return. The other (Saudi Arabia) was a kingdom that crushed democratic protests during the Arab Spring in Qatif (where the third graders had been lashed for trying to cheat on a test), and then sought to ensure that democracy would be definitively toppled in Egypt too. As a reward, the Kingdom received billions more in weapons deals and even firmer diplomatic support from Western capitals.

Shortsighted pragmatic minds routinely beat out democratic hearts in the West. The royalists outgunned the reformers. Perhaps that was the path that ensured stability. But how long can you control a despotic medieval system that rests on the cracking foundations of a badly damaged economy and authoritarian repression that is increasingly rejected by its own people? Saudi Arabia is starting to fray in the face of low global oil prices. Analysts now speak about the Kingdom's impending collapse. In the meantime, the Wahhabist royal family exports terrorism, which has spread into Europe and the United States.[28] Egypt is little better, with a fragile military despot at the helm. We are left with a ticking despotic time bomb.

The Saudi Arabia Effect involves actively supporting strategically important dictatorial regimes in pursuit of competing agendas that do not prioritize democracy. The Madagascar Effect involves prodding less strategically important regimes toward democracy, but only pressing them to clear an embarrassingly low bar of democratic quality. Both phenomena are key culprits in the twenty-first-century decline of democracy. They help explain how and why the world's champions of democracy are also accomplices in imperiling it.

This book is certainly not an anti-Western diatribe or a tale of conspiracy theories. The West has, until recently, been the only international force in the world for actively spreading democratic government. It's the only group of nations that invests its limited resources in pursuit of that admirable goal. That's remarkable. It's laudable. And it's well intentioned. The West's efforts have often paid off, too. Japan, Germany, and South Korea are democracies at least in part due to critical and generous Western support. Western foreign policy has helped democracy flourish in some parts of Africa and much of Eastern Europe—regions that had been under the yoke of tyranny throughout most of their history. More recently, Western governments have pushed democracy forward in countries as diverse as Ghana, Estonia, Mongolia, and Tunisia. So rather than bashing the West, this book is focused on how the West could do better, while acknowledging existing Western efforts to promote and support democracy worldwide. But the same forces backing democracy in the West are now failing to make the world more democratic—sometimes by design, because other priorities are deemed more important, and sometimes because Western standards for democracy are far too low for other countries, where what's "good enough for them" is not the same as with "what's good enough for us."

I do not believe that combating democracy is the prevailing goal in any of these cases. There is no conspiracy—just complex, messy and sometimes contradictory foreign policy realities. Dictators and savvy counterfeit democrats are not easy to deal with. Nor are fragile democracies. Every interaction is fraught with peril. To navigate this complexity, there is an entire Western democracy support industry—which has its share of failings—but is nonetheless composed of well-intentioned, hard-working people who try to help democracy germinate across barren dictatorial dirt and the fickle soils that lie between dictatorship and democracy.

These technical experts and their work should be celebrated. But they need more help. Far too often, the millions spent on low-level democracy support on the ground are rendered almost meaningless, derailed by the high-level diplomatic agendas that so often imperil democracy. What do we expect in spending millions on programs ensuring women's representation in Jordan's parliament, if the West simultaneously helps ensure that the parliament remains the king's puppet? As millions are disbursed for Jordanian "democracy", Western governments pump in billions of dollars' worth of weapons that ensure the survival of the friendly Jordanian monarchy. Technocrats teach women how to be elected to a sham parliament while smiling Western presidents pose for photo ops with King Abdullah II. Diplomatic support for the kingdom at the high level undermines technical training and support at the low level. Uncoordinated, conflicting agendas doom democracy.

There is one major case in recent history where high-level diplomacy and low-level local democracy support have worked together: Tunisia since the Arab Spring. What was the result? The country received the 2015 Nobel Peace Prize for its democratic success—the only Arab Spring country where democratic governance took root.[29] There is, of course, no guarantee that Tunisia will remain democratic, particularly with myriad threats ranging from economic woes to terrorist attacks. But the Tunisian example demonstrates what can be possible in countries where local leadership is eager to democratize and willing to work in tandem with Western presidents and diplomats who coordinate their efforts with the technical support on the ground.

If democracy is possible in places like Tunisia, why does the West so often act as an accomplice to despots? There is no simple answer. These questions are difficult, and even well-intentioned diplomats who firmly believe in democracy and hope to promote it abroad are forced to consider serious tradeoffs. For example, how should the United States have interacted with Pakistan's military government in 2002 when Pakistani intelligence cooperation was perceived as vital to success against the Taliban and the search for Osama Bin Laden? Cozying up to a brutal post-coup military regime is ugly business, but so was the prospect of taking the democracy high road: shunning the military government but making it more likely that mass murderers responsible for 9/11 would go free. Unreflective support of democratic principles—no matter the costs—can be as damaging as an outstretched hand to dictatorship while turning a blind eye.

Making the world more democratic requires walking a delicate tightrope. The stakes couldn't be higher. Getting it wrong would not only continue making the world less democratic but could also cause the world to fall into further terrorism, war, or needless political volatility. Nonetheless, in this book, I provide my best attempt to answer several profoundly difficult but crucial questions.

Is the devil we know better than the devil we don't? Is the West at least partly to blame for the world's crisis of democracy and the last decade of democratic backsliding? Can democracy be spread with force? How can we deal with countries that would be even more staunchly anti-Western if they were to democratize? Should we provide golden parachutes to entice dictators to leave power as we hold our noses at our sense of injustice in doing so? Can digital technology be a weapon used against dictators and despots? And, most important of all, what could be done differently to reverse the current trend and return to a global resurgence of democracy?

These are enormous questions fraught with strategic and moral considerations. I nonetheless set off to answer them by conducting research around the globe—bringing me to places as diverse as the whitewashed Mediterranean villas of Tunis, the bustling streets of leafy Bangkok, the post-Soviet grayness of Minsk, and the post-civil war West African boomtown of Abidjan.

After years of exploring democracy and despotism in Africa, Asia, the Middle East, and Eastern Europe, and after hundreds of interviews with politicians, diplomats, generals, coup plotters, rebels, journalists and academics, I'm convinced that simple answers do not exist. Ideologues claiming to have them are unhelpful. But I've nonetheless come away more certain than ever that democracy—true democracy—is not just an admirable value, but one that makes the world richer, safer, and more stable.

I find it too difficult to stomach the notion that Saudi bloggers should resign themselves to being lashed or even having their head chopped off for speaking their mind, simply because that government is the West's strategic ally on the global stage. But I also firmly believe that Western foreign policy must further Western interests. In this book, I argue that there is room to reconcile both sides. Western hearts and diplomatic minds can work together. We can wean ourselves off a counterproductive alliance with barbaric states like Saudi Arabia and we can also expose the absurdity of democracy peddlers like the "pro-values" political party in Madagascar. Over the long term, Western interests are served far better by genuine democratic partners than by the mirage of stability provided by dictatorial allies like Saudi Arabia or the illusion of political freedom conjured up in counterfeit democracies like Madagascar. The path toward democratization is a perilous and long one, but will ultimately reduce the threat of terrorism, cool down possible conflict hotspots, and drive stronger economic growth. Boosting democracy around the globe is the right thing to do, but it also benefits the West and its citizens.

In this book, I explore why democracy is in retreat and suggest solutions to get it on the march again. In doing so, I've found that the protagonists in the stories of global democracy are often bizarre. Their tales are frequently unbelievable. There's the birth of democracy in Athens that can be traced to a fateful incident involving gay lovers; or the failed Cold War CIA plot to assassinate a Congolese politician with poisoned toothpaste; or the backfiring "democracy war" quagmires in Iraq, Afghanistan and Libya; or Rwandan hitmen plotting to assassinate pro-democracy critics in London; or the results of an election in Azerbaijan being released on an iPhone app the day before voting took place; or the tragicomic blowhard Donald Trump blustering about how he has himself as his primary foreign policy adviser because he "has a very good brain" and he's "said a lot things"; or even the story of how a Turkish court was forced to enlist "Gollum experts" to determine if a pro-democracy activist comparing the authoritarian President Erdoğan to the *Lord of the Rings* character was, in fact, insulting him.

Curious and occasionally amusing tales aside, the crisis of democracy is real and it is dangerous. In the coming chapters, I explain how the West is aiding and abetting the decline of global democracy, and provide ten principles that can guide us instead to its resurgence. Following them will help create a safer, richer, and more just world.

But first, to understand the future of democracy and its spread around the world, we need to understand its past and its principles.

1

# A CONCISE BIOGRAPHY OF DEMOCRACY

I believe in democracy.

I grew up in Minnesota, the state that produced the "Minnesota Miracle" of world-class schools while giving America the wholesome, principled leadership of Walter Mondale and Hubert Humphrey. It's the kind of place that instills in you a staunch belief that politics can truly be a force for good and that democracy works. Minnesotans genuinely believe—in the words of the late Minnesota Senator Paul Wellstone—"We all do better when we all do better." In spite of my biased "statriotism", nobody would dispute that Minnesota truly is a shining example of how collaborative democratic politics can yield impressive results.

Yet as long as democracy has existed throughout history, there have been those very un-Minnesotan characters that would abuse the system for personal gain and power. For every genuine democrat, there are usually several demagogues or dictators who pretend to be democrats. That, in a nutshell, is the long-term history of democracy. It has ebbed and flowed across continents and across centuries, from Ancient Greece and Rome, to modernizing Europe and the Americas, and now across the globe. But whenever a new incarnation of democracy is born, someone, somewhere, inevitably attempts to break free from democratic constraints and take advantage of democracy's intrinsic weaknesses.

It didn't take long for that to happen in the storied birthplace of modern democracy, Ancient Greece. According to Greek mythology, the end of the Trojan War had one silver lining for the great surviving warriors of the time: the prize of Achilles' armor—an eternal symbol of heroic martyrdom. The only way to fairly award it, in accordance with early Greek democracy, was with a vote. Like many elections, it quickly became clear that there were two main contenders: Ajax and Odysseus. Both leaders eloquently made their case, in an ancient form of the modern-day stump speech. Then, ballots were cast. Odysseus won narrowly, though Ajax insisted that his rival had been a "thievish maker of votes," rigging the election somehow, perhaps with pre-marked leaves, or behind-the-scenes deals.[1]

As Sophocles tells it, the consequences of history's first stolen election were severe, at least for Ajax. Driven mad by defeat, he entered a hallucinogenic state induced by Athena, and began slaughtering sheep and cows that he mistakenly believed to be supporters of his rival, Odysseus. As madness finally receded, shame at his own brutality and dishonor flooded in. Ajax impaled himself on his sword and died.[2] This mythic parable—of manipulated democracy and its tragic consequences—fits rather well with the risks of democratic government throughout history, even without the intervention of vengeful goddesses.

Yet it's not just a problem of democracy being hijacked by "thievish makers of votes." While it's taboo to admit it, democracy has some innate flaws and dictatorship has some innate strengths. Just after the world's few democracies banded together (along with the Soviet Union) to win World War II, Winston Churchill was nonetheless a reluctant champion of democracy, saying: "Democracy is the worst form of government except for all those other forms that have been tried."[3] Churchill was right; democracy—when done well—is imperfect, but it is the best way to organize societies and govern countries. But a twenty-first-century Churchill, confronted with the all-too-common toxins of rigged elections, predatory politicians, and intense political violence in the world's so-called "democracies" might qualify his statement, adding that: "Democracy done badly can be one of the worst forms of government, including all those other forms that have been tried."

In the West, it's difficult to imagine permanently living in a society without any measure of political freedom. But it's perhaps equally difficult to imagine that people who live without democracy may be less troubled by that fact than we might assume. For most people in the world, the struggles of daily life significantly overshadow the desire for political freedoms. This is not because they don't want democracy, but rather because democracy often falls further down on their list of personal priorities than, say, clean water, a stable income, quality health care for their kids, and other necessities that are easy to take for granted in Western economies.

Nonetheless, any genuine democracy is always preferable to the worst dictatorships (such as those of Stalin, Hitler, or Mao), but "bad" or counterfeit democracies can in fact be worse than "good" authoritarianism. After all, dictatorships may offer stability but no voice for the people. Sham democracies with rigged elections usually offer neither.

Most of us would be willing to give up our democratic freedoms for the right price. This does not negate the value of democracy. But, if you were faced with a contrived choice between being poor in a democratic society or comparatively rich under an authoritarian regime, would you exchange your right to vote for a salary that was five, or ten, or 100 times larger than your current income?

We don't deal with these tradeoffs in the West because we have the luxury of living with economic riches and political freedom. But, if we had to choose, most people—myself included—would rather be born and live in authoritarian Singapore than the electoral democracy of Benin. After all, the average Beninese worker would need to toil for sixty-eight years to match the annual salary of the average Singaporean. Voting seems a rather sorry consolation prize for the urban poor of Cotonou.

This is, of course, a false choice. For decades, conventional wisdom in political science and economics touted the myth that authoritarian regimes were better for economic growth than democratic governance. Now, the preponderance of evidence suggests that a few outliers skewed earlier studies to draw incorrect conclusions. Most scholars now agree that, at least on a global scale, there is no systematically obvious economic drawback to democracy and no economic edge for dictatorship. There are rich authoritarian countries and poor democratic ones.[4] The opposite is true too. Eight of the ten largest economies are democracies.[5] However, in per capita terms, six of the ten richest populations live under authoritarian regimes, though almost all of them are rich because of oil.[6] The majority of the world's countries are not rich, whether they are democratic or not. For every Singapore, there are several Eritreas and for every Norway there are several Nicaraguas. But even though there are multiple pathways to riches, the economic potential of democracies is often greater than the economic potential of authoritarian states. For the moment, though, let's take the statistics at face value and consider it a wash.

Aberrations, outliers, and flukes can skew statistics. There are, however, intrinsic strengths and weaknesses to both democracy and dictatorship. Democracy's strongest asset is inclusion, putting everyone in the same boat, which creates a buy-in of shared benefits and shared responsibility. Whether in China, Japan, Russia, or the United States, citizens are more likely to engage constructively with a regime that they feel takes their voices seriously. Democracy maximizes that feeling. In turn, the government must ensure at least a minimal baseline of wellbeing for the people, or face being replaced in elections. Nobel Prize-winning economist Amartya Sen has demonstrated the virtues of this asset, arguing that this connection between the government and the governed is why no modern democratic state—including his birthplace, democratic India—has had a famine.[7] Mao's Great Leap Forward in China alone provides 15 million counterexamples on the authoritarian side of the ledger.

Moreover, the broader democratic "marketplace of ideas" that accompanies citizen participation allows the best ideas to swim while the worst ideas sink. When Libya's longtime dictator Muammar Gaddafi had a bad or bizarre idea (like ordering his military to shoot down a civilian airliner or employing an impractical horde of Amazon-style virgin fighters as his presidential guard), those ideas became reality without question—sometimes almost instantly. Even authoritarian, oligarchic China has recognized the drawbacks of this style of dictatorship to a limited extent, which is why Chinese state policies are crafted by collaboration, drawing on a wide array of party officials, rather than by an all-powerful despot at the top (demonstrating that even authoritarian regimes that don't base their decisions on the overall voice of the people still "borrow" aspects of democracy).[8] Beyond state policies, the free exchange of ideas in democracies spurs private innovation, a boon not only for growth but also for developing novel government approaches to existing problems. Democracy, by definition, is inherently more collaborative and more willing to consider alternatives before launching new policies—a crucial advantage.

Dictators are also weakened over the long-term because they do not face substantial costs when they make mistakes—even catastrophic ones. Take Turkmenistan's former longtime dictator, Saparmurat Niyazov. Many of his decisions were highly eccentric but mostly harmless—such as changing the word for bread to the name of his mother (Gurbansoltan), or banning smoking because he was personally trying to kick the habit, or outlawing beards and lip-syncing nationwide because he hated both.[9] But in 2004 and 2005, Niyazov unilaterally fired 15,000 rural health workers and shut all the hospitals outside the capital with the reasoning that sick people should enjoy the opulent city of Asghabat during their care.[10] Mobility is not the strong suit of most severely ill people, so his absurd policy surely killed thousands. That death toll later rose, as he severed the pensions of a third of the nation's elderly citizens, and then had the audacity to make them pay back two years' worth of payments that they had already received—to settle debts incurred by "crucial" state expenses like the Neutrality Arch, a $12 million, 246 foot tall gold statue of Niyazov himself that rotates to always face the sun.[11]

In a democracy, these mistakes may still be possible (gold statues of Donald Trump seem more plausible than ever, after all), but at least such state abuse would likely result in a change of government with impeachment or at the next election. Instead, Niyazov stayed in power until his death in 2006. Democracy, by its very nature, would have allowed the Turkmen people the opportunity to replace their dictator (and perhaps openly lip-sync a farewell song while doing so).

But sometimes, authoritarianism shines beyond the glimmering statues. In May 2003, the SARS outbreak in China threatened to spread into a global pandemic. The crisis was largely averted because authoritarianism allowed China to act without consulting society or abiding by "pesky" labor laws. The government built a 1,000-bed hospital facility dedicated to SARS patients in eight days.[12] They broke ground on a

Tuesday and patients were ready to move in by the following Wednesday. 7,000 people worked day and night until it was done. The outbreak was contained. By contrast, groundbreaking for the New Stanford Hospital in Palo Alto, California took place in 2013 for the 600-bed facility, which will not house patients until early 2018. Of course, these facilities are not comparable, and China's labor strategy for the SARS hospital was appalling. But, the red tape of democracy—which often prevents bad ideas (like closing rural hospitals in Turkmenistan) from gaining steam—also slows down, or can derail, progress. This can be a critical difference during crises, when government response time is essential.

Democracy has other Achilles' heels. Transparency is a key feature of truly democratic states. But too much transparency can be a bad thing. How could the 2015 Iran nuclear deal, averting a dangerous foreign policy crisis, have been successfully negotiated if both Iranian and American diplomats were forced to brainstorm a compromise on live television? Closed doors shielded diplomats from public scrutiny and allowed them to entertain bridge-building ideas during negotiations that would have been unpopular with their respective domestic constituencies. It worked.

Likewise, too much accountability can be a weakness. Knee-jerk overreactions to comparatively small events like a localized, low-casualty terrorist attack are far more likely to occur in democracies as leaders are forced to respond to citizen fear. Such concern on the part of the electorate, a definitive feature of Western democracy, paradoxically derails the West's commitment to democracy elsewhere. Short-term election cycles breed shortsighted politics. Presidents and prime ministers are often less concerned with democratization over the next quarter-century than they are with stability in the present. It's easier to convince Theresa May to pursue a strategy that will help her poll numbers than to invest in a political gift for her successor by troubling the short-term waters. Insulated autocrats, on the other hand, can stay the course (even if the course is usually not a very pleasant one).

None of these reasons are sufficient to reject democracy and become a cheerleader for some form of supposedly benevolent dictatorship. Without an exceptionally paternalist mindset, it is difficult to argue in principle against the core tenet of democracy: that citizens should have a meaningful say in how they are governed. In the meantime, however, China and Russia are eager to capitalize on these weaknesses. Both states present themselves as alternative models to the world. That message is potent, and it's a key reason why we have seen democracy recede globally rather than in just one region. In the last decade, South Korea, Taiwan, South Africa, Indonesia, Ukraine, Colombia, Venezuela, Ethiopia, Indonesia, Thailand, Mexico, Turkey, and Egypt (to name but a few) have veered away from democracy. These cases overshadow the rare success stories, like Chile or Tunisia.

Democracy is an "essentially contested concept," meaning that there are unending disagreements over what is democracy and what is not.[13] There is no "one size fits all" approach. But some aspects of democracy—like elections—are so central that they are present in all its varieties. Elections are, of course, not enough. For any genuine democracy to survive and thrive, there need to be three legs to its system: state power, citizen participation, and the rule of law.

Like a tripod, knocking off any one of these legs makes the whole thing collapse. The first leg (state power) allows governments to get things done; without effective state power, even the most well-intentioned democratically elected leader cannot provide for the country's citizens. The other two legs work to constrain state power, ensuring that the government avoids the mistakes and abuses of authoritarian rule and is responsive to the people while protecting the rights of the minority. Without engaged citizen participation, the people cannot rule. Without the rule of law, citizens can never be treated as equals in decision-making.[14]

Without the *demos* (the people), democracy loses its soul. But without the *kratos* (power or authority), democracy loses its effectiveness. Put differently, if democracy is supposed to be government "of the people, by the people, and for the people," even the best weak democracies (or authoritarian states masquerading as democracies) often fall tragically short of being "for the people." This is where there is room for a dictatorial state with plenty of *kratos* to run circles around a well-meaning cadre of earnest democrats lacking it. It's why the procedural system of democracy alone is no panacea. It's why I'd rather live in authoritarian Singapore than democratic Benin.

Around 2,500 years ago, Athenians made the same argument, in reverse. This is where the history of democracy usually begins. Athenians proudly proclaimed why they would rather live in democratic Athens than dictatorial Persia. They pointed to their major military victories against the Persians at sea (Salamis) and on land (Marathon) to illustrate their superiority. To the Athenians and their allies, democracy bred their victory; tyranny was a weakness and a shamefully backward form of governance.[15]

It wasn't always seen that way in Ancient Greece. Many who study the period credit Solon's reforms as a necessary precursor to democracy in Athens. But the history of recognizable democracy also began, strangely enough, with a homosexual lovers' quarrel in the sixth century BC. For Athenians, the lovers—Harmodius and Aristogeiton—were the equivalent of what George Washington represents for Americans. According to popular Athenian legend, democracy was, in effect, born because Hipparchus, the brother of the ruling tyrant, tried to seduce Harmodius. This angered Aristogeiton, who convinced his lover Harmodius to assassinate both Hipparchus and his tyrant brother, Hippias. Lovers scorned, tyrants toppled.

As Thucydides chronicles, the two young lovers concealed their daggers beneath their cloaks and pounced at the opportune moment. Their daggers struck Hipparchus in the heart, striking him down in a pool of blood during a public celebration. But Hippias escaped, as his guards killed Harmodius during the assassination attempt before arresting and torturing Aristogeiton. Harrowed by the brazen attack, Hippias cracked down on internal dissent, intensifying the ruthlessness of his tyranny. As a result, the *demos* rallied against his rule and overthrew him, with the help of Sparta.[16] The downfall of tyranny paved the way for Cleisthenes, who would usher in a democratic constitution in 507/8 BC. Harmodius and Aristogeiton nonetheless remained the revered symbols of democratic martyrdom for Athens.

Athens was arguably not the first democratic system. However, it was the most prominent and most representative in the ancient world. Thousands of years earlier, proto-democratic forms of government had been tested in Ancient Mesopotamia, perhaps most notably in the Kingdom of Ebla, where kings were elected rather than selected and nobility was not strictly limited by lineage. Similar proto-democratic practices were sprinkled throughout the ancient world.[17] However, none went nearly so far as Athens, where a stunningly radical form of direct democracy first graced the world's political stage.

In practice, a citizen assembly largely decided the affairs of Athens. Women, slaves, and foreigners were not allowed to participate. Still, political decisions being left to an assembly of up to tens of thousands of people was a remarkable break from the tyranny of the one. The larger assembly was assisted by the Council of Five Hundred, which recommended possible ideas for approval by the larger body. Voting was often done by a show of hands. For some votes, including whether to grant citizenship, votes were done by casting small pebbles—black for no and white for yes—into an urn (giving rise, eventually, to our modern usage of the term "blackballing").[18] For other votes, preferences were recorded on broken pottery shards, leaving historians with a wealth of surviving ancient ballots.[19]

With this inclusive system of consultative government, Athens became the pre-eminent Greek power, founding the Delian League of Greek city-states in 477 BC. Its intellectual life flourished, as debate and discussion produced Socrates, Plato, Aristophanes, Sophocles, Herodotus, Thucydides, Pericles, and eventually Aristotle.

Democracy produced greatness. It also destroyed it. In 404 BC, the Athenians' main Greek rivals, Sparta, backed a group known to history as the Thirty Tyrants, who sought to wrestle democratic control from Athenians and establish an elite oligarchy. They succeeded. Socrates had taught one of the leaders of the group, Critias. The oligarchy did not last, and was overthrown after just over a year in power. As the popular tide turned against the tyrants, Socrates fell under suspicion. He was put on trial, convicted by the majority vote of a citizen jury, and then sentenced to death—again by a vote. He was given the poison hemlock, which he willingly drank, provoking endless historical debate as to whether he did so in protest against the injustices of democracy, in order to become a political scapegoat that could heal Athens, or because he believed in abiding by the rule of the people.[20] Whichever interpretation is correct, democracy created one of the world's greatest philosophers, but devoured him too.[21]

The Athenian prototype for direct democracy, at least until the advent of modern communications technology, required a physical presence. That limited the sizes of Athenian-style democracies severely—to a few dozen square miles at most. By contrast, Durack district in Western Australia, which is home to just 90,000 voters today, covers

613,000 square miles. If the electoral district were a country, it would be the eighteenth largest in the world, sandwiched between the vast territories of Iran and Mongolia. One MP, Melissa Price, represents the entire area. "During the election campaign, I slept in a different bed every night," she recently told me. To drive the 1,804 miles to meet voters from one end of her district, Geraldton, to the other, Kununurra, Price would need to set aside twenty-nine hours. Thankfully, she can fly to about ten of the 300 towns in the area she represents. The advent of electronic communications and e-newsletters has made her job easier. Those are necessary workarounds; if you distributed the land in Durack between all of Price's voters equally, each would get 3,388 football fields' worth. Even with such a giveaway, Kununurrans probably wouldn't be too excited about the prospect of driving for two or three days to scrawl their preferences on a pottery shard, or to put a pebble in an urn. For that reason, "We don't do a lot of door knocking," Price explained.[22] An innovation was needed to make democracy over such vast distances possible.[23]

That innovation was representative democracy. If the Athenians popularized a rudimentary form of direct democracy, the Romans popularized a prototype of indirect, or representative, democracy. But, except for in Antiquity, the idea never really took root until the twilight years of the Dark Ages (which were particularly dark for democracy). During that time, the divine birthright of kings was an accepted fact, and representative democracy was an absurd concept. As John Keane put it, that idea survived until people began to challenge the fallacy that "sperm was the carrier of good government."[24]

If a love triangle of scorned lovers indirectly gave birth to democracy, a dribbling epileptic arguably revived it. Alfonso IX of Léon grew up known as *baboso*, "the slobberer", either due to fits of uncontrollable epilepsy or because he foamed at the mouth when he was particularly angry (accounts differ). This was only one step above Bermudo the Gouty or Henry the Impotent in the hierarchy of unflattering medieval royal nicknames, but Alfonso earned respect in other ways.[25] Still a teenager, the young king found himself at war and in need of support. He summoned representatives not only from traditional power centers such as the bishops and the aristocracy but also from the urban middle class. Cities supplied a spokesperson—usually without a birthright—

for their community's views. In 1188, the *cortes* of Léon met for the first time, and agreed upon a slate of legal codes that constrained the king's power but created a shared sense of governance from groups that had previously been mere subjects of royal authority. This was arguably the first modern parliament.[26]

With the slobberer showing the way, parliaments spread. They all lacked teeth. When push came to shove, kings reigned supreme over the people's representatives. That all changed during the English Civil War in 1649, as the people of England ended that era of royal supremacy by severing Charles I's head with an axe. Sentenced to die, the king approached the execution platform in two heavy shirts so as to ensure that the crowd would not confuse his shivering for fear. Then, he proclaimed, "I go from a corruptible to an incorruptible crown," politely asked the executioner, "is my hair well?" and met his bloody end.[27]

The execution of King Charles ushered in parliamentary sovereignty, and marked the beginning of the end of ruling monarchs in England. Though the United Kingdom of Great Britain came into being sixty years after the execution, the monarch increasingly became sidelined, subjugated and replaced by the will of (representatives of) the people. This was, of course, a process that took time. The balance of power was still being recalibrated under the reign of King George III, who, in the late eighteenth century, witnessed the birth of the world's most consequential democratic experiment from his throne across the Atlantic Ocean.

The story of America's democratic birth is well known. What is less well known and often lost in the popular mythology is how suspicious the Founding Fathers were of democracy as a concept. This was clear from the proceedings themselves, which were conducted with utmost secrecy behind closed doors. During the Constitutional Convention, George Washington chastised his peers after one delegate dropped his notes on the floor: "I must entreat Gentlemen to be more careful, lest our transactions get into the News Papers, and disrupt the public repose by premature speculations."[28] Had they been allowed in, the reporters from the "News Papers" would have likely reported discussions where "democracy" was considered a bad word. They preferred to call it a "republic."

James Madison, one of the pre-eminent architects of American democracy, felt democracy in the Athenian sense would be a recipe for disaster. In *Federalist Paper Number 10*, he argued: "Democracies have ever been spectacles of turbulence and contention; have ever been found incompatible with personal security or the rights of property; and have in general been as short in their lives as they have been violent in their deaths."[29]

Yet, 240 years later, America is still the world's most successful democracy. Clearly, the framers got something right. Most scholars of democracy would agree that the United States' innovation with regard to institutionalized constitutional checks and balances was a major step forward in representative democratic government. Even at its core, though, some contemporaries considered constitutions to be an anti-democratic constraint, as the majority in one generation was pre-committing the next to sets of rules and regulations that would effectively ensure that majority rule could not always be carried out.[30] Ultimately, though, this was the right choice, as the constitution has been a powerful tool for ensuring that the majoritarian pendulum does not end up being a wrecking ball for democracy in times of crisis, when popular opinion is at its most malleable.

Yet, there should be no illusions: early American democracy was neither a "pure" nor an inclusive democracy. Women could not vote. Slaves, who were considered property, could not either. In fact, slaves were a particular bone of contention at the convention, because population figures were to be used to determine apportionment of seats in the Congress and also to divide up tax obligations by state. Ironically, then, northern states that tended to find slavery an unsavory institution argued that people of African descent were not full persons, or at least should not be considered as such for the purposes of the constitution. Southerners argued the opposite, insisting on the humanity and personhood of their slaves. The dispute was resolved by the infamous "three-fifths compromise," which held that population figures would be counted "excluding Indians not taxed, [and] three fifths of all other Persons."[31]

With that horrifying detail out of the way, the Convention turned to figuring out how to set up a legislative body. The Great Compromise, also known as the Connecticut Compromise, dealt with the seemingly unresolvable dispute over representation between large and small states. Under the solution, the upper house of Congress—the Senate—

would be comprised of two representatives from each state, while the lower house—the House of Representatives—would have seats proportionally allocated according to population. Keep in mind, however, that until the Seventeenth Amendment was enacted in 1913, the Senate was elected by state legislatures rather than by citizens directly. Nonwhite men were given the right to vote in 1870; women secured that hard-fought right in 1920. Congress adopted further protections to ensure Native Americans had the right to vote in 1924. Protections for other minorities (particularly African-Americans) were passed in 1965. American democracy was and is, as all political systems are, a living work in progress.

Shortly after the American model was built in Philadelphia, the French established their rival model in Paris, ushered in by the gruesome sound of the guillotine. When the blood dried, France had built a new, albeit shaky, democracy across the channel from the parliamentary United Kingdom. However, democracy was not just enlisted for people in Europe and the United States. In the 1800s, thousands of miles from Philadelphia, Paris, and London, democracy began to take root in the southern hemisphere for the first time.

Simón Bolívar, the liberator of Latin America, spoke of democracy in the region in unflattering terms, saying, "We elect monarchs whom we call presidents."[32] He was referring to the rise of the *caudillos*, the Latin American strongmen and the early adopters who figured out how to use counterfeit democracy as a populist weapon to wield power throughout the region in the nineteenth and twentieth centuries.

There were, of course, some genuinely democratic elements to these regimes. For example, in the Colombian province of Vélez, women were granted the right to vote in 1853—more than fifteen years before the first American state (Wyoming).[33] Unfortunately, the Colombian Supreme Court struck down the provision before women of Vélez ever voted, but democratic sentiments were spreading across Latin America, even if they were often limited in practice.

These bright spots were pinpricks of light in the darker shroud of a brutal form of early counterfeit democracy. *Caudillos* were ready and willing to use violence to get their way, often bullying and—if necessary—slaughtering indigenous peoples in the process. Few were as effective at using the language and trappings of democracy in support of an authoritarian agenda as the Argentine *caudillo*, Juan Manuel de Rosas.

Rosas, the Red Despot of Buenos Aires, ruled like a dictator but cloaked himself as a man of the people, sworn to bring democracy to Argentina. As many future autocratic wolves in the wool's clothing of democrats would mimic, Rosas used fraudulent elections to legitimize this image. The elections were a joke. As is usually the case in counterfeit democracies, the voting looked good from the outside. All free men over the age of twenty had the legal right to vote—a comparatively open arrangement for its time in the early nineteenth century. There were no literacy or property qualifications. People were free to pick from a slate of candidates.

All of this was, however, carefully managed. Rosas handpicked the slate of candidates. Justices of the peace were sent to ensure that the "right" candidates won. Voting was done verbally and openly, so state officials could use intense intimidation to ensure that nobody voted against the approved list. In the March 1835 election, Rosas won 99.96 per cent of the vote. Four people were reported to have voted against him and I cannot imagine they found the aftermath of doing so pleasant.[34] Rosas used this illusion of a popular mandate to get his way, at times ruthlessly. But this innovation—of wielding the veil of democracy as a weapon to masquerade as a man of the people—was made even more dangerous by the same defense of despots that continues to derail democracy today: that they bring stability.

Rosas presented himself as a force that transformed lawlessness into law and order. He eschewed criticisms of his authoritarian rule by pointing to the success of his harsh tactics in reducing crime, and Western observers bought into the narrative. William MacCann, an Irish doctor who rode through Los Pampas of Argentina in 1851, applauded Rosas, saying that criminals were "sure to suffer the extreme penalty of their crimes, [but] robbery and outrage are almost unknown."[35] That basic formula—of a dictator first using democracy to pretend to be a man of the people, and then deflecting criticism by pointing to the virtues of stability and order instead—would be a successful tactic to secure Western backing for the next 165 years. The illusion of democracy, it turned out, could be used as a very powerful weapon domestically and abroad.

It also turned out that weapons could be used by democracies in support of democracy. Sixty-five years after Rosas was eventually toppled in Argentina, Woodrow Wilson addressed a joint session of the US Congress and called for the country's involvement in the Great War. His grand argument, a novel one at the time, was that "the world must be made safe for democracy."[36] He put forth this argument as a principled ideology, a stand for an idea rather than for self-interest, proclaiming: "We seek no indemnities for ourselves, no material compensation for the sacrifices we shall freely make. We are but one of the champions of the rights of mankind. We shall be satisfied when those rights have been made as secure as the faith and the freedom of nations can make them."

Less than a year later, Wilson followed up that speech with another, the Fourteen Points, which incorporated the notions of democracy and self-determination for colonized peoples into American foreign policy. For the first time, a major international power had made it an explicitly stated goal to pollenate democracy abroad.[37]

There were, of course, democratic success stories in the twentieth century advanced by Western intervention and support. The tragedy of World War II eventually gave rise to two international pillars of democracy, Germany and Japan. But regardless of the overall historical verdict on Wilson's ideals, the ethos of those speeches permeated American foreign policy, at least rhetorically, for the next 100 years. As we approach the centenary of the "make the world safe for democracy" speech, two watershed moments stand out in the extension of Wilson's self-righteous view.

In 1963, only a few months before his assassination, Democratic President John F. Kennedy spoke to throngs of Berliners (the people, not the jam doughnuts) about the promise of democracy at one of the tensest moments in the Cold War. "Freedom has many difficulties and democracy is not perfect," he said, "but we have never had to put a wall up to keep our people in."[38]

Twenty-five years later, President Reagan also spoke of walls, with doors embedded in them that were open to the people of the world yearning for freedom, as he repeatedly invoked the image of America as a shining "City on a Hill." In Reagan's rhetoric, America was a beacon, not only an example of democratic prosperity, but a friend to democracies around the world.

Unfortunately, for the people of countries caught in the grip of Cold War rivalry—particularly in the era between Kennedy and Reagan—America did not always act as a friend to democracy. Rhetoric and reality were divided. From Iran to the Congo or Chile, the Cold War era crystallized a trend that was difficult to buck: when push came to shove, the strategic imperative to deal a blow to the Soviet Union always trumped Wilsonian idealism. Democracy, it seemed, would have to wait.

2

# SPOOKING DEMOCRACY

In the past, the West has occasionally actively undermined democratic governments, setting up "our" despots in their place abroad as a strategic weapon against the Soviet Union, for instance. During the Cold War, the spread and retreat of global democracy often took place in the shadows, as the real-life James Bonds in Western intelligence services played a pivotal role in overthrowing or supporting democratically elected regimes.

Western foreign policy was far more myopic during the East-West, Soviet-American showdown than it is today. In order to understand modern pitfalls in the realm of spreading and supporting democracy elsewhere, it is crucial to understand the checkered history of the concept. During the Cold War, a friendly pro-West dictatorship was typically preferred to an unfriendly pro-Soviet democracy. In pursuit of that foreign policy, the West was willing to take such extreme measures to ensure that nations did not end up in the communist camp that the action needed to be covert.

Fascinatingly, Washington was sometimes more worried about democratically elected leaders who gravitated toward the Soviet Union than about autocrats who did the same. After all, pro-Soviet dictators could be explained away as corrupt despots who set their foreign policy with evil empires against the will of the people. But if a democratically elected leader tilted away from Washington and toward Moscow, it would be hard to argue that the leader was illegitimate. It would also provide a pro-Soviet democratic model for other states to follow suit. As a result, in some diplomatic circles, it was clear that Western governments could not allow any flourishing of democracy in a place that sympathized with the USSR.

This foreign policy priority had devastating results for the peoples of Iran, the Democratic Republic of the Congo, and Chile during the 1950s, 1960s, and 1970s respectively.

Typically, when the West intervenes against democracy abroad, there is usually one of three justifications involved: economic self-interest, ideology, or stability and security.

In 1953, the West saw Iran threatening all three. The elected prime minister, Mohammed Mossadegh, had nationalized the Anglo-Iranian Oil Company (the precursor to BP) in 1951, provoking extreme anger, as this threatened the economic interests of the London establishment.[1] The American government saw no reason to weigh in one way or another—until, that is, the British made the highly dubious accusation that Mossadegh was rapidly tilting toward the Soviet Union. The clear implication was that if Washington did not intervene, Iran would soon be communist and a Soviet ally.[2] The seed of that idea was sufficient to flip President Eisenhower, who subsequently saw Iran as a major emerging threat in his quest for ideological "containment". Finally, Mossadegh's bold move against its former colonizer's oil stake served as a possible model for others in the crumbling Empire to emulate; inaction against Iran, the British believed, would lead to a series of nationalizations, uprisings, and volatility in each of Britain's colonial jewels. Such a doomsday scenario was perceived as a critical security threat, at least as much as an economic or ideological one. In Washington and London, it was agreed: something had to be done to take out Mossadegh.

The intelligence operation the two powers hatched still reverberates in Iran's broken relations with the West six decades later. It was code-named Operation Ajax—an inadvertently appropriate reference to the mythical scorned warrior who went mad in the face of a democratic vote for a valuable prize.[3]

The man responsible for Operation Ajax was an unlikely character. On 19 June 1953, Kermit Roosevelt—the grandson of former American president Teddy Roosevelt—slipped across the Iranian border under the pseudonym "James Lockridge."[4] He was charged with a mission: to overthrow the democratically elected Mossadegh, and install a pro-London, pro-Washington puppet instead.

Bags of cash in tow, Roosevelt began orchestrating a systematic campaign to provoke a coup. The CIA Art Group began producing anti-Mossadegh cartoons. Newspaper editors and media officials were paid off, with one editor receiving the startling sum of $45,000 to play ball. By the CIA's own estimation, in the weeks and months preceding the implementation of Operation Ajax, they controlled or held sway with 80 per cent of Iranian media outlets.[5]

Beyond propaganda, the CIA also spent heavily to ensure the support of key political figures. $135,000 was dished out to General Fazlollah Zahedi, the CIA's handpicked successor, ready to pick up the pieces and become prime minister once Mossadegh was toppled. $11,000 per week was allocated for bribing members of Iran's flawed but nonetheless somewhat democratic parliament, the Majlis. Washington's deep pockets bought a lot of influence.

As this was a covert action, secrecy was paramount. If anyone in Mossadegh's loyal inner circle discovered the existence of a plot, the plot could not only fail, it could backfire and provoke even more aggressive anti-Western Iranian foreign policy. This was a delicate balance fraught with risk.

By his own account, Roosevelt nearly blew the mission's cover on multiple occasions, exclaiming "Oh, Roosevelt!" when he missed shots during regular tennis matches held at the Turkish embassy. When asked to explain why a man named Lockridge had developed such a strange curse phrase, he coolly replied that any self-respecting Republican would do the same given the hideous presidency of Franklin Delano Roosevelt.[6]

But Roosevelt's boyish exclamations belied a much more sinister plot. With the cooperation of the Shah, the CIA obtained two *firmans*, royal decrees that would be used to provide legitimacy to the post-coup government. The plot was set in motion.

The idea was simple. A cohort of troops loyal to the anointed successor would travel first to the home of the military commander, General Riahi, and arrest him, then to Mossadegh's house, where they would do the same. With both men in custody, the dissolution of the government was to be announced, followed immediately by the proclamation of the Shah installing General Fazlollah as a replacement prime minister. Roosevelt had selected a mid-ranking officer, Colonel Nasiri, as the man for the job. He would lead the column of troops and instigate the coup.

On the night of 15 August 1953, the coup plotters arrived at General Riahi's home. Nobody was there. This should have raised red flags, but Colonel Nasiri thought little of it and stuck to the plan, directing his troops to continue to the next waypoint: the home of the democratically elected prime minister. Little did they know that General Riahi had been tipped off and was himself leading a cohort of troops—at the exact same time—to Mossadegh's house to protect him and arrest the disloyal plotters.

While all this was unfolding, Roosevelt and his colleagues were in a safe house celebrating what seemed to be a surefire victory. They drank expensive imported vodka and sang Broadway show tunes. They belted out "Luck Be a Lady Tonight" from *Guys and Dolls*, hoping that luck would be on their side rather than on the side of Iranian democracy.[7]

Two columns of troops raced toward Mossadegh. The government would survive if Riahi arrived first; it would fall if Nasiri arrived first. Unfortunately for Roosevelt and the CIA, Nasiri came a close second, beaten to the punch by General Riahi and his loyal entourage. When the CIA's proxy force showed up, they were arrested. The plot had failed. Mossadegh took to the airwaves shortly thereafter, triumphantly announced that an insidious coup plot—launched by the Shah in coordination with "foreign elements"—had been foiled. After hearing the broadcast, the Shah roused his family, hopped into the personal airplane that he himself routinely piloted, and set a course for Baghdad. All seemed to be lost. Mossadegh would remain in power. The Shah was disgraced, fleeing into exile. Suspicion fell heavily (and correctly) upon the notion that the "foreign elements" concerned were a scorned West, angry to fight back against nationalization of their economic assets.

CIA orders to Roosevelt grudgingly accepted Operation Ajax's failure, advising him, "If you're in a jam, get out so you don't get killed. But if you're not in a jam, go ahead and do what you have to do."[8] Roosevelt decided to work his way out of the jam. First, he distributed $50,000 to buy the participation of an unruly ragtag mob to pose as angry supporters of Mossadegh. The aim was to use provocateurs to create blowback against the regime. As they reached the main square in Tehran, they began to get out of control, rioting and shouting slogans against the widely popular Shah. Authentic anti-Shah elements, particularly from the communist-allied Tudeh Party, spontaneously joined the demonstrations, further playing into the CIA's hands. Showing some of his democratic stripes, Mossadegh ordered the police and armed forces to allow them to demonstrate. Ironically, this liberal gesture would initiate the spiral that led to his downfall.

The protests sharply divided Tehran, creating the polarized atmosphere that the CIA knew would be most ripe for a coup. With popular opinion turning against Mossadegh as a result of the CIA-manufactured mob rioting against the Shah, it was now time to orchestrate its inverse—a CIA-manufactured mob rioting in the Shah's favor.

But this was not to be any old mob. It was a literal circus. The CIA, with the help of key Iranian agents, had identified low-income street performers and athletes to be the protest's vanguard. Broad-chested weightlifters marched alongside acrobats and jugglers.[9] Many wielded clubs. Others wielded knives. Some—the jugglers in particular—performed, tossing pins into the air while the mob danced around them. At the edges of the mob, thugs waved ten rial notes to onlookers. The ranks quickly swelled to thousands, marching as they chanted, "Long Live the Shah!" Soon, the circus-like atmosphere morphed into a serious threat. Soldiers began to join the thronging crowd, adding tanks and an official veneer to the demonstration. This created a tipping point; it was time to put the final act of Operation Ajax into motion.

Anti-Mossadegh soldiers, including many that had been paid off by the CIA, raced yet again toward Mossadegh's house to arrest him. Other loyalists had already sensed the turning tide and had barricaded themselves inside, ready to defend their prime minister to the death. The assault began late on 19 August, and sporadic but fierce fighting left the streets outside Mossadegh's home covered in blood. Mossadegh fled after a single tank shell exploded into his house, but he was captured and detained shortly thereafter. The Shah, who had been waiting in Rome to see how things unfolded before returning to the country he purported to rule, flew back to Tehran accompanied by CIA director Alan Dulles. Democracy had been subjugated. General Fazlollah became the government's new chief, backed by the authoritarian and hereditary Shah. "Our" autocrat was in place.

The plot continues to poison Iranian-American relations to this day. Scholars struggle to explain the 1979 Iranian Revolution without considering it at least partly as a response to the 1953 coup. But this incident also shows a broader pattern during the Cold War: when the spread of communism seemed possible, democracy was a distant secondary concern. Hard-nosed geopolitical pragmatism inevitably trumped democratic idealism. On the Cold War chessboard, the loss of pawns in the Third World (like Iran) was viewed as an unacceptable blow, one that would ensure the ruthless advance of the existential threat posed by the rival and aggressive queen moving freely about the board, the Soviet Union. The chess masters in the West let their cynical minds ignore the beating of their democratic hearts as they manipulated the board to their advantage around the world.

The Cold War chessboard extended everywhere. The West's moves were particularly important in Africa in 1960, just seven years after the CIA plot had toppled Mossadegh in Iran. Sixteen former African colonies became independent states in 1960 alone, and nobody knew how they would situate themselves in global politics. One of them was the former Belgian Congo, renamed the Democratic Republic of the Congo after breaking with its colonial masters in Brussels. In May, the country held its first democratic elections. Men over the age of twenty-one cast ballots, selecting 137 Congolese leaders to constitute the country's first elected Chamber of Representatives. This was a sharp break from its colonial past; it ushered in an optimistic euphoria that was simultaneously sweeping across the continent from Senegal to Somalia.

The real winner of the elections was Patrice Lumumba, a former traveling beer salesman and postal worker who was elected to be the nation's first prime minister after his party won over voters. Before later changing his name, Lumumba had been born with the surname Okit'Asombo, or "heir of the cursed", with Okit' meaning "heir" and Asombo referring to "cursed or bewitched people who will die quickly."[10] The prophetic patronymic was to be fulfilled shortly after Lumumba ascended to power.

The wave of independence in Africa forced each new nation to choose its orientation: West, East, or neither. Would Lumumba gravitate toward the Soviet Union or the United States? Or, would he try to walk a non-alignment tightrope between each, playing a savvy game to exploit maximum concessions and sponsorship from both?

Lumumba made a fateful decision early on when he faced an insurrection in Katanga province during the transition to Congo's independence. Backed into a corner, he approached the Soviet Union and asked them to provide him with weapons, food, and medical supplies. A thousand Soviet advisers arrived almost immediately. For Washington, this was clear evidence: Lumumba was a communist sympathizer who could set a dangerous precedent for other newly independent former colonies.[11] For Belgium, Lumumba seemed dangerously eager to distance Congo from its former colonial power—and their intertwined interests. In a variety of Western capitals, it was agreed: the democratically elected Congolese prime minister needed to go, so that the Congo would become an ally of the democratic West.

Rather than making the world "safe for democracy", the CIA—likely in conjunction with SIS, the British overseas spy service popularly known as MI6—yet again hatched a plot to eliminate an elected head of state in pursuit of competing security interests. Unlike Mossadegh, who had been placed under house arrest after being toppled, Larry Devlin, the CIA station chief in Léopoldville (now Kinshasa), received orders to kill Lumumba. In pursuit of that goal, President Eisenhower authorized a covert operation to provide Devlin with a poisoned tube of toothpaste, which local operatives were to slip into Lumumba's bathroom.[12]

The toothpaste arrived in Léopoldville, but it was never used. Devlin later said that he tossed it into the Congo River, discarding it because it was no longer necessary.[13] Lumumba, fearing for his life and realizing that the West was conspiring against him, had fled. Soldiers loyal to an ambitious mid-level officer, Joseph-Desiré Mobutu, used intelligence gleaned from the Americans, Belgians, or British, and quickly captured Lumumba.

Lumumba was arrested and beaten publicly on 17 January 1961, almost exactly seven months after he had been elected by the people of the Democratic Republic of the Congo. After the public beating, Lumumba was strapped in place on an airplane and flown to Elizabethville (now Lumumbashi). Katangan and Belgian officers tortured him, transported him to an isolated spot in the countryside, and executed him with a firing squad while Belgian officials looked on. The Belgian report noted with characteristic matter-of-factness that he had been executed between 9:40 and 9:43pm local time.[14] Careful to ensure that his body would never be discovered, the Belgians and Katangans worked together to dispose of his remains. Lumumba's body was dismembered, his bones dissolved in sulfuric acid.[15] The stench was so bad that the Belgians drank whiskey trying to cope; they got drunk as they dissolved Lumumba's body.[16] The promise of democracy in Congo also dissipated that night, as Colonel Mobutu would eventually ascend to power in a coup, only to rule the country as a megalomaniac dictator for nearly four decades. He fleeced the devastatingly impoverished country, flying in lunches from Paris on Concorde jets while crushing all political opposition with a ruthless iron fist. Congolese democracy has never recovered.

This is, of course, not to say that the Democratic Republic of the Congo would have lived up to its democratic namesake without Western intervention. The young Congolese state may have turned equally despotic under Soviet influence. Democracy was imperiled across Africa at the same time even in the absence of Western manipulation. Therefore, while it is naïve to believe that interventions and plots by the United States, the United Kingdom, and Belgium derailed a democratic system that would otherwise have flourished, the Western-backed assassination of Lumumba certainly did usher one of Africa's worst despots into power.

The Congolese and Iranian cases were spawned by the same myopia: Western diplomats in this era tended to sport blinders that kept their focus on anti-Soviet containment. This created a paradox: while Western (and particularly American) leadership regularly spoke of the virtues of democracy compared to the vices of communism, they were simultaneously willing to go further than ever to topple unfriendly democratic regimes across the globe.

During the Nixon years, however, this patchwork foreign policy strategy took on stunning coherence under a new architect, Secretary of State Henry Kissinger. As a German Jew born in Bavaria during the Weimar Republic, Kissinger was fifteen years old when his family fled the burgeoning Nazi regime. They escaped to New York by way of London. Kissinger then returned to Germany in an American uniform, serving as a counterintelligence sergeant during the Allied advance through his former homeland—when German language-speakers were at their highest premium. After the war, Kissinger established himself as a shrewd scholar of international affairs at Harvard, and landed himself a job within the highest echelons of the United States government, first as National Security Adviser, and later as America's top diplomat, the Secretary of State.[17]

Kissinger's vision for foreign policy revolved around *realpolitik*, an amoral approach to diplomacy that stressed state interests and power over ideology or principle. The development of democracies abroad was, in Kissinger's view, sometimes a bonus, but certainly not a critical interest for the United States. This view was hugely influential during the presidencies of Richard Nixon and his successor, Gerald Ford, as Kissinger had the ear of both men.

While Kissinger is perhaps best known for his role in the Vietnam War, he is equally infamous—at least in Latin America—for his cynical strategy to rid Chile of its democratically elected socialist leader, Salvador Allende. The aim was to replace Allende with a pro-Western leader, a strongman who could do Washington's bidding rather than giving the Soviet Union another foothold in the vicinity of Cuba.

Just eight days after the democratic election ushered Allende into power, President Nixon met with Kissinger. At the conclusion of the short meeting, Nixon ordered the CIA to "make the economy scream," as a means of conditioning Chile for an eventual coup d'état.[18] This economic sabotage accompanied another stream of CIA activity in Chile, as Washington tried to stop Allende from ever taking power by blocking his inauguration. To do so, a CIA-backed operation successfully assassinated the Chilean commander-in-chief of the armed forces, General René Schneider, but to no avail.[19] Allende was inaugurated and continued down his socialist path, which was deemed an unacceptable provocation toward NATO interests in the Western hemisphere.

In an illuminating document (since declassified), Kissinger's rationale for intervention in Chile shows how these issues can be debated at the highest levels of Western government. They are not taken lightly, as some conspiracy theorists might suggest, but are instead the carefully thought-out strategies of competing interests with the highest stakes imaginable.

"The election of Allende as president of Chile poses for us one of the most serious challenges ever faced in this hemisphere," Kissinger wrote to Nixon. "Your decision as to what to do about it may be the most historic and difficult foreign affairs decision you will make this year."[20] Kissinger stressed, of course, that a billion dollars of US investments was at stake, but was more worried about the effects that Chile could have on other similarly placed nations across the globe. To that end, he warned Nixon that there could be an "insidious model effect," as there would be no way to undermine Allende's legitimacy after his demo-cratic election—precisely the route to power that Washington vocally supported in the lofty and idealistic rhetoric routinely broadcast from the White House. A pro-Soviet democratic success story in the Western hemisphere was intolerable. Either the regime had to fall, or it had to be made to fail. Otherwise, Kissinger warned, "The example of a suc-cessful elected Marxist government in Chile would surely have an impact on—and even precedent value for—other parts of the world." Even as he was strongly urging Nixon to covertly depose Allende, Kissinger's memo noted: "Allende was elected legally, the first Marxist government ever to come to power by free elections. He has legiti-macy in the eyes of Chileans and most of the world; there is nothing we can do to deny him that legitimacy or claim he does not have it."[21]

Yet there were dissenters who believed that Kissinger was overstat-ing the Chilean threat. Viron Vaky, a top deputy to Kissinger, wrote a classified memo to him suggesting that the plan to overthrow Allende was not only likely to provoke "widespread violence and even insurrec-tion," but that it was also deeply immoral. "What we propose is patently a violation of our own principles and policy tenets... If these principles have any meaning, we normally depart from them only to meet the gravest threat to us, e.g. to our survival. Is Allende a mortal threat to the US? It is hard to argue this."[22]

Vaky's words, written in 1973, echo my overarching argument in this book. There is, of course, a calibration that needs to be made between core short-term geostrategic interests that cannot be ignored and the long-term ambition to shape the world into a more stable, prosperous, and democratic place where people have a meaningful say in their governance. Vaky believed that the calibration in Kissinger's diplomatic strategy had been badly skewed, assessing minor threats as major ones, conflating annoyance with existential risk. Where to draw this line is a difficult question, but in hindsight, most contemporary scholars, policymakers, and diplomats would agree that Kissinger was the architect of a plot in Chile that overstepped the appropriate bounds of Western foreign policy.

Kissinger, however, was under no illusions. This was going to be a coup to remove democracy from a nation that, as he saw it, had foolishly brought intervention on itself. As Kissinger explained in yet another classified memo: "I don't see why we need to stand by and watch a country go communist due to the irresponsibility of its own people. The issues are much too important for the Chilean voters to be left to decide for themselves."[23]

Like the actions in Iran and the Democratic Republic of the Congo that preceded it, the CIA mission in Chile was a covert attempt to undermine a sovereign and democratically elected leader. Like the others, it succeeded.

The CIA, with direct backing from President Nixon, began to reach out to military officers within Chile, threatening to withdraw all military aid if a coup didn't happen, but offering to pour further resources into Chile if a coup did take place. It paid off political opponents of Allende, financing them to organize destabilizing mass protests and strikes. Anti-Allende propaganda was spread throughout Chile, notably by buying influence with a major newspaper, *El Mercurio*.[24]

On 11 September 1973, the covert action paid off. The coup took place in a matter of hours. Dozens were killed in fighting. Cornered, President Allende shot himself with an AK-47, and with a single gunshot, ended democracy in Chile for the next seventeen years. Kissinger had achieved his goal, and lamented in a private phone call with President Nixon that the West would not be able to publicly take credit for its covert role in the coup.

While Kissinger may have overstated the threat that Chile posed to Western interests, it is hard to overstate the damage wrought by the CIA-backed coup. In just a month after taking power, General Augusto Pinochet killed thousands of leftists who had supported Allende. These killings were ordered directly by the regime. The "Caravana de la Muerte" (Caravan of Death) was established as a targeted vengeful death squad, killing ninety-seven people in the span of less than a month after the coup.[25] 40,000 members of the political opposition were imprisoned in Chile's national stadium. Torture was rampant.

Pinochet's military regime was terribly despotic, repressive, and damaging. The West was integral not only to its arrival in power but also to its longevity; the CIA continued to put key regime figures on its payroll, including the head of Chile's notorious secret police force, the DINA.[26] Such people were effectively used not only to marshal Chilean politics away from the orbit of the Soviet sphere, but also to encourage a resumption of key American business interests, such as Anaconda Copper or General Motors operations in the country.

All three camps of objectives were therefore achieved. Chile's economy continued to act in favor of, rather than against, Western economic interests. In ideological terms, Pinochet was firmly in the West's camp, and spoke disparagingly of the Soviet Union and its sympathizers within Chile. And the security dimension was no longer a threat, as the "insidious model" of an "elected Marxist government" had been toppled, serving more as a warning to other states than a model to be followed. On the criteria with which Kissinger evaluated foreign policy, *realpolitik*, the coup in Chile was a resounding success.

Today, Chile has turned a page and is a thriving democracy. Since the return of democracy in the late 1980s, Chile's economy has soared, outpacing virtually every other economy in Latin America (other than Uruguay, which is the only other country in the region that is considered a fully consolidated democracy). In other words, the short-term success of the West's policy in authoritarian Chile overshadowed decades of lost long-term potential that has finally shown itself under a fledgling democratic state. We still don't know how much potential has been lost in Iran and the Democratic Republic of the Congo because neither is a functioning democracy.

This introduces the difficult rub at the heart of the democracy promotion paradox. The West has been stubbornly reluctant to promote democracy unless it perceives it to serve its short-term strategic interests. However, when short-term national interests override long-term considerations, then democratic principles routinely fall by the wayside as a result of competing geopolitical ambitions. In Iran, Congo, and Chile, the democratic principles articulated by Wilson and echoed by every president since were undercut by the prismatic view of global politics during the Cold War struggle. The dictatorial devil on our side seemed better than the democratic devil on theirs. It was a misguided and shortsighted approach.

The Cold War is, of course, over. The tactics of CIA toothpaste plots have largely fallen by the wayside too. In the majority of instances, Western efforts to support democracy abroad have emerged from the shadows, either through overt military action (in Iraq, Afghanistan, or Libya), rather than covert plots, or through technical assistance from government-funded entities, such as the American overseas development funding organization, USAID.

However, old habits can sometimes die hard, and Cold War politics can re-emerge in bizarre forms. In 2010, less than five years before American president Barack Obama took the historic step of shaking hands with Cuban president Raul Castro and six years before his historic visit to Havana, Washington developed a creative throwback to an earlier era when Cuba was one the leading bogeymen of the Cold War. The 2010 plan was a bit more sophisticated than poisoned toothpaste (or the infamous botched "exploding cigar" plan tried against Fidel Castro half a century earlier), but it was nonetheless aimed at provoking insurrection in Cuba.

Joe McSpedon, a US government official with USAID, worked on a secret program to create a Twitter-like social media platform called ZunZuneo (a Cuban colloquialism for the sound of a hummingbird's tweet). This Cuban Twitter would lure in users with soccer scores, music reviews, and hurricane updates. But then, once a critical mass of young Cubans was using the platform, the app developers envisioned using it to provoke a "smart mob" during times of crisis. The idea was to drastically exacerbate unrest during any time of political volatility, funneling anti-government messages to young people rather than keeping them up-to-date on the Manchester City vs. Arsenal score.[27]

However, unlike previous initiatives against Mossadegh, Lumumba, or Allende, this effort was aimed at ushering in democratic change to a country that had long avoided democratic rule. The stated aim of the ZunZuneo project was to "get the transition process going again towards democratic change."[28]

In March 2011, ZunZuneo had attracted 40,000 active users. A year later, the service was discontinued. USAID claimed that the covert app disappeared because funding ran out, but there are suspicions that its true nature was uncovered and deemed a risk to American public relations at a time when US-Cuban relations were beginning to show signs of a thaw.

This intervention in Cuba offers two lessons. First, diplomatic history casts a long shadow: tiny Cuba continued to be perceived as a disproportionate threat in Washington for decades beyond the Cuban Missile Crisis. Second, modern-day diplomacy aimed at promoting democracy around the world has not completely dissociated itself from bizarre plots straight out of a James Bond film, a sort of misguided GoldenHashtag sequel to Goldeneye or Goldfinger.

Yet in all the cases mentioned above, from Iran to the Democratic Republic of Congo to Chile or Cuba, the perceived threat was exaggerated and overblown. As Viron Vaky argued in 1973, Chile did not pose an existential threat to the United States and it was not necessary to perpetrate such an egregious act of unprincipled diplomacy. The same was, of course, true in Cuba during 2011. These were not truly vital interests.

However, such disproportionate missteps are easy pickings for critics of Western foreign policy. Sure, Washington did not act admirably at all times during the Cold War. That is not exactly a revelation. The more difficult and important question, however, lies at the core of a central dilemma in democracy promotion: how can the West actively promote democracy when it so often conflicts directly with core economic or security interests of Western governments? This is an exceptionally difficult question, and the debate to which we now turn. To begin, we must navigate a tricky foreign policy minefield by traveling back in time to Pakistan in 2002, as the United States decides whether to support a post-coup military regime in order to improve the odds of capturing or killing Osama Bin Laden and his associates.

3

# TUNNEL VISION

*Principle 1: Think long-term*

Promoting democracy consistently is not easy. It requires tough choices and a truly long-term vision in a system that rewards short-term thinking. But far-sighted thinking can pay big dividends.

The morning of 12 October 1999 began like any other Tuesday morning in Pakistan. It ended with a different government in power, as General Pervez Musharraf toppled the elected civilian prime minister, Nawaz Sharif.[1] That morning, General Musharraf was in Sri Lanka, when word leaked to him that Prime Minister Sharif and Pakistan's intelligence chief, General Ziauddin, were plotting to force Musharraf into an early retirement, sidelining him for good. Musharraf immediately hopped on a Pakistan International Airlines flight back to Karachi, and set the wheels in motion on a coup plot to sideline the prime minister and his inner circle instead.[2]

As soon as Pakistani intelligence detected troops emerging from the barracks and got word that Musharraf was returning to Karachi, Prime Minister Sharif ordered air traffic control to divert the plane, forcing it to land in Nawabshah, 275 kilometers northeast of Karachi. The president's security team would be waiting to arrest Musharraf. The plane was not given permission to land and was told to re-direct.[3]

Musharraf's contingent of troops surrounded air traffic control, and Musharraf himself entered the flight deck and spoke directly to the controllers on the ground, demanding permission to land. Air traffic controllers finally agreed as soldiers approached their tower. It was just in the nick of time, as the circling jet was down to just seven minutes' worth of fuel in its tank—which would have been harrowing news to the more than 200 civilians on board at the time. Shortly after landing, Musharraf dismissed Prime Minister Sharif and successfully took power in a military coup.[4]

Democracy, which was already flawed in Pakistan, disappeared. Under a state of emergency, Musharraf's regime detained political prisoners without charge, banned public rallies, and made political parties impotent. Rana Sanaullah Khan, a government critic, was whipped, beaten, and tortured in custody.[5] This was unsurprising; military regimes are not bastions of good governance or human rights. They are also rarely counterfeit democrats. It's one of their very few virtues. With military despotism, what you see is usually what you get.

At the time, Westerners were enjoying seemingly unstoppable economic growth. There were few immediate security threats. Pakistan was therefore not vital to Western interests. In the final months of President Clinton's administration, Washington gave Musharraf the diplomatic cold shoulder and urged him to return power to elected civilians. Then, 11 September happened.

As Thomas Carothers, a vice president at the Carnegie Endowment for International Peace, explained in a 2003 *Foreign Affairs* article, "The cold shoulder that Washington turned toward General Pervez Musharraf after he seized power in 1999 has been replaced by a bear hug."[6] Suddenly, the West needed Pakistan. Its cooperation was no longer just a diplomatic bonus; it had become vital for Western security. Without it, the war in Afghanistan would be logistically impossible and the prospects for defeating the Taliban or capturing Osama Bin Laden would grow much slimmer.

The White House quickly canceled $1 billion of Pakistani debt, pledged $3 billion in new aid (split evenly between civilian and military expenditures) and shipped off hundreds of millions of dollars to the notorious ISI, Pakistan's military intelligence service; it is even widely believed that American funds helped build ISI's new headquarters.[7] US sanctions that had been implemented due to Pakistan's nuclear program (and to protest against Musharraf's undemocratic coup) were quietly waived. Deputy Secretary of State Richard Armitage made the change in policy even more direct, by telling Musharraf that as far as US-Pakistan relations were concerned, "History starts today." All would be forgiven if he played ball now, regardless of past differences. Musharraf agreed.[8]

Just a few years later, General Musharraf even appeared on the hit late-night American comedy show, *The Daily Show*, hosted by Jon Stewart. In a surreal interview, Pakistan's military despot joked and laughed with an amused American audience, including a jarring light-hearted moment where he was offered a Twinkie, contrasted against the backdrop of an appropriate but pointed question about public enemy number one: "Where is Osama Bin Laden?" This lightheartedness would have been unthinkable in 1999, when Pakistan—Musharraf most of all—was seen as an international pariah that needed to be shunned and shamed back to democracy. Nothing about Musharraf had changed, but the international context was drastically different.

Even with Musharraf formally on board with the West's War on Terror, it's not easy to control despots. There is credible evidence that Pakistan's government may have had some knowledge of where Osama Bin Laden had been hiding. The US-backed ISI (Pakistani intelligence) may have been aware of his whereabouts well before he was killed in his compound in Abbottabad, literally under the noses of the officers at the prestigious Kakul Military Academy.[9]

This is a classic case of the tunnel vision that routinely plagues democracy promotion. Democracy promotion cannot be effective if short-term geostrategic concerns are allowed to dictate Western foreign policy, because democracy needs a sustained commitment to grow and take root. The necessity of garnering Pakistan's military cooperation after 11 September demonstrates how easily core democracy promotion principles can fall by the wayside when the geopolitical context changes. But if Western governments do not believe democracy promotion to be in their short-term interest, they are far less likely to pursue it as a central strategy. In other words, for democracy promotion to take place, it usually has to exist in a framework that guarantees it will fall by the wayside anytime that competing interests come into play—as they almost always do. The United States urged the military government to return to democracy in 1999, but then needed to ignore Pakistan's undemocratic ways in order to fight terrorism just three years later. This, like many reversals of democracy promotion, had the inadvertent effect of killing off pro-democracy forces in Pakistan with friendly fire from the West, as Washington cozied up to a despot. But could the United States have afforded not to do so in that crucial moment? These are the types of foreign policy dilemmas that Western presidents, prime ministers, and diplomats routinely face.

In diplomacy, the safe but unprincipled bet often wins. Across the globe, being a despot's adversary rather than an accomplice requires a willingness to take risks. In 2002, Washington was not prepared to risk it with so much at stake in the region and in the global fight against terrorism. At most, the State Department occasionally prodded Musharraf privately with boilerplate human rights talk. That seemed to pay off. Left unprovoked, Pakistan hit back at the West less than it might have. Musharraf was never going to be a democrat, but in the eyes of Washington, he was at least "our" dictator (or more so than he would have been had the West pressed him more aggressively).

This risk-averse attitude to democracy promotion is, ironically, an outgrowth of Western democracy itself. Spreading democracy takes a principled long-term commitment, but democratic electorates reward pragmatic shortsighted victories. Even if Presidents Bush Junior and Obama had wanted to stand up to Musharraf regardless of the challenges it would present to the war effort, they also knew that public support for the war in Afghanistan was already tepid at best. Because Western foreign policy was being formulated in a democratic environment, under the watchful eye of skeptical voters, both presidents needed to keep Pakistan's government on their side to avoid further volatility half a world away provoking an electoral backlash—and, ultimately, defeat at the polls.

Western democracies frequently succumb to this critical short-term bias in formulating foreign policy for two reasons, and both undermine the long-term march from dictatorship to genuine democracy.

First, electoral cycles give "credit" to leaders that make demonstrable progress toward the national interest during their time in office. If President George W. Bush had helped set Pakistan on a long-term course toward democratic reform but ushered in greater volatility in the short term, he would suffer politically while his successor might be able to take credit. Convincing a politician to hurt himself or herself while rewarding an opponent or successor is not an easy task. The risk/reward calculus therefore usually favors co-existing with despots over the much longer project of trying to get rid of them.

Political scientists refer to this as having a short "time horizon."[10] In a dictatorship, by contrast, the leader can look further into the future, knowing not only that he or she is likely still to be in power, but that successful long-term reforms might actually prolong that tenure and prevent a revolution or a coup. Term limits in democracies undercut any similar incentive; Bush Junior knew the exact date of his departure from the White House, whether his foreign policy was a success or not, so his time horizon largely ended on 20 January 2009, when President Obama took over.[11]

Second, and related, democracies have to be responsive to constituent concerns, which are often knee-jerk reactions to global events rather than sustained foreign policy commitments. In 2002, President Bush may have articulated a vision for spreading global democracy, but he did so knowing that his prevailing policy imperative was to look tough and effective against al-Qaeda.[12] That overriding policy necessity made pressing Musharraf's regime on democratic reform unfathomable to the Washington establishment, and understandably so. Its extremely likely that all modern commanders-in-chief, from Reagan to Obama, would have made the same hard-nosed, pragmatic calculation as the Bush administration in their post-9/11 dealings with Pakistan.

Still, Bush let the pendulum swing too far; the West obviously needed Pakistan, but Pakistan needed the West too. That dynamic gave rise to a missed opportunity, as more pressure could have been leveraged against Musharraf in that moment. There was a middle ground between isolating Pakistan completely on the one hand, and embracing a military ruler, showering him with American tax dollars, and cheering him on a late-night comedy show on the other. This is where the first principle for reversing democracy's retreat comes into play: think long-term.

Democracies are not designed for long-term planning, but they can achieve it. Whether it was JFK's vision for a man to reach the moon during the 1960s, or the prolonged NATO commitment to containment during the Cold War, or France's sustained and privileged diplomatic ties with its former colonies, Western democracies can make long-term foreign policy priorities stick for good or ill, weathering the ups and downs of finicky electorates and soundbite-driven news cycles. But this requires leadership, articulating a vision that overrides bumps in the road, and provides a clear roadmap forward. It also requires consensus across party lines, so that democratic reformers know that they won't be left out in the cold after an unfavorable election in a Western partner nation.

Long-term thinking is therefore the key to overcoming democracy promotion tunnel vision. Thankfully, there is a consensus in Washington, London, Paris, Berlin, Tokyo, and Brussels that a more democratic world generally serves Western interests—in terms of trade, peace, stability, and diplomatic soft power (the ability of governments to cajole rather than coerce their way to making their imprint on the world). A stable democratic Pakistan would likely be better for democracies elsewhere, from Brazil to India and everywhere in between. But the ideal outcome rarely happens in foreign policy, particularly when it comes to spreading and supporting democracy abroad. For that trend to be reversed, short-term geostrategic interests need to be incorporated into a long-term framework that puts democracy promotion much higher up the ladder of Western imperatives on the global stage. Only then can the retreat of democracy transform back into a liberating advance.

In other words, for the Bush administration in 2002, the worst outcome was a dictatorial and uncooperative Pakistan, a lose-lose scenario that let the Taliban roam free while suppressing democracy. The second worst option was a dictatorial but cooperative Pakistan, a lose-win situation. The best scenario would have been a cooperative democratic Pakistan, but the Washington establishment completely lost sight of that ultimate ambition. As a result, when there was an opening for that win-win option, as widespread protests broke out in favor of democracy in Pakistan during late 2007, the Bush administration stood by Musharraf rather than supporting the grassroots movement. Musharraf was ousted against Washington's wishes, and the democratic West's image suffered for having backed the unpopular general, who had badly overstayed his welcome in the eyes of the public. For Pakistanis who abhorred Musharraf, the West was his accomplice. Was it worth it?

Between 2002 and 2010, the United States alone sent $18 billion in economic and military aid to Pakistan, but the relationship was severely damaged once Musharraf fell.[13] The funds had bought reluctant, temporary cooperation rather than a long-term partner. It's questionable whether it was a good investment, as spending on Pakistan alone rivaled the United States government's total global expenditures in support of democracy over the same period. The return on investment would have been far greater had the United States made clear to Musharraf's government—and the Pakistani people more generally— that the cooperation on security did not give the regime a free pass on democratic reform, good governance, and respect for human rights. Seeing those long-term imperatives as central rather than secondary concerns would have paid considerable dividends, likely without imperiling the overall relationship—which was ultimately uneasy for both sides. Chasing short-term victories that create long-term problems is the current strategy but it is not the right one.

There is, unfortunately, considerable reason to believe that American taxpayers directly funded a gift to the survival and entrenchment of authoritarian institutions in Pakistan during this pivotal period. Proponents of foreign aid often speak of it as buying leverage, using financing to prod countries to reform. In this view, foreign aid should help shore up democracy where it already exists, and push authoritarian states more toward democratic rule. Instead, scholarly research has demonstrated the existence of an "amplification effect", meaning that foreign aid has limited transformative power, but instead typically serves to perpetuate existing political institutions. It is not usually the case that government-to-government financial support for "bad" governments provides effective leverage in turning them into "good" ones. Put simply, aid causes democracies to become more democratic, and dictatorships to remain unflinchingly dictatorial.[14] Foreign aid is no magic wand, and it may be more of a curse than a blessing when misspent on a military regime—as it was in Pakistan.

I'll be the first to admit that "think long term" is not the most precise policy advice, but it is a crucial and forgotten bit of wisdom in democracies as they formulate foreign policy priorities. The controversial Bush Doctrine was simply swept away by President Obama's arrival in the Oval Office, as Bush's failed evangelical strategy of democracy promotion by the sword morphed into a pragmatic firefighting approach to foreign policy crises, with no coherent direction. President Obama admitted as much himself, boiling his foreign policy doctrine down to a single unscripted phrase while aboard Air Force One in 2014: "Don't do stupid shit."[15] In the following nine chapters, I provide more direct guidance, with nine further principles for how to make the world more democratic, but none of them would be effective without long-term thinking. Without a long-term vision, it's inevitable that the West will do stupid shit, trading pyrrhic short-term security for long-term volatility, blowback, and a less democratic world for the next administration to inherit.

Short-term thinking doesn't just pervade the White House, Downing Street, the Élysée Palace, or the Sori Kotei in Tokyo; it pervades the corridors of the democracy promotion industry itself, the very people responsible for the actual nitty-gritty of making the world more democratic day to day. Those low-level, on-the-ground interventions are also failing, for a simple reason: making the world more democratic has become a business, a cottage industry that is built to best thrive on reinforcement of the status quo.

It may seem surprising that the democracy promotion industry is, to varying degrees, a business. Non-profits often act like businesses, particularly the alphabet soup of groups like the National Endowment for Democracy (NED), the International Republican Institute (IRI), the National Democratic Institute (NDI), USAID, the UK's overseas development agency (DFID), the Netherlands Institute for Multiparty Democracy, the German Konrad Adenauer foundation, and the European Partnership for Democracy (EPD). But there are also literal businesses in the game. For-profit democracy promotion businesses—yes, there are companies that are paid by governments and foundations to spread democracy—include firms like Chemonics and DAC, among others.[16]

Whether profits are involved or not, democracy promotion organizations have two common needs and both reflect short-term priorities. The first is government money. Without government grants, the operating costs that pay for employees, democracy promotion programs, and administration go unpaid and the democracy promoters have to close up shop. The second is a space to work in; if democracy promoters anger the host government too much, they'll be expelled from the country. "On-the-ground" democracy promotion is hard in a country where you can't operate.

The combination of these two imperatives has forced democracy promoters to gravitate toward "tame democracy promotion." As Sarah Bush argues in her book *The Taming of Democracy Assistance*, these organizations are no longer confronting dictators but are instead focused on around-the-edges reforms that, by design, do not tip the scales toward democracy in any meaningful way.[17]

Tame democracy promotion has three main features. First, the strength of democracy promotion is inversely proportionate to the geo-strategic importance of the country in question. Because Bahrain hosts the United States Fifth Fleet, it receives exceptionally tame democracy promotion messages from the United States government. Madagascar, by contrast, may receive a comparatively strong pro-democracy message because it has virtually no strategic importance for the West (something of which I had to remind my contacts in Madagascar, who repeatedly suggested that I was a CIA agent scoping out the island for some sinister plot). These different standards based on the strategic importance of each country are derived from the same logic at the core of the tunnel vision that derails democracy promotion.[18]

Second, because NGOs compete for government grants, they have gone overboard in trying to quantify their measures as a means of showing "value" for their activities. Value is a difficult concept to imagine in this industry, when the ultimate goal is a transition to consolidated democracy. Should we really fund groups based on the number of luncheons they run for pro-democracy activists? If the regime becomes more authoritarian, but dozens of MPs have been briefed on how to strengthen a political party, is that evidence of a successful program? These questions are not abstractions; they are genuine conundrums that funding organizations confront in an industry gone mad with quantifying progress into "measurable" results.

Sometimes, the results are tragically comical. A USAID program operating in Cambodia during 1997 claimed that it had "exceeded expectations" on all of its pre-selected benchmarks for democracy— even though a coup d'état had eliminated Cambodian democracy that year. As Sarah Bush argues, this competitive quantification of democracy promotion can get out of control: "In Armenia, competition for democracy assistance was so fierce that it drove NGO leaders to call each other 'grant chasers,' 'grantrepreneurs,' and even 'prostitutes.'"[19]

The reason for this is simple; once organizations get a taste for grants, it's hard to go back. As one democracy promoter explained, "One of my friends runs a $50 million organization and so he has to generate $50 million to keep everyone employed. It means that you have to go where the money is."[20] This grant chasing on the ground mirrors the shortsighted approach to democracy promotion in diplomacy and Western government policy.

Third, dictatorships resist democracy promotion, forcing democracy promoters to weaken their activities simply so they can stay in business. Each NGO needs government permission to enter the country and work on democracy promotion within its borders. As you may imagine, democracy promoters are not always the most welcome guests of dictatorial regimes. As a result, they have been tamed out of necessity; provoke the regime too much, and they'll kick you out. In July 2015, Russia banned the National Endowment for Democracy, expelling its workers with immediate effect.[21] China is considering following suit, and dozens and dozens of countries have passed laws banning local NGOs from receiving foreign funding, effectively tying the hands of Western democracy promotion organizations. For more creative despots, democracy promotion NGOs find themselves hit with hundreds of building code violations or extensive and onerous investigations into the minutiae of their paperwork. Sometimes, as is often the case in Jordan, the intelligence services attend training workshops in an "observational" capacity; unsurprisingly, fewer and fewer participants show up each time. The only way for Western NGOs to avoid such restrictions is to tame themselves and work around the authoritarian regime without ever challenging authoritarianism itself.

This means that, by design, democracy promoters can only create programming that is tolerated by the regime—anything that could actually meaningfully change the political dynamic is often out of bounds. This is why "low-level" democracy promotion can never be effective on its own; it can only be part of the equation, in tandem with high-level diplomatic pressure from Western governments.

Belarus provides an excellent example of the tunnel vision that can create rapid and counterproductive shifts that undermine democracy promotion. Shortly before Christmas in 2015, I traveled there, hoping to understand why the European Union was starting to cozy up to a dictator. I found myself in an empty café in Minsk interviewing Mikalai Statkevich, a former Belarusian presidential candidate turned political prisoner. Statkevich spent nearly five years in prison for organizing a peaceful pro-democracy protest against President Alexander Lukashenko, often called "the last dictator in Europe."[22]

As he was telling me about his ordeal, a young woman walked into the café. Rather than sit at any of the dozens of empty tables, she made a beeline for the booth directly next to ours. She sat down opposite me, took out her phone, held it to the side of her face, and pretended to read. Statkevich paused, leaned forward and whispered: "I picked a café without any microphones hidden in the tables, so they have to do it the old fashioned way."[23]

The "they" he was referring to was almost certainly the Belarusian KGB, which, unlike Russia's FSB, still uses the antiquated Soviet acronym. This is fitting. Belarus is a living museum for the Soviet Union. Its economy is still 70 per cent state-run and its politics just as ruthless.

Since he consolidated his authoritarian grip in the mid-1990s, Lukashenko has, like many dictators, tried to legitimize his system of governance by demonstrating popular support with rigged elections. As one senior political analyst—who wished to remain anonymous for obvious reasons—explained to me quietly at a bar in Minsk, "Lukashenko instructs everyone as to what percentage he wants. Maybe it's 76 per cent. But then, his aides don't want to get in trouble in case someone fails to deliver. So they tell the regional staff to ensure that it's 79 per cent just to be safe. Then the regional staff tell the local staff to make sure Lukashenko wins 83 per cent. Then, everyone delivers, and Lukashenko gets 83 per cent."[24]

This dynamic explains why Lukashenko may be the only president in modern history to have publicly admitted to rigging an election, claiming that he actually rigged the 2006 vote downward in order to seem more plausible to outsiders.[25] For precisely the reasons the analyst explained, he believes this may genuinely be true.

Moreover, in the 2010 election, several presidential candidates were beaten in the streets by Lukashenko's thugs. On a cold, dark afternoon in Minsk, I asked Uladzimir Nyaklyayew about his ordeal when he ran for president. The cost of that candidacy, he explained to me, was nearly death, as he was attacked during a peaceful political rally in the capital: "I was beaten, nearly to death in the street. Then, as my wounds were still healing, I was abducted from the hospital and taken to prison. Change can only happen if the West finds the line where help to Belarus begins and help to Lukashenko ends."[26]

That is a tricky line to find, but it needs to be found to transform this ruthless regime. Otherwise, more political prisoners will face beatings and long prison sentences for their political views. Back in the café, sipping his coffee as the KGB agent pretended not to listen, Statkevich told me what it was like to be incarcerated for nearly five years, simply for standing up to Lukashenko:

> All the time, they asked me to confess and beg for forgiveness from the president. If you sign this document, they told me, you can go home tomorrow. I refused. After years of pressure and isolation, they tried a new approach. Rather than isolate me, they forced me to share a cell with a certified psycho. I shared a cell with him for two months. I was only allowed to meet with my family once a year, for two hours each time, behind glass. I was only allowed out of the cell one hour per day to go for a "walk" but in a closed space. I measured it. It was thirty-five steps long. But I still refused to sign.[27]

Being told these harrowing stories while also being followed by KGB agents is a little unnerving. I woke up in my Minsk hotel room the day after arriving to a series of automated alerts from Skype saying that my account had been targeted by a hacking attempt. My account was shut down; it had been compromised. But during my visit, I was reassured by one of my contacts, a pro-democracy dissident, in startlingly frank language: "don't be afraid—while the EU is processing some grants for Belarus, you can feel safe here as I do." A diplomat I spoke to echoed that sentiment: "Don't worry. You're a twofer: you're an American that teaches at a prestigious British university. They're not going to want to piss off two governments and make headlines while they're reconsidering sanctions." A precarious reassurance, but one I was happy to have. Put differently, I was safe and avoided arrest because democracy promotion had fallen by the wayside and the West had recently decided to cozy up to Lukashenko in pursuit of other short-sighted geopolitical goals.

For much of the 2000s, Western governments took a principled pro-democracy approach to Belarus. The European Union issued a visa ban to "persons who are directly responsible for the fraudulent elections and referendum in Belarus on October 17, 2004 and those who are responsible for severe human rights violations in the repression of peaceful demonstrators in the aftermath of the elections and referendum."[28] This was followed by an asset ban targeting Lukashenko and his entourage in 2006. The United States was on board too. In 2004, President Bush signed the Belarus Democracy Act, authorizing direct government assistance to pro-democracy forces in Belarus working to undermine Lukashenko's dictatorship. It also effectively prohibited any form of non-humanitarian aid to Belarus so long as Lukashenko failed to implement democratic reforms. Waves of sanctions soon followed, biting into the nation's prosperity.[29]

In response, Lukashenko cracked down on local pro-democracy NGOs, claiming that all of them were puppets of the West. He raided their offices and used every available opportunity to cripple their activities. Before long, democracy promotion was tamed; substantial pressure was not tolerated, so the only NGOs that did operate did meaningless work while claiming to be promoting democracy.

For this period, though, the West's approach to Belarus was a full-throated defense of democratic principles. This was possible because of geopolitics. At the time, Lukashenko was angering the West in two main ways. First, there was credible evidence that Belarus had provided weapons support to countries supporting terrorism (including Saddam Hussein's Iraq). In fact, while the Ba'ath party loyalists were trying to escape Iraq undetected after the US-led invasion, several—including Saddam's sons—were found with authentic Belarusian passports furnished by the government.[30] Second, Belarus was a close ally of Vladimir Putin's Russia. Both of these aspects meant that opposing Lukashenko was perfectly in line with supporting a democratic uprising; the dictatorship was the West's enemy already. In such instances, tunnel vision isn't a problem, because the short-term geostrategic interests are aligned with the long-term democracy promotion goal. That can quickly change if the geopolitical situation shifts. What would happen if courting Lukashenko somehow became more attractive than shunning him?

Three developments in 2015 and 2016 altered the West's geopolitical calculations—and all three ensured that the West would pursue competing shortsighted strategic interests in Belarus rather than backing a long-term push for democracy.

First, the Belarusian economy began to fall apart rapidly in 2015 contracting by roughly 4 per cent in just one year.[31] State-run Soviet enterprises dominate economic activity but they are drowning in inefficiency. Second, the Russian economy is also trudging through a deep economic slump; Vladimir Putin can no longer afford to bail out Belarus. Third, the volatility ushered in by crises in neighboring Ukraine and Crimea—and the souring of Russia's relations with the West—have transformed Belarus in the eyes of Western diplomats, from a place that urgently needs democracy and human rights, to a place that just needs to remain stable. Hoping to avoid further upheavals, the West has no appetite for anything other than business as usual in the governments ruling the region—even if this means working with a despot rather than working for democracy.

There is therefore little reason for optimism that Lukashenko, a ruthless political dinosaur stuck in the Soviet past, will let his authoritarian system go extinct anytime soon. So, there was much speculation about how the West would behave in the immediate aftermath of the (yet again) rigged October 2015 elections. President Lukashenko was "re-elected" in a predictable landslide victory, winning an announced 83 per cent of the vote. In the past, Europe and the United States had responded to Belarus' blatantly rigged elections by reading off the same stale foreign policy script: first, they condemned the election in predictable language ("The presidential election indicated that Belarus has a considerable way to go in meeting its OSCE commitments for democratic elections").[32] Then, Western governments either strengthened or at least maintained sanctions against the regime. Next, Lukashenko would slink back toward his political patron Vladimir Putin, and the two would continue their relationship, born more out of economic necessity and security cooperation than any true personal affinity. The end result was always the same: Belarus stays in Russia's camp, democracy remains a pipe dream, and the West has limited leverage to do much of anything.

That script was crumpled up and tossed after the October 2015 vote. Of course, the quality of the election was no different; Lukashenko's victory was as rigged and undemocratic as ever. "The government let us 'observe' the vote tallying from 50 metres away with a group of regime thugs blocking our view. All we could see was a bunch of butts from 50 metres—so obviously we couldn't see if the ballots were being counted correctly," one Western ambassador told me. What had changed, however, was the international context. Isolated from the West, Lukashenko used to rely on Putin's deep pockets and trade with Russia to survive (nearly half of Belarusian exports go to Russia).[33] Now, with both the Belarusian and Russian economies in trouble, Putin's pockets are no longer so deep. Belarus therefore has a fresh incentive to try to reconcile with the European Union and the United States instead.

Some form of uneasy reconciliation has been made possible by token and marginal reforms (such as a handful of political prisoners including Statkevich being released in August and nobody getting beaten close to death like Nyaklyayew during voting in October). Those gestures would not have been enough to placate the West's disdain for dictatorship in Belarus in 2010, but seem to be enough to change the dynamic now. In February 2016, the European Union suspended its sanctions against Belarus.[34]

This seems unthinkable given the dismal Western relationship with Belarus during the 2000s, when Brussels and Washington colluded against Lukashenko. But since the 2010 election, Russia has annexed Crimea and destabilized Ukraine. Further afield, the ostensibly democratic Arab Spring revolutions have imploded into chaos everywhere but Tunisia. As a result, Western diplomats in Belarus have gravitated toward a thinking grounded in stability and pragmatism rather than principle. For Washington, London, and Brussels, the prevailing wisdom today is to live with the dictatorial devil they know in Lukashenko, rather than risk yet another crisis. And, as an added bonus, luring Belarus away from being Putin's pawn would be a foreign policy victory on the global chessboard.

Russia won't let that happen so easily. In late 2015, President Putin began pressuring Lukashenko to build a Russian airbase on Belarusian soil.[35] This move irritated Lukashenko as an affront to his sovereignty but also prodded the West to see Belarus in even starker security terms. Now, in addition to worrying about a democratic revolution and the volatility it could bring, Western diplomats also needed to worry about Russia's military expansion, just a two-hour drive from the European Union's eastern edge. These are real concerns that cannot easily be dismissed.

To avoid these cataclysms, the West is reducing pressure on Lukashenko. But diplomats know that any thaw in foreign relations will not usher in real change for Belarus or a return to democracy. Twenty-five years after the Cold War, the country is being viewed as just another chip in this post-Soviet East vs. West poker game. This high-stakes gambling is perfectly, poetically symbolized by the geographic juxtaposition of the American Embassy and the Russian ambassador's residence. The two buildings share a common wall, their dueling flags towering above a bleak Minsk neighborhood, as each camp vies to peel Belarus away from the other. As the two sides spar, Belarusian pro-democracy forces are caught in the diplomatic crossfire.

The overall victim of such high-stakes gamesmanship is genuine reform and democratic change. Diplomats that I spoke to lamented the need to prioritize stability over democracy, a policy that will almost certainly entrench the dictatorial status quo.

This is the problem with tunnel vision: any Western push for democracy falls by the wayside when it no longer aligns with the short-term geostrategic interests of the West. Inevitably, Lukashenko's regime will eventually crumble. His ruthlessness, combined with the regime's inability to provide for the people, will one day catch up with him. When that happens, the transition could be extremely damaging to Western interests in the region, as the pro-democracy forces within Minsk bite the hand that used to feed Lukashenko's despotism from afar. Now, many of the pro-democracy activists and opposition leaders I spoke to see the West as an opportunistic snake, Lukashenko's friend when it suits and his foe when it doesn't.

In my view, the recent thaw in relations is a shortsighted blunder that will do more harm than good in the long run. With a long-term vision, and a recalibration of priorities that reflect policy goals in the next decade rather than in the next several months, Belarus could be pushed toward democracy much more quickly. In subsequent chapters, I outline specific strategies that can be used to prod, rather than force, despots toward democracy. But for now, the play-it-safe West is ensuring that the last dictatorship in Europe continues to survive. On 15 February 2016, the European Union fully withdrew sanctions.[36] There had been no reforms to justify the shift.

Ultimately, it seems that a thaw between Belarus and the West ironically worsens the prospects for Belarusian democracy. As the West warms to an unreformed Lukashenko out of a perceived security necessity, pro-democracy forces in Belarus are likely to be left out in the unforgiving Minsk cold—perhaps shadowed by a young woman pretending not to follow them.

But at least what is happening in Belarus is better than the biggest blunders of democracy promotion in the last fifteen years: the misguided "democracy wars", backfiring quagmires that made the world less democratic and never should have been attempted in the first place. It's time, then, to leave Minsk behind and focus instead on Kabul, Baghdad, and Tripoli.

# 4

# THE "SAVAGE WARS OF PEACE"

*"I don't think our troops ought to be used for what's called nation-building. I think our troops ought to be used to fight and win war."*

George W. Bush, 11 October 2000

*Principle 2: Stop trying to impose democracy with war*

Rudyard Kipling's poem *The White Man's Burden*, written in 1899, captures the ethos behind the West's recent quagmires in Iraq, Afghanistan, and Libya:

> Take up the White Man's Burden, the savage wars of peace…
> Take up the White Man's burden, no tawdry rule of kings.

Kipling's poem, which was interpreted by some as a satire of colonialism and by others as an endorsement of it, nonetheless speaks to the notion that Western governments have a duty and an obligation to spread good government to the "backwards" peoples of the rest of the world. Some critics will inevitably make the argument that my defense of democracy promotion as a concept generally falls into the same patronizing trap. But whether you generally believe in the enterprise of democracy promotion or not, there are undoubtedly bad ways and better ways to pursue it. Today's "savage wars of peace" have not, of course, brought peace or democracy to Afghanistan, Iraq, or Libya.

Instead, they have imposed broken counterfeit democracies that are struggling to avoid complete state collapse.

This gives rise to a crucial lesson of the twenty-first century: democracy wars simply don't work. They are expensive, create intense blowback against the West, spill much blood, and ultimately don't create lasting democratic systems. Moreover, they undermine peaceful democracy promotion tools, as an increasing number of regimes now see "democracy promotion" as a euphemism for "regime change" led by America's armed forces. Democracy wars need to be exorcised from the possible repertoire of diplomatic tools aimed at spreading democracy abroad.

In 2009 Afghans went to the polls—some of them at least. The vote took place almost exactly eight years after the launch of Operation Enduring Freedom—a reference to the democratizing justification of the counterterrorism assault—in the wake of 11 September. The election posed extensive logistical challenges. Rural polling stations were so cut off from population centers that American helicopters were necessary to transport ballot boxes.

Six days after polls closed, an American Chinook helicopter dropped into the valleys of the rugged mountains in Nuristan, a remote northeastern province bordering Pakistan. Soldiers loaded up fifty ballot boxes in a "sling load" hanging from the chopper, took off, and set a course for a central vote-processing center. Not long after take off, the sling malfunctioned, sending half of the ballot boxes—twenty-five in total—tumbling to the valley floor. Upon hitting the ground, they burst, scattering thousands of ballots into the wind.[1] The image of ballot boxes falling from a military helicopter and exploding is an effective metaphor for the woeful state of democracy in Afghanistan, Iraq, and Libya today. It probably wouldn't have mattered that much if the twenty-five ballot boxes had reached their destination; the election was rigged from the start, and the lost votes had likely been bought or stuffed anyway.

Mullah Tarakhel Mohammadi, an MP representing eastern Kabul, provides a window into the fraudulent Afghan democracy that so many, Westerners and Afghans alike, have died fighting over. From his outpost in Kabul, Tarakhel allegedly engineered a sophisticated scheme to churn out ballots for the incumbent president in the 2009 election, Hamid Karzai.

When the polls opened, an election official (who wished to remain anonymous) arrived at his assigned polling station in Pul-i-Charki village, to the east of Kabul. He found the ballot boxes already full, stuffed to the brim with votes for Karzai. Tarakhel, who proudly accepts his nickname of "Crazy Tarakhel," denied that the ballot boxes had been stuffed, telling a *New York Times* reporter that the overflowing ballot boxes resulted from a a higher than anticipated turnout.[2] Yet when a British journalist arrived at the village polling location just an hour after voting had begun, there were no voters to be seen, even though twelve boxes had been filled with ballot papers and the official tally showed that 5,530 voters had already come and gone. That was, of course, impossible.

The election official tried to cry foul and report the fraudulent ballot boxes. When word of this reached Tarakhel (who controlled the other election officials in the area), the Mullah telephoned the rogue election official and instructed him to drop his protests and certify the results. When the stubborn official refused, Tarrakhel dispatched four armed bodyguards. They forced the official into their car and drove off. He was released eventually, but only after polls had closed and the ballot boxes had been certified. This happened across the country, on all sides. The election was largely meaningless, and some election monitors alleged that at least a third of all ballots were fraudulent.

Political spin-doctors in the West saw the silver lining and many praised the vote as an important step toward democracy. In reality, the election made a mockery of democracy, entrenching fraud and affirming that the rigged political system would continue to dictate Afghanistan's future.

In the subsequent 2014 election, leaked covert audio recordings of election officials captured a conversation between a senior election official and an accomplice, with the official instructing his counterpart to "Take the sheep into the mountain and bring them back stuffed." The two men then lament the rising price of buying off voters and local officials: "The price of goats and sheep has gone up these days."[3]

You can't bomb your way to democracy. And, while the United States and its coalition partners did genuinely try to support democratic institutions in Afghanistan after toppling the Taliban-led government in 2001, the polarization resulting from the war, the lack of functioning institutions, historic divides, battling local warlords, and a series of policy blunders doomed the effort.

It was equally doomed in Iraq and Libya. Part of the failure there can be attributed to avoidable gaffes that seem bizarrely amateurish and naïve in hindsight. In May 2003, shortly after US-led coalition forces toppled Saddam Hussein's Ba'athist regime, L. Paul Bremer III—the American viceroy of Iraq—issued two orders that would doom Iraqi democracy for the next decade and beyond. "Order 1" disbanded the ruling Ba'ath Party and barred any of its former members from "positions of authority and responsibility in Iraqi society." With a pen stroke, Iraq's most powerful elites—the only people who had any experience in running the country—were wiped off the political map. Legally, the only people who would be allowed to serve in a new regime would be those that had never served in government since Saddam Hussein took power in 1979. By alienating Iraq's powerful political class and scrubbing clear their crucial expertise from the transition, political reconciliation was doomed from the start. "Order 2" disbanded the Iraqi military, leaving 400,000 trained, armed men suddenly unemployed. Many found "work" in the fledgling insurgency.

If the goal was to create chaos, it's hard to imagine two other orders that would sow disorder and violence with greater effect.[4] In the span of a few months, Western intervention transformed Iraq from a functioning dictatorship to a collapsed state with no effective institutions and a burgeoning sectarian civil war. This happened because the West took a wrecking ball to what had been built previously in Iraq, rather than trying to co-opt existing institutions in service of democracy.

Panaceas are rare in politics. It's difficult to convincingly argue that Iraq would be a democratic paradise free from violence if L. Paul Bremer had exercised restraint and avoided those two blunders. But the decision to try to build something completely new in place of an authoritarian system that had been in place for decades was misguided and dangerous.

Part of the problem was that Iraq hosts three sectarian groups within its borders, which were drawn (for geostrategic reasons by Britain and France) in the aftermath of World War I. There could just as easily have been three nation-states within the current borders: one in Baghdad, one in Basra, and one in Mosul. That doesn't mean that democracy was or is doomed in Iraq. Many diverse societies with historical sectarian divides have overcome them in order to create a functioning government that has at least a precarious democratic peace. Democracy could still take root, even if it seems a long shot now. But, as Thomas Carothers of the Carnegie Endowment for International Peace has argued, democracy promotion in Iraq failed because it was overly technical and not sufficiently thought through from a "big picture" perspective. Rather than attempting to bridge major schisms in society, the coalition authority poured money into advisers and technical assistance on how to write a constitution and how to design a parliamentary system rather than how to simply co-exist with perceived sectarian enemies. For Carothers, this was like building a new house for three quarreling families, forcing them to move in together, and expecting them to leave their squabbles at the door. The house itself wasn't the problem that needed to be addressed first.[5]

At least, though, the West did not abandon Iraq after the old system was destroyed. While some scholars argue that an occupying force prolongs violence during transitions, it is also true that Western taxpayers bankrolled an array of ambitious programs aimed at supporting democracy from Mosul to Basra. The United States spent an estimated $1.82 billion on programs aimed at directly supporting democracy in post-Saddam Iraq. The figure is much higher if other programs are included, such as efforts to establish the rule of law or fight corruption. However, an independent watchdog auditing the American-led rebuilding effort in Iraq documented that more than 50 per cent of those funds were spent on "security and overhead costs."[6] When other costs are tallied, the total bill for the West's intervention in Iraq approaches $2 trillion by some estimates, but is certainly above $800 billion—which is roughly thirty times the total of the United States' spending on promoting democracy everywhere else in the world during that same period.

Ultimately, the Western invasion of Iraq, and all the blood spilled and treasure spent, only created a system that can best be described as a dysfunctional state at risk of collapse. Iraq's political institutions act as a counterfeit democracy at best and a milder version of Saddam's authoritarianism at worst. All in all, post-occupation elections are nearly as flawed in Iraq as they are in Afghanistan. Nouri al-Maliki, who governed Iraq from 2006 to 2014, entrenched sectarian strife while ruling as a sort of Saddam-lite, including brazen assaults on local Iraqi journalists and other similar despotic abuses. Most people in the democracy promotion community—and the political establishment in the West—agree that the wars in Afghanistan and Iraq have been back-firing quagmires, no matter the benchmark.

In late 2015, the disaster of Iraqi democracy—which is closely intertwined with security in the country—came full circle, as destabilization devoured 300 election officials who were murdered by the so-called Islamic State (ISIS). They were rounded up and killed by firing squad in Mosul, while another group was knifed to death in a different part of the city:[7] yet more victims in Iraq's seemingly quixotic struggle for democracy, mistakenly initiated at the barrel of a gun.

Hawkish critics of my argument might object here, arguing that democracy wars can work, even though they did not work in Iraq and Afghanistan. To an extent, they are correct. After all, two pillars of global democracy today—Japan and Germany—both emerged as such in the wake of destructive conflicts with the United States. However, those conflicts diverged in significant ways from their more modern counterparts in Iraq, Afghanistan, and even Libya.

As Francis Fukuyuma argues, "the United States and other occupying powers did relatively little state-building in either country: both Germany and Japan possessed powerful state bureaucracies that survived the war weakened but structurally intact."[8] Even though political purges were attempted, the occupying forces recognized the necessity of re-incorporating people with technical know-how into government operations. This was about re-legitimizing existing institutions within a new democratic framework, rather than taking a wrecking ball to the entire political system. In Afghanistan, by contrast, the Western intervention effectively created a political vacuum without a functioning state.

Moreover, there is an important distinction between post-war "reconstruction" and post-war development. The West is much better at the former than the latter. In Japan, all that was needed was reconstruction, as effective institutions already existed. The economy was damaged severely by the war, but it was salvageable. This differed from Iraq, Libya, and Afghanistan, where functioning state institutions divorced from the dictator's personal entourage had to be created from scratch.

Moreover, Germany and Japan had a common characteristic shared by very few societies targeted in today's democracy wars. There was no major social divide; German and Japanese society both had a level of cohesion that is rare in conflict-prone dictatorships today. This is not to say it is non-existent, but there are a vanishingly small number of cases that present, simultaneously, the yoke of tyrannical government, united societies, and a strong and functional bureaucracy.

Transitions to democracy are difficult by their very nature. Bombing campaigns and invasions make them even more difficult, except in the absolute best circumstances—which are exceedingly rare. As two prominent political scientists put it, "Governing a society that is democratizing is like driving a car while throwing away the steering wheel, stepping on the gas, and fighting over which passengers will be in the driver's seat."[9] When the transition is done by force, the car is destroyed, the passengers feel victimized, and an occupying force is in the driver's seat. It rarely plays out well.

Some scholars have, however, suggested that internal war can be a democratizing force even if international wars (especially Western interventions) do not work. Since World War II, some democracies have emerged phoenix-like from the ashes of conflict. But similar examples have been few and far between since the end of the Cold War. Croatia (1996) is perhaps the only convincing contemporary example of a war having a clear democratizing effect.

The prevailing reason for this is simple. Wars don't just damage infrastructure and kill people. They also divide societies. Expecting warring factions to simply resolve their differences through the ballot box when fighting ends is as naïve as imagining that democracy will arise from bomb craters. The challenge, therefore, is to create a democratic system out of an undemocratic means of defusing tensions: power-sharing agreements. These can be immensely helpful in forcing both sides of a conflict to work toward a lasting peace; after all, if each side has a meaningful say in the country's future, neither will have as strong an incentive to destroy that future with further conflict.

However, power-sharing agreements can also be exceptionally undemocratic, substituting the will of the majority for a system that simply declares both sides winners for the sake of expediency. When that happens, democracy may remain exceptionally flimsy, ready to regress back to fighting as soon as the next election, political crisis, or security challenge rolls around. Afghanistan's 2014 power-sharing agreement and subsequent collapse back into fierce fighting offers a clear example of the perils of such agreements.

At other times, even power-sharing agreements become impossible, as reconciliation is out of reach for viciously fighting camps with radically different visions for the country at war. This is the case now in Libya, where Western intervention created a political vacuum so forceful that it has sucked the life out of any meaningful attempts at national unity—and doomed democracy in the process.

The West's intervention in Libya has been disastrous. The decision to use Western-led airstrikes was justified as a means to depose Muammar Gaddafi and "pursue the broader goal of a Libya that belongs not to a dictator, but to its people," in the words of President Obama.[10]

Gaddafi, who was killed in the aftermath of the airstrikes, truly was one of the more bizarre dictators in modern history. Due to a crippling fear of heights, he refused to mount more than thirty-five steps. He loathed elevators, which is part of the reason why he traveled with a flowing but bulletproof multi-colored Bedouin tent, to sleep in on his travels abroad. Most of the time, the tent would be filled with camels; he would drink their milk to prove to guests that he had not forgotten his roots as a tribesman even though he was one of the richest despots in the world. The tent was routinely guarded by his private Amazonian bodyguard detail, forty fierce virgins who took a vow of chastity when they pledged their service to Gaddafi's protection.[11]

But even if the bodyguards didn't tempt Gaddafi, other high-profile women did. The erratic Libyan despot reportedly showered former US Secretary of State Condoleeza Rice with $200,000 worth of gifts—including a lute—during her visit to Tripoli in 2008. Even though she was part of an administration that advocated Western-initiated regime change in the Arab world, overthrowing dictators by force, Gaddafi was smitten. When he finally fell from power in 2011, rebels found a carefully composed photo album in his palace, featuring picture after picture of Secretary Rice. Perhaps this shouldn't have been a total surprise; after all, like a creepy stalker, the Libyan despot told Al-Jazeera in 2007, "Yes, Leezza, Leezza, Leezza... I love her very much."[12]

Gaddafi was clearly unhinged. His reign was oppressive, brutal, and vindictive. Clearly, Libya could do better with a less erratic leader. However, Libya in 2016 is without any leader at all.

The Western intervention in Libya involved nineteen countries, and not just the usual suspects. While France, the United Kingdom, and the United States conducted most combat flights, Norway and Denmark combined to drop 700 bombs during the air campaign. Several Arab states also backed the intervention. Between 19 March and 31 October 2011, coalition forces flew nearly 30,000 "sorties" in an attempt to tip the scales against the dictatorship and in favor of rebels painting themselves as committed democratic reformers.[13] As John McCain glowingly noted, "[The rebels'] Prime Minister got a doctorate at the University of Pittsburgh. Their Finance Minister was recently teaching economics in Seattle...others are lawyers, doctors, women activists."[14] British Foreign Secretary William Hague also chimed in, insisting that NATO air raids would produce a democratic Libya: "These people at the top of this organization are genuine believers in democracy and the rule of law. It is quite inspiring."[15]

Either the West was being fooled, or the rebels' commitment to genuine democracy was much weaker than the internal rivalries over who would wield power in a reconstructed Libyan state. This is the problem with sudden, militarized pushes for democracy from the outside: it is never clear what will take the despot's place, and there is little time to ensure that it's not just chaos.

Shortly after Gaddafi was killed, Libya began to spiral out of control. By 2015, the Libyan state had splintered, with two governments— one in Tobruk and one in Tripoli—each proclaiming control.[16] In reality, the on-the-ground control lies with militia commanders and warlords who hold the politicians in both capitals hostage. Taking advantage of the lawlessness, migrants have flooded out of Libya and into Europe. Extremists have entered Tunisia, prompting Libya's neighbor to build a wall along the length of its eastern border. But most importantly, the basic functions of the Libyan state have collapsed. It is a power vacuum, a politically anarchic abyss just a few hundred miles south of Europe. The promise of democracy hinted at by those pushing Western intervention has been replaced by the insecurity and volatility of a failed state.

This, of course, was certainly not the exclusive fault of the West. Libyans themselves did not learn from the mistakes made in Iraq. The Libyan "Political Isolation Law" mirrored de-Ba'athification attempts in Iraq, removing from Libya's political future anyone with any level of expertise, because they were considered "tainted" by Gaddafi, who had been in power since 1969. Moreover, the Central Bank of Libya has inexplicably continued to pay salaries to militiamen, effectively incentivizing young unemployed men to join warring factions, all while the bank funds both sides.[17] This truly bizarre situation shows precisely who the power-brokers in today's Libya are: the men with guns, the true forces behind dueling sham assemblies from Tobruk to Tripoli.

Anarchy is a dangerous thing in a world susceptible to terrorism. Osama Bin Laden gravitated toward Afghanistan like a moth to an ungoverned flame, knowing that a weak state would allow his operations a degree of anonymity and peace and quiet. Today, ISIS is using the same logic to set up footholds not only in Syria and Iraq but also in Libya. By early 2016, an estimated 6,500 ISIS fighters were based in Libya, a number that is steadily growing at the time of writing.[18]

This is the trouble with trying to spread democracy through the barrel of the gun. Just as shoppers are on the hook to purchase anything they break in a store, the West is on the hook to clean up the aftermaths of failed democracy wars abroad. "You break it, you own it" is a mantra that the West has learned the hard way in Iraq, Afghanistan, and Libya. While the West took that obligation seriously in Afghanistan and Iraq (even though their efforts have ultimately failed), similar support for Libya has not been forthcoming. Instead, the West tried to destroy the state from the air and then fly away. This doesn't work, which is why Western governments are now being enticed to engage in further airstrikes against ISIS within Libya, cleaning up the mess that they helped to make.

This is not to say that Western interventions at least tangentially driven by a democratizing agenda are evil attempts to destroy other countries for the fun of it—far from it. Many of the brave soldiers who gave their lives in each intervention understood their mission as a means to bring a better and freer life to an oppressed people. The conflicts' architects did not hope to sow chaos and provide a foothold to terrorists. But the inadvertent consequences of democracy wars are impossible to stomach. The number of analysts, politicians, and diplomats who think these three wars have had a net positive effect on the country in question are dwindling by the week as more bad news spills out of each quagmire. Unfortunately, the lesson that Western governments seem to have learned from these experiences is to shy away from democracy promotion altogether, preferring the devil we know. This is a mistake. Democracy cannot be spread with military force, but it can still be spread. However, now that the Pandora's Box of these three disastrous democracy wars has been opened, despots around the world are using those failed interventions to crack down on peaceful democracy promotion within their borders, claiming that it is just a pretext for democracy promotion with bombs. In that way, failed democracy wars have done extensive damage to democracy around the globe, not just to hopes for democracy in Afghanistan, Iraq, and Libya.

On 26 February 2016, the 2016 Republican presidential hopefuls squared off in a debate in Houston, Texas. Donald Trump, the frontrunner, delivered a blistering attack on military interventions aiming to establish democracy and instead defended Muammar Gaddafi and Saddam Hussein: "We would be so much better off if Qaddafi were in charge right now … and we had Saddam Hussein and if we had Qaddafi in charge … we would have been better off if the politicians took a day off instead of going into war." The fact that a US presidential candidate could heap backhanded praise on despots and dictators shows exactly how much damage these interventions has caused in Western thinking. The discourse of a decade ago couldn't have been more different. The twenty-first century's democracy wars were so disastrous that they risk Americans following Trump's seductive logic: if you can't get rid of them with force, then we should embrace them. That's absolutely the wrong approach, even though military interventions to support democracy are usually dangerous fool's errands.

The use of military force is always going to be a contentious topic. It is one of the most fateful decisions any country can make. But the evidence of the last fifteen years is crystal clear: spreading democracy with war does not work. Democracy does sometimes arise naturally from the aftermath of war, but Western governments are foolhardy to try to impose it externally. That doesn't mean that we should cozy up to despots and counterfeit democrats around the globe. It does mean that the justification for any future military interventions should be clearly dissociated from any stated aim to impose democracy with the sharp end of the West's very sharp stick. Only then can we move away from the "savage wars of peace" and toward a more meaningful and lasting democratic peace.

# 5

# THE CURSE OF LOW EXPECTATIONS

*Principle 3: Insist on real democracy and coordinate low-level and high-level diplomacy*

Since the end of the Cold War, a new norm has developed: rulers now have to at least pretend to be democratic. This is an important shift and it has, in some places, been a crucial force in advancing democracy. Sometimes, by going through the motions, countries do become more democratic.[1] For the most part, however, that progress has stalled and slipped backward. We are currently seeing a "hollowing out" of global democracy as countries around the world become empty shells, places where the pageantry of democracy looks attractive, but the substance is lacking. The West, unfortunately, is fueling this trend with two misguided policies.

First, there is what I call the Madagascar Effect, or the curse of low expectations: countries are routinely pressured to do only the bare minimum for democracy, and no more. Second, there is the West's gift to dictators and counterfeit democrats: the lack of coordination in Western foreign policy between high-level diplomacy and low-level, technical democracy promotion. Sometimes this takes the form of rosy statements by diplomats and higher-level government officials overshadowing election observation reports—which are often accurate, technical assessments of election quality. At other times, it occurs when low-level democracy promotion programs are undermined by much more powerful diplomatic support for the authoritarian regime. This mismatch plays into the hands of despotic governments, giving them a chance to legitimize their authoritarian rule by capitalizing on low-level reforms rather than any substantial changes to the system itself.

Both these policies need to change if the retreat of meaningful democracy is to be reversed. Azerbaijan showcases the effects of both. In 2013, Azerbaijan was the eleventh most authoritarian country in the world. Put differently, 94 per cent of the world's countries were more democratic than Azerbaijan at that time (the proportion is roughly the same in 2016).[2] The president, Ilham Aliyev, was and is, like his father before him, a caricature of a dictator. Corruption is so rampant that in 2010, the president's son—an 11-year-old boy—purchased nine waterfront mansions in Dubai worth a total of $44 million. The average citizen of Azerbaijan would have to work for 10,000 years to afford the mansions. This was difficult to explain for the president, who officially subsists on a salary of around $250,000. When reporters asked the reasonable question, "How was it that an 11 year-old is able to afford nine waterfront homes when his father claims to have a modest head-of-state salary?", the presidential spokesman responded, "I have no comment on anything. I am stopping this talk. Goodbye."[3] This is typical Azerbaijan—opaque governance and slammed-down phones, because transparency would expose the inner workings of a dictatorship run on cronyism rather than popular legitimacy.

As a result, everyone knew that, yet again, the 2013 elections would be a charade. But nobody expected them to be such a blatant joke— one that probably wasn't funny to the people of Azerbaijan.

In the run-up to the election, the opposition coalesced behind the Oscar-winning film director Rustam Ibragimbekov. As a director, Igrabimbekov had created the cult Soviet classic *The White Sun of the Desert* (1966) which, to this day, is screened for cosmonauts as a good luck omen before they blast off into space. But his challenge against Aliyev was much more short-lived than his film's cult legacy; Aliyev's regime quickly disqualified Ibragimbekov because he had both Azerbaijani and Russian citizenship. As a result, the campaign proceeded with only token opposition as usual.

The election was scheduled for 9 October 2013. In anticipation of the big day, the Aliyev regime had decided to showcase its technological savvy by creating an iPhone app that would provide up-to-date vote tallies as returns came in after polls closed. The app was released and ready to go. But then, something strange happened. The day before the election, people who had downloaded the app were surprised to find that it had updated results from the election that was supposed to take place the following day—complete results for all the candidates, including turnout by district. Nobody had voted yet. The government spokesman tried to cover-up the absurd gaffe by claiming that it was simply reiterating results from the previous election. That didn't convince many people, because the candidate names had been updated and the results and turnout figures were different from the previous election's results. The ridiculous spectacle of Azerbaijan's rigged elections had been exposed. The results had been decided (and inadvertently announced) before the polls had even opened, as the government boasted about precisely how many Azerbaijanis had deemed it worth their time to vote for their dictator. Comically, after the gaffe had been made public, the regime attempted to cover up its mistake by releasing different official results the following day—with an even larger landslide victory than the app had suggested.[4]

The iPhone blunder exposed the worst-kept secret in Baku—that Azerbaijani elections were always a complete sham. Nobody was really surprised to have those suspicions confirmed. What was surprising, however, was the Western reaction to an election that was stolen before polls even opened.

The rigging had started well before election day: the main opposition candidate had been excluded; the opposition had been given extremely limited media time; and intimidation (against voters and candidates alike) was rampant. On election day itself, foreign observers in 58 per cent of polling locations documented serious fraud or manipulation.[5] Observers actually witnessed thirty-seven instances of ballot box stuffing right in front of them. The number of ballots cast rarely matched the official tally. This was a textbook example of how to rig an election.

Every step of the way, the technical, on-the-ground experts robustly documented how the entire vote was deeply flawed from the start. They did their job. But the high-level message coming from the West was completely different. A Congressional delegation from the United States fawned over the quality of the election. Former representative Michael McMahon, a Democrat from New York, said the election was "honest, fair, and really efficient." He was impressed by the short queues of voters (perhaps because a lot of people weren't actually voting, but were having their ballots stuffed into ballot boxes). A contingent from the Parliamentary Assembly of the Council of Europe and the European Parliament echoed these flowery sentiments, saying, "Overall around Election Day we have observed a free, fair and transparent electoral process... From what we have seen, electoral procedures on the eve and on Election Day have been carried out in a professional and peaceful way."[6] It is probably true that the ballot box stuffing was done peacefully, and the henchmen who did it are certainly pros, but that doesn't mean it was free or fair. It was neither.

Azerbaijan holds strategic importance for the United States for its position as an oil transit point from the Caspian Sea. Moreover, Aliyev helped the West by deploying a limited number of troops to assist with the wars in Iraq and Afghanistan. He allowed coalition bombers to refuel on Azerbaijan's airstrips. So there are reasons why the West might want to airbrush the election's extensive blemishes. Even so, this was a remarkable show of hypocrisy at the high level, even while the low-level assessment was spot on. The bar was set so low that even Azerbaijan could clear it, and then mixed international messages allowed Aliyev to seize the positive comments to paint his "re-election" in a positive light, all with the help of Western apologists.[7]

This schizophrenic message from the West, with ground-level democracy promotion tools (like the election monitors' reports) condemning an election and international diplomacy voicing little concern, is a problem. Not only does such behavior entrench dictators but it also leaves pro-democracy reformers caught in the crossfire of mixed messages between high-level diplomacy and low-level technical assessments. Furthermore, it provides absolutely no reason for autocrats like Aliyev to change. After all, he carried out one of the most obvious election riggings in modern history, and still received praise from top-level Western figures. If that's not a recipe for business as usual, I don't know what is. The West was complicit in undermining democratic reformers in Azerbaijan.

This hasn't, however, stopped the West from its quixotic spending to promote democracy in Azerbaijan. United States taxpayers have dumped $55 million in democracy promotion on Azerbaijan since the early 1990s. From 2007 to 2011, USAID spent $5.6 million to "enhance the overall effectiveness" of Azerbaijan's parliament.[8] This included a training initiative to "solidify [the parliament's] own sense of identity." It was a colossal waste of money because the parliament is a meaningless rubber stamp for Aliyev. A candid government assessment of the program found that the funding for training had no effect on Azerbaijan's democracy, or even on the functioning of the parliament. Low-level democracy programming was rendered useless by high-level diplomatic support for the regime.

Azerbaijan is not necessarily a representative case, however, because it could be categorized under the "Saudi Arabia Effect": geostrategic interests reduce Western pressure for democratic reforms. What happens in countries on the global periphery? Is the experience the same for nations that have absolutely no strategic value for the United States and its Western allies? Surely those are the cases where a high bar can be set and principles can trump pragmatism; after all, it should arguably be easier to be principled when there are so few core interests at stake.

In 2012, I took the first of many trips to Madagascar, the world's fourth largest island and a place that is as isolated politically as it is geographically. Many Western diplomats have probably never even heard of the capital, Antananarivo. When I called my bank to let them know not to block my debit card if I bought something on the island, the cheery customer service representative said, "Madagascar? I thought that was a children's cartoon. Are you sure that's a country?" I assured her that the cartoon was named after the country, not the reverse, and that it is a very real country that 23 million individuals call home, even though very few people take any notice of them.

Madagascar is also a paragon of counterfeit democracy. The nation has elections, and those elections even sometimes result in peaceful transfers of power. But the elections themselves are severely flawed. Illicit money buys campaigns. Coups and coup attempts are regular occurrences. In 2006, a major opposition candidate was denied the opportunity to stand in the election after the president stopped him from coming home by unilaterally closing down the island's airports—

just as his plane was about to start its descent. The flight was turned around several times as it approached the airport, as the president toyed with his opponent.[9] This is a place that looks like a democracy from the outside, but is obviously not one once you take a closer look inside (if, unlike the opposition leader, you can make it in).

To understand why Madagascar always seems stuck between dictatorship and democracy, I found myself calling General Desiré-Philippe Ramakavélo, a retired Malagasy general who had previously served as minister of the armed forces and continues to have major sway over the island's politics. I'll never forget that phone call, which taught me plenty about the ways that informal power and strongmen, much more than formal political institutions, dominate politics in Madagascar. We were speaking in French, but here's what was said:

"Hello, yes, General Ramakavélo—I'm hoping to speak with you. I'm a researcher studying democracy in Madagascar and—"

"Hello. Don't say stupid things. There is no democracy in Madagascar."

"Okay, well, I'd still like to speak to you about the lack of democracy then. Would that be possible?"

"Breakfast. 8am. Tomorrow. My house."

"Oh, okay, sure that sounds great. Could you give me directions or maybe a landmark to—"

"Are you taking a taxi?"

"Yes."

"Just tell them you want to see General Ramakavélo. They'll know what to do."

And then, with a click, he was gone.

The next morning, bewildered, I flagged down a passing taxi and told the driver, somewhat sheepishly it must be said, that I wanted to see General Ramakavélo. He nodded simply, and fired up his 1960s Citroën Deux Chevaux, a car that resembles the vintage Volkswagen Beetle in both style and age. The motor hummed to life. I got in, and was surprised to find that there was no floor on the passenger side. The driver pointed to two metal rails that were the remains of a collapsed footwell, and I put one foot on each, straddling the gaping hole. We set off, and I watched the colonial-era cobblestone streets of this forgotten capital city pass below the car as we lumbered Fred Flintstone-style up and down Antananarivo's dusty hills, en route to see the fabled general.

Soon, we arrived at the base of a steep hill. The taxi driver pointed to an imposing house at the top. As I approached the house, General Ramakavélo—a distinguished-looking man with swept-back peppery gray hair—emerged and welcomed me warmly. After the phone call, I didn't know what to expect. But whatever I was hoping for, I was not disappointed. After shaking my hand, General Ramakavelo got right down to business: "Ask me your questions," he said.

I opened with a question about Western support for democracy in Madagascar—whether it had been effective, whether it was useful, and whether he was pleased to see the West helping his country. The general paused, got up from the couch, grabbed a small leather bound book, and sat back down. "I think," he said, "that the only way to answer your question, is with one of my poems."

He proceeded to read several to me. They were all beautifully written. But the one that stuck out was called *Langouste*, "the rock lobster". The gist of it was that Madagascar was a rock lobster, a spiny creature that walks backward in the eyes of the West, which couldn't care less which way it walked. "It doesn't matter that it walks backward, so long as you can get its succulent meat," he explained as he finished reading. "The West cares about democracy in name only here. As long as we have elections, they can go back to business. If we have a coup, they get worried, they complain, and eventually, we hold elections. It doesn't matter if they are any good. Then the cycle repeats itself."

General Ramakavélo does acknowledge, however, that Western pressure has changed political dynamics in Madagascar. When I asked him how Western pressure had shifted the island's politics, he had his answer ready to go.

"Do you know what I did when we had a political crisis in 1991?"

"Refresh my memory," I replied.

"You see the hotel at the base of the hill, the Panorama? Well, back then, just like now, we had some politicians that wouldn't get along. I picked them up, made them come with me, forced them both into the hotel, locked them inside, and told them they could leave when they signed an agreement. They signed what became known as the 'Panorama Convention' in that hotel. It ushered in Madagascar's first multi-party elections. Unfortunately," he finished with a sigh, "you can't do things like that anymore. They would condemn it immediately."

The "they" he was referring to was Western governments, and he's almost certainly right; if a general in a geopolitically unimportant country like Madagascar kidnapped civilian political leaders and locked them in a hotel for a few days in 2016, it would conjure up a wave of condemnation from across the Western world. Today, particularly in strategically unimportant places, there may be more of an appetite for actually enforcing baseline democratic principles (which is why coups are bluntly condemned in Madagascar but swept under the rug and called something else in Egypt). However, being geopolitically unimportant is, in some ways, the worst of both worlds. The West will insist on democracy (what is there to lose?), but will force halfhearted democratization. The principled approach is only committed to an extremely low baseline of democratic procedures. As long as it looks like a democracy from a distance, that's often good enough. Countries like Madagascar (rightly) feel the ire of the West when they clearly gravitate toward authoritarianism, but then are given every incentive to create only a counterfeit democracy. This helps to trap countries between dictatorship and democracy.

Part of this halfhearted baseline comes from something that I call "electoral grade inflation." In universities and colleges, professors often lament grade inflation, wherein the average score gravitates toward an "A" to avoid dooming students' career prospects—even if their work actually deserves a "B" or "C". The same thing happens all the time in elections, particularly as the lexicon of election monitoring does not allow for much nuance. Pick up a newspaper after an important election has happened in an "emerging democracy" (itself a terrible euphemism) and I'll bet you that the words "free and fair" appear in the story. Occasionally, the words "not free and fair" appear, but that is rare.

This dichotomy is problematic for two reasons. First, having a pass/fail approach to elections is counterproductive. Try comparing elections in Iceland with elections in Sierra Leone. Now grade them with the same rubric. Do both pass? Does one fail? Their political systems are vastly different. Sierra Leone is in the nascent stages of democratization while Iceland has a democratic heritage that spans more than a thousand years, but the prevailing language that observers have to work boils down to "free and fair" or "not free and fair."[10] It doesn't make sense. There needs to be a better way to show progress without outright condemnation and some way to show regression without outright praise. That nuance, which exists in most election reports, is lost at the journalistic and diplomatic level. Those are the messages that make a political splash, not the lengthy, technical election reports.

Second, when elections are considered "not free and fair," it can tie the hands of Western governments that have admirably formed a political determination not to dispatch foreign aid to countries that have fundamentally unfair elections. As a result, election observers—which are a huge force for democratization around the globe generally—may sometimes nonetheless hesitate to condemn an election outright, knowing that their classification could doom the country to an economic recession; in places like Madagascar, the loss of foreign aid is a crushing blow that will wipe out much-needed economic growth for years. Western governments may also hesitate to certify such a classification, particularly if they have ongoing aid operations or trade links with the country in question. As a result, for an election to be condemned it usually needs both to be egregiously and blatantly rigged and to take place in a country that either holds no geostrategic interest for the West, or is a perceived enemy of the West.

I served with the Carter Center as an election observer in Madagascar's 2013 poll. The election was blighted by many undemocratic warts. Two major candidates had been excluded from participating, and one had previously taken power in a coup. Illicit funding was the main source of campaign financing with no transparency or oversight.[11] And, perhaps worst of all, the last population census was undertaken in 1993—twenty years before the election—which meant that millions of voters were kept off the voting rolls.[12] To try to address the problem, Madagascar sent a patchwork group of officials door-to-door in an attempt to register voters; it was uneven at best and left large parts of the island uncovered. Imagine something similar happening in France, Japan, or the Netherlands, and people saying that, yes, a few million people were denied the right to vote, but overall it was a good election. It would be unthinkable. But it's what happened in Madagascar.

The Carter Center, to its credit, avoided a caricature of Madagascar's elections; it is the Center's policy to avoid phrases like "(not) free and fair" in its reports. In 2013, it documented flaws carefully and systematically; such reports are hugely important weapons against despotism. But others fell into the usual traps of false dichotomies and excessive praise. The EU's chief election observer, María Muñiz de Urquiza, declared the elections "free, transparent, and credible" after just a few hundred ballots had been counted.[13] It's hard to see how the vote was credible, when the margins between candidates were exceedingly narrow while millions were left off the voter rolls. "Free, transparent, and credible" are words that would never be used for a similarly dubious election if it happened in Ireland or Belgium, but such lofty phrases were regularly bandied about in Madagascar after a severely flawed vote.

There is one surprising reason for this—yet another case of good intentions that produce bad results. One election official from the EU mission told me that they had been instructed to endorse the election "unless lots of people got killed." This was because the EU had already earmarked hundreds of millions of dollars of aid to Madagascar, but the funding had not been disbursed since 2009 because the government had been toppled in a coup, whose leaders were isolated by the EU in a principled, pro-democracy stance. The EU never expected, however, that the coup government would stay in power for nearly five years. In order to help Madagascar, the logic went, the election had to be endorsed—no matter its quality. Several monitors I've spoken with in diverse elections have told me that they routinely experience some form of pressure to focus on the positives. This is particularly likely in observation groups funded by or affiliated with governments that have serious diplomatic "skin in the game."

This shows the full circle of Western activity in a non-strategic country—from a principled approach post-coup to later sweeping electoral scabs under the proverbial rug as a means to re-legitimize the government in order to disburse long-earmarked foreign aid. Ultimately, the outcomes in Azerbaijan and in Madagascar were similar, even though their geopolitical positions are different. The curse of low expectations gave no incentive for further improvements beyond the pitifully low benchmark for democracy set by Western governments. Keep in mind, too, that elections are just one component of functional democracy, though elections are given disproportionate influence in Western foreign policy assessments. Often, what happens after an election is equally, if not more, important for the democratic health of a nation. The fetishization of elections helps further entrench low expectations once the dust has cleared from voting.

In particular, the time between elections is when the democracy promotion industry is critical. These are the programs that you rarely hear about but that do important work: training to help the political system become more inclusive; technical assistance to political parties by demonstrating models that other countries have used to develop party manifestos; or showcasing possible models drawn from all over the world for writing a democratic constitution. These are important and necessary features of any Western attempt to support and spread democracy abroad. But they are not working, at least not nearly as well as they should be. They are far too often the victims of contradictory high-level diplomacy that ends up bolstering despots rather than prodding them to reform and embrace democratic change.

Rwanda showcases this problem brilliantly. The tiny landlocked country is not Azerbaijan—there are no major Western strategic interests at stake in Kigali. So, as with Madagascar, you might mistakenly expect the West's democratic bar to be high in Rwanda. As in Madagascar, you would be disappointed.

Known as the Land of a Thousand Hills for its rugged terrain, Rwanda is infamous for playing host to one of the grisliest genocides of modern times. Some 800,000 ethnic Tutsis were hacked to death by Hutus wielding machetes. Often the perpetrators and their victims were even neighbors or friends, pushed to despicable acts by ethnic demagogues. After the initial killing stopped in Rwanda, it spilled over into refugee camps across the border, in the Democratic Republic of the Congo, sparking one of the greatest mass-casualty conflicts in African history. Hutus and Tutsis alike died on a tragic scale.

When the dust settled and a precarious peace returned, Paul Kagame—the former military commander of the Rwandan Patriotic Front Tutsi rebel group—was the man at the top. He ruled through a puppet until 2000 and then formally took power. Since taking charge, Kagame has turned the country's economy around with impressive results, but he did so as a despot with virtually no tolerance for opposition or resistance. Kagame has been masterful at using low-level democracy promotion (programs aimed at forcing democratic reforms on the ground) to ensure that he doesn't have to reform at all. In other words, he has taken the West's agenda and turned it around to undermine the West's stated goals. Kagame has co-opted the low-level activities adopted by Western governments to support democracy in Rwanda and used those efforts as tools to entrench his authoritarian regime.

For example, groups like the National Democratic Institute (NDI) and USAID have spent heavily on encouraging Rwanda's government to include women in politics. That is an excellent goal, not to say a lesson that the donor countries should heed themselves. However, Kagame has used this pressure to create further strength for his savvy brand of authoritarianism. In response to Western cajoling and foreign aid investments, Kagame has helped ensure that Rwanda leads the world in terms of its representation of women in parliament. Women hold fifty-one out of eighty seats in Rwanda's lower house (nearly 64 per cent, far better than the United States, on 19 per cent; Sweden is the best Western country by that metric, with 44 per cent).[14] Rwanda's success on this front has allowed the country to continue extracting tens of millions of dollars of "democracy and good governance" aid from the United States alone, not to mention similar investments from donors across Western Europe.

This matters because Kagame is one of Africa's premier spin-doctors, marrying aspects of "good governance" that the West prizes (like women's representation in parliament) with strong economic growth, guided by his firm and despotic hand. As a result, he can point to those important and real achievements, while being dismissive of more substantive critiques of his dictatorial reign. The correct way to see female representation in Rwanda is as follows: it's wonderful that an enfeebled parliament has a lot of women in it, but it's still an enfeebled parliament that inevitably must bow to a single male despot. Is that true progress? What really matters is whether parliament has a voice, not the gender of the people who are silenced within it.

Regardless, Kagame's gender equity masterstroke has worked brilliantly. And that's the problem. Admirable and well-intentioned democracy promotion programs get overshadowed and ultimately undermined by diplomacy that parrots Kagame's lines about being a reformer, when he is truly nothing of the sort. Kagame actually uses the low-level democracy promotion as a rhetorical tool to defuse and deflect meaningful pressure. Western leaders have taken the bait, hook, line, and sinker. Tony Blair called Kagame "a visionary leader."[15] Bill Clinton fawned that he was "one of the greatest leaders of our time."[16] Bono, U2's frontman, routinely presents him as a model for other leaders in developing countries. Consequently, he has been referred to as "the global elite's favorite strongman."[17]

There are two sides to President Kagame the despot: one positive, one negative. Both present difficult conundrums about the merits of democracy and dictatorship in post-conflict zones that need, some may argue, economic growth and stability more than anything.

On the positive side, Kagame's leadership has arguably produced the greatest economic turnaround in any post-conflict country since the Cold War. It is certainly the most striking achievement in sub-Saharan Africa, as he took a war-torn basket case with 800,000 bodies in the streets and churned out steady economic growth that, at times, approached double digits. His success comes from a micro-manager's attention to detail, using authoritarian methods to insist on achieving clear results. For example, Kagame's *imihigo* program forces government officials to sign contracts for the results they are expected to deliver, and all of them are meticulously benchmarked. This is not just about big initiatives; local officials even sign contracts to ensure that they will produce the correct number of inseminated cows in their district … or else.[18] With this method, Kagame delivers. Aid agencies—which are almost always focused on measurable outcomes—tend to love him. Money comes in. Results come out.

This invites a deeper question. Is the price of democracy worth it? Rwanda was war-torn; now it's peaceful. The economy was broken; now it's thriving. Hutus and Tutsis were butchering each other for years; now they co-exist. Maybe Kagame is onto something. This is the seductive logic that has allowed superficial democratic "reforms" to obscure Kagame's true face as a despot, all with the support of fawning Western diplomats. Are Rwandans better off as a sort of African Singapore? Are we certain that similarly powerful economic results would be impossible under a more democratic system?

Kagame's micro-managing attention to detail isn't always a good thing. In banal ways, it infringes on basic freedoms; dirty clothes are outlawed and sharing straws is prohibited (both laws are enforced). Alice Muhirwa, a member of the opposition, explained to *The New York Times*: "It's like there's an invisible eye everywhere… Kagame's eye."[19]

Beyond the straws and the inseminated cows, though, Rwanda's despotic elite silences dissent in more meaningful ways, sometimes viciously. There have been an alarming number of politically motivated abductions in recent years. Some jailed dissidents have mysteriously died in custody. For ordinary Rwandans, these tales are enough to teach them that free speech does not exist in the Land of a Thousand Hills. Amazingly, though, it doesn't exist for Rwandans abroad either, as many of the government's opponents who have slipped through the net and gone into exile have later been assassinated. The story of these hit squads would have been covered up, swept under the rug like so much in Rwanda, had it not been for the brave journalism of Judi Rever and Geoffrey York of Canada's *Globe & Mail*.

In 2011, Colonel Dan Munyuza, the director of Rwandan military intelligence and a close adviser to Kagame, contacted Robert Higiro, a former Rwandan military officer living in exile. Higiro was asked to do a job: kill two enemies of President Kagame—Colonel Karegeya and General Nyamwasa. Higiro agreed, sensing that this was more of a threat-based order than a request. However, rather than proceed, he tipped off the intended targets and recorded the phone conversations with Kagame's right-hand man: "The price is not a problem. We will show our appreciation if things are beautifully done. They will be rewarded." Higiro asked for $1.5 million to carry out the hit; Munyuza suggested $1 million instead. The men agreed. The point, the intelligence chief insisted, was to ensure that nobody else talked badly about Kagame in the future. "If we managed to hit both of them ... others would shut up."[20]

Though Higiro tipped off Colonel Karegeya, it was to no avail. When Higiro didn't go through with the plot, the government found someone else. Karegeya was strangled to death with a towel in an upscale Johannesburg hotel room. Two Rwandans had booked rooms across the hall from the colonel; they flew back to Kigali the morning after Karegeya had been murdered. The other target, General Nyamwasa, is still alive—barely. He has a bullet lodged in his spine from a previous assassination attempt in South Africa, and has escaped three other attacks miraculously unharmed.

Kagame's reach extends well beyond South Africa. In March 2011, he was a guest on a BBC radio program. Rene Claudel Mugenzi, a Rwandan activist living in exile in the United Kingdom, called into the show and asked whether an Arab Spring-like revolution might happen in Rwanda, as a popular uprising toppled the authoritarian regime. Just weeks later, Mugenzi received a letter—hand delivered by the Metropolitan Police—warning that "Reliable intelligence states that the Rwandan government poses an imminent threat to your life." Mugenzi is thankfully still alive, but British intelligence doesn't issue such warnings lightly, and the threat still exists. At a minimum, Mugenzi received a powerful message from Kagame's shadowy entourage.[21]

In Rwanda, political opponents disappear, are abducted, or jailed. Should we still be thrilled that there are a high proportion of women in its rubber-stamp parliament?

Western governments seem to think so. The West is funding Kagame's administration, even though they try to claim that they do not fund despotic regimes. 30 to 40 per cent of all Rwandan government spending comes from foreign aid. And, as political scientists and economists have demonstrated convincingly, even earmarked aid slated for specific purposes is "fungible," meaning that money from Western governments can simply free up existing funds for use in indirectly financing clientele networks, repression, military arms, and other nefarious efforts.[22] Kagame certainly takes advantage of precisely that. Western tax dollars are bolstering the Rwandan government's efforts to oppress its citizens, stifle dissent, and even kill its enemies.

This strategy is counterproductive to Western interests. Kagame's rule has left a sizeable portion of Rwandans disillusioned with their government. Because of his ruthless intolerance for dissent, their grievances are simmering below the political surface, held under Kagame's tight lid. But when the transition comes away from Kagame, as it eventually will, Western backing of his authoritarianism could backfire, provoking far greater instability and strife than would otherwise occur. Helping an authoritarian ruler stay in power beyond their popular welcome almost never ends well; it usually produces more volatility and conflict.

Moreover, think of what Western support for Kagame does for other leaders in the region. If you were the president of Burundi, or the Democratic Republic of the Congo, and you saw Western leaders falling over themselves trying to tout Kagame's leadership, wouldn't you feel like mimicking him was a good idea? Leaders of both nations have begun to do exactly that, most recently by moving to unilaterally extend their time in office beyond the constitutional limits, a tactic learned from their despotic neighbor. In late 2015, Kagame's regime also changed Rwanda's constitution, allowing him to extend his rule as far as 2034. If he can last that long, nearly forty years will have elapsed since anyone but Kagame held power in Rwanda.[23]

Now, for the first time since 1994, Kagame's status as the West's darling is beginning to come under fire. At last, there are signs that high-level diplomats are removing the wool from their eyes and seeing the bigger picture. In mid-2015, with the constitutional referendum pending, President Obama offered a pointed (and not so subtle) jab at Kagame's leadership: "When a leader tries to change the rules in the middle of the game just to stay in office, it risks instability and strife... And this is often just a first step down a perilous path."[24]

Obama's more pointed rhetoric may provide hope after all that democracy promotion efforts in Rwanda could be unusually harmonious, with low-level programming and high-level diplomatic rhetoric marshaled in pursuit of a genuine democratic goal. But if the preponderance of evidence around the globe in recent years is any guide, Rwanda is unlikely to face a truly high bar for what constitutes democracy. Instead, it is likely that Western governments would be contented with bare-bones reforms, perhaps bringing Rwanda closer to the Madagascar model, where the illusion of democracy at least looks good from the outside and international assassination plots come to an end. Until then, though, Rwandans—like billions of others around the world—will continue to be cursed by the West's low expectations.

6

# BACKING THE WRONG HORSE

*Principle 4: Do not directly intervene in foreign elections*

One of the annoying things about democracy is that other people often don't feel the same way that you do. Worse still, sometimes those people outnumber you. Democracy forces people with radically different opinions to co-exist in the same society. In international relations, that's an unavoidable problem. In order to truly support democracy, Western governments have to support the integrity of the electoral process—even if it could result in a government that the West finds abhorrent, reckless, and even terroristic. Respecting that people should have a choice in selecting their government necessarily means respecting their ability to make their own choice.

For many Western governments, that inevitable price of democracy is too high. Rather than risk it, they intervene, trying to influence the outcome of the election—sometimes covertly—in order to stop their enemies from coming to power. Trying to pick winners and losers is almost always a case of backing the wrong horse, because it's illegitimate and undemocratic for foreign governments to actively manipulate another government's internal affairs. Governments are completely free to indicate their support for a certain party, or politician, in foreign elections. They are free to suggest that diplomatic consequences may follow if a certain party wins. The line is crossed, in my view, when foreign intervention involves critical funding for one party at the expense of another, aiming to sway the election from how it would have unfolded in the absence of foreign intervention.

That's the liberal foreign policy side of my brain talking. But even to the *realpolitik* side, it is becoming clear that preferential backing in foreign elections often backfires, gift-wrapping the election for the very party that Western governments were hoping to undermine. In other words, even if you don't care about the normative value of non-interference in foreign elections, it's worth considering how it can often be counterproductive to Western interests. And, as was the case in the 1953 coup in Iran, meddling in the internal affairs of other governments can sometimes seem like a good idea at the time, only to create an enemy that endures for decades. Even in hard-nosed conceptions of foreign policy, election interventions are therefore not usually a good long-term foreign policy strategy.

Nonetheless, regional or global powers have been backing allies in key elections for decades. The CIA worked aggressively to derail the Italian left in the 1948 elections.[1] The United States likely helped sway the vote against Nicaragua's Sandinista president Daniel Ortega in 1990.[2] Western advisers also worked with the Serbian opposition to help in their fight against Slobodan Milošević.

Intervening in elections is not, however, a phenomenon exclusive to the West. India aimed to influence the 2008 elections in Nepal, swaying Nepalese voters to support parties that would uphold India's key foreign affairs priorities.[3] In Lebanon's 2009 elections, a key battleground in the Middle East power rivalry between Iran and Saudi Arabia, the Saudi government alone spent hundreds of millions of dollars in the race (even though Lebanon is only home to 4 million people). The money was used to bankroll a massive vote buying campaign, with foreign financing driving up the average cost per vote to above $800. Foreign governments also provided free plane tickets to expatriate Lebanese to return home to vote, on the condition that they back the "right" party.[4] In other words, Western governments certainly do not have a monopoly on meddling in elections abroad.

However, this strategy has increasingly been viewed as a viable option in the West, especially in the twenty-first century. As the failed and hugely costly interventions in Iraq and Afghanistan dragged on,

realists in the Western foreign policy establishment began to see intervention in elections as a sort of "bargain" form of regime change: all the
perks, with none of the costly clean-up—or so the thinking went.

In 2002, just a year after taking office, President Bush articulated a
new approach for resolving the Israel/Palestine conflict. The strategy
revolved around a new push for Palestinians to hold credible elections.
It was essential, President Bush argued in a speech, to forge "a working
democracy for the Palestinian people."[5] It took three and a half years,
but Bush's vision came to fruition in early 2006. It became a classic
foreign policy case of "be careful what you wish for".

For the United States, Israel, and Western allies with similar interests
in the region, the elections were an unmitigated disaster. On 25 January
2006, Palestinians voted in a poll that was considered by most international observers to be highly credible. There may have been some "electoral grade inflation" at play, of course, but generally, the elections were
not heavily flawed. In the eyes of the United States, the same could not
be said of the winner. Hamas, a militant, Islamist party, won the elections
with a clear mandate from the Palestinian voters. This was highly unwel-
come news for the United States. Now an organization that was officially
designated as a terrorist group was in power, and it could claim the
mantle of popular legitimacy derived from a genuine election. That same
legitimacy was now lost for American's preferred partner, the Fatah faction of the Palestine Liberation Organization (PLO).

Fatah had made itself unpopular. The party allowed its members to
engage in sustained political corruption that tainted its image with voters. Hamas capitalized on this, displaying a superior level of party discipline and "clean" politics. Hamas rode its anti-corruption message all the
way to victory. But corruption alone did not create the stunning electoral
rebuke of Fatah. The United States helped ensure it, with its biased (and
arguably counterproductive) partisan electoral support for Fatah in the
years, months, and days before Palestinians went to the polls.

Political scientists have classified two types of foreign (and particularly Western) involvement in elections abroad. The first type is partisan engagement, wherein a foreign power actively backs a specific
party or candidate at the expense of others. The second is process
engagement, wherein the foreign power takes an even-handed approach,
supporting democratic institutions and processes (such as the indepen-

dent election commission) rather than weighing in on a particular side. In preliminary research, scholars have found evidence that partisan engagement can damage democracy by polarizing the electorate and crippling moderates—a group of people who are usually critical to the success of any sort of democratic consolidation. Without moderates, the risk of a democratic reversal increases substantially. Process engagement doesn't necessarily help much, but it does less harm.[6]

In the 2006 Palestinian elections, the United States decided on a strategy of polarizing partisan engagement rather than supporting the democratic process more broadly. In Washington, there was a clear view: Hamas could not be allowed to win the elections, as this would deal a deadly blow to prospects for peace in the region. A terrorist group could not become the legitimately elected representative of the Palestinian people. This was an understandable perspective, and I have absolutely no love for Hamas. However, by actively and directly supporting Fatah in the election campaign, the United States likely fueled a Hamas victory.

As it became clear that the Palestinian Authority was heading toward elections, the Bush administration scaled up aid to President Mahmoud Abbas' Fatah-led government. In 2004, the United States provided roughly $75 million to the Palestinian Authority to help it govern. But in the year leading up to elections, that figure more than tripled to $275 million (accounting for more than 7 per cent of all Palestinian Authority expenditures that year).[7] This was not a solely American intervention. Adding in funding from the EU, hundreds of millions went to help the Fatah faction "meet their payrolls, field their security forces, make welfare payments and build infrastructure."[8] This was intended as a sort of trickle-down diplomacy, hoping that Western-funded governance successes would translate to electoral victory for Fatah.

But the intervention went beyond simply bolstering Fatah's ability to govern; the Bush administration also stripped an earmarked expenditure of $45–75 million that had been slated for a desalinization plant in the Gaza Strip.[9] This was a shrewd move, because Gaza was (and is) known as a Hamas stronghold and a weak point for Fatah. By stripping funding from that area and reallocating it to the West Bank, the United States was using clean water as an electoral weapon, aimed at making it easier for Fatah to provide for the population at the expense of

Hamas. The thinking in Washington was that such a move could only bolster Fatah's credibility going into the elections.

That longer-term financial support was also matched with a critical pre-election push, as the Bush administration also quietly disbursed $2 million in emergency pre-election funding to Fatah just before the election. Bizarrely, those American tax dollars were used just before voting began to pay for a Palestinian youth soccer tournament, a tree planting ceremony, and a last-minute street cleaning initiative.[10] Each basically functioned as a high-profile Fatah rally linked to a project that enjoyed widespread popular support. The projects coincided with a major US-funded publicity campaign showcasing these initiatives—and others from the previous year—as a means to highlight Fatah leadership in the Palestinian Authority.

Critically, however, the US broke its own rules in spending these emergency funds. When USAID spends money, the organization is supposed to publicize that funding as a means of generating public awareness that American taxpayers are helping another country in a time of need. Yet in this case, the United States government recognized that such publicity would almost certainly backfire; only about a fifth of Palestinians held a favorable or somewhat favorable view of the United States at the time, so linking President Bush to Fatah would have been an obvious blunder. The decision to ensure that USAID would not publicly be associated with Fatah's electoral campaign was justified euphemistically as a "temporary paradigm shift."[11]

Unfortunately for the United States, the story broke before the elections. The United States, in yet another instance of Orwellian double-speak, attempted to claim that it was not taking sides when it was doing precisely that. James A. Bever, the director of West Bank and Gaza operations for USAID, explained: "We are not favoring any particular party... But we do not support parties that are on the terrorism list. We are here to support the democratic process."[12] In other words, "We are not supporting any particular party... But we do not support Hamas. We are here to support the democratic process so long as Fatah wins."

Palestinians can read between the lines. They knew that the US was actively backing Fatah and actively working against Hamas, and had spent $2 million in emergency disbursements to sway the vote. While $2 million pales in comparison to other Western disbursements in the

Palestinian Territories, it dwarfed local spending by the political parties themselves (one estimate suggests that Hamas spent less than $1 million during the campaign). Many people who were on the fence may have been swayed against Fatah, with its image even more tarnished by its unpopular Western allies. It would be impossible to prove that American support for Fatah ensured a Hamas victory, but it is likely— particularly as the margin of victory was narrow.

Hamas won. The peace process stalled then regressed. A week after the election results were announced, someone fired a Qassam rocket into a kibbutz south of Ashkelon; four people, including a one-year-old baby, were injured as the rocket caused a roof collapse.[13] Intelligence sources indicated that Hamas had likely sponsored the attack—one of many more to come.[14] The electoral result took Washington completely by surprise. Condoleeza Rice, the American secretary of state (and long-shot object of Muammar Gaddafi's affections) spoke of the elections blindsiding the administration: "I've asked why nobody saw it coming. It does say something about us not having a good enough pulse."[15] Perhaps, but it may also be a case of a misguided electoral intervention backfiring at a critical time—a time when the narrowest of margins could be swayed by the perception of foreign influence run amok in a highly sensitive political climate.

Another post-mortem of the election offered a different take. Martin Indyk, a seasoned Middle East negotiator from the Clinton administration, argued that "There is a lot of blame to go around. But on the American side, the conceptual failure that contributed to disaster was the president's belief that democracy and elections solve everything."[16]

Indyk's argument is a broader critique of democracy promotion and one that I do not share. I believe that the Palestinian people have every right to elect their leadership, even if it results in a regime that I (or my government) do not agree with. I certainly do not agree with Hamas—I abhor their violence, and I would prefer if they were a deeply unpopular fringe group among the Palestinians. Yet I picked this example precisely because it's one of the hardest ones to defend. To maintain consistency, I have to believe that genuinely free and fair elections are a good thing, even if the elected regime deals a setback to the peace process. It's hard to stomach, but I think it's correct, at least in the long run.

In this way, support for democracy is akin to support for free speech. If only widely popular speech is protected, then the notion of freedom of speech is rendered meaningless. The power of free speech arises when unpopular attitudes are protected. Likewise, if the democratic process can only be supported when it produces the West's preferred result, then democracy is meaningless. If we believe people should have a choice, we have to respect them enough to let them make that choice without foreign interference. There are, of course, limits. Once an elected leader starts to antagonize Western interests, then it is entirely legitimate to use all the carrots and sticks of traditional diplomacy. Once Hamas took power, the United States had every right to try to isolate it. But Palestinians deserved a chance to have their voice heard, rather than having it drowned out by American funding in pursuit of Western interests.

Moreover, non-intervention in elections in also usually in the West's self-interest, at least in the long run. I believe that principled intervention in support of democratic institutions, regardless of the players involved, can help empower moderates, even if the outcome of the election doesn't tilt in the West's favor. Over the long term, however, continued interference in foreign elections on behalf of a specific party is virtually certain to backfire, as a polarized political system is far more volatile than one built on consensus.

Of course, Hamas might have won the elections anyway. Nobody can be sure, and I certainly believe that the most critical actor in those elections was the Palestinians themselves—even if the United States may have tipped the scales. Either way, Hamas's victory was a major setback for peace, in my view, but a setback I would have been willing to accept if it was clearly the legitimate will of the Palestinian people, free from external coercion or influence.

The US and European states had every right to publicize the planned foreign policy consequences of a Hamas victory; they had every right to impose sanctions, or refuse to cooperate with a Hamas-led government if it didn't renounce its aggressive stance toward Israel; and, of course, they had every right to sound the alarm bells and impose external costs on the new regime if it took steps to ensure that future elections would not take place, or would become meaningless. After all, the clichéd refrain that Hitler was elected democratically doesn't make him a democrat, nor does it call into the question whether it was legitimate to actively oppose him once he was elected. It most certainly was and he obviously should have been more strongly opposed earlier on. Electoral victories don't give leaders carte blanche, but the elections themselves shouldn't be meddled with. In other words, democracy is a moral good, but democratically elected leaders shouldn't get away with other moral violations just because they won the most votes.

In the interest of both *realpolitik* and the principle of spreading meaningful democracy, the 2006 contest in the Palestinian Territories shows the damaging blowback of electoral interference that was more of a self-inflicted wound than a viable democracy promotion strategy.

There is, however, one way that Western governments (in conjunction with the United Nations) can help enforce democracy, after allowing the process to play out "naturally." When elections take place, and the prevailing view is that they were clean, credible, and reflected the genuine will of the people, I believe it is legitimate for a short-term, multi-national force with an exceptionally strict mandate to ensure that the electoral victor is able to take power. Otherwise, what can one do when an incumbent loses an election but refuses to leave power? In my view, this, along with post-conflict peacekeeping, is a rare instance when military force may be a useful tool in pursuit of democracy abroad. Yet the conditions for such an intervention are limited; it's only worth pursuing if the losing candidate does not have the backing of a powerful military force and there is a reasonable chance that the use of force will not spark further destabilizing conflict. Those are big ifs.

With such narrow scope for success, this type of intervention is not used frequently. But sometimes, it can be implemented to great effect. The most successful military intervention to install an elected president in recent years occurred in 2011, in Côte d'Ivoire, the cocoa-rich and repeatedly war-torn West African nation.

The 2010 elections in Côte d'Ivoire were meant to close a chapter of warfare rather than start a new one. The previous elections, held in 2000, helped spark a low-intensity civil war that lasted between 2002 and 2007. The 2010 vote, which pitted the two warring factions against each other, was intended to resolve the conflict peacefully, allowing the Ivoirian people the chance to turn the page and move on with a legitimately elected government. The two protagonists in this tragic tale were Laurent Gbabgbo of the Front Populaire Ivorien (Ivoirian Popular Front) and Alassane Ouattara of the Rassemblement des Républicains (Rally of the Republicans). Gbagbo, the incumbent president heading into the 2010 contest, largely represented the southern, Christian half of the country; Ouattara's stronghold was in the Muslim north.

Western governments tended to favor the rebel-backed Ouattara over the incumbent President Gbagbo—partly because Gbagbo was starting to shift contracts toward Chinese firms rather than Western (and mainly French) ones, and partly because Ouattara had previously worked at the top echelons of the International Monetary Fund. Ouattara was therefore seen in the West as the reformer Côte d'Ivoire needed to turn around a broken economy, battered by years of civil war.

However, unlike in the 2006 Palestinian elections, there was no evidence to suggest that Western governments directly tampered with the actual process of campaigning, voting, or tabulation. Côte d'Ivoire's Independent Electoral Commission certified that Ouattara received 54 per cent to Gbagbo's 46 per cent. The United Nations' parallel vote tally certified that result, confirming Ouattara as the clear victor. International observers agreed.

Rather than accept defeat, however, Gbagbo called on the Constitutional Court—a court that he had stacked with allies—to "revisit" the results. Their "revised" tally showed a clear Gbagbo victory, flipping the results. Nobody in the international community bought this, but Ivorian politics had reached an impasse. As the standoff continued, fighting broke out between Gbagbo loyalists and Ouattara's rebel militias. In Gbagbo's strongholds in the capital, Abidjan, pro-Ouattara supporters were stopped at impromptu checkpoints and condemned to die under a so-called "Article 125" verdict, named because gasoline cost 100 francs, and matches cost 25 francs. They were set alight in the street, leaving black grease stains charred into the ground for months to come.[17]

Ouattara's rebels sprung into action as the brutality became rampant in Abidjan and Gbagbo continued to resist calls to step down. They swept across the country in a lightning-quick assault, capturing most of the national territory in three days. Their takeover was tainted by horrific revenge attacks. In the town of Duékoué, Ouattara forces went house to house, AK-47s in hand, rounding up the men and systematically executing them. Witnesses recount the soldiers' chants of "You voted Gbagbo! We are going to kill you all!" as they fired their rounds. They left behind 800 bodies rotting in the streets.[18]

Even after such grisly violence on both sides, Abidjan was still a battleground after the rebel offensive. It quickly became clear that street-to-street fighting was heading toward a bloody, prolonged stalemate. In the midst of fighting, the UN Security Council—including China and Russia—backed Ouattara as the legitimate victor and called for targeted sanctions against Gbagbo until he relinquished power. When that didn't work, the UN pressed for further action.

French troops, under the banner of the United Nations, intervened to enforce the democratic will of the Ivoirian people. French helicopters attacked Gbagbo's guard towers. Western bombs fell on crucial ammunition depots. Then, French troops swooped through Abidjan, leading Ouattara's forces literally to Gbagbo's doorstep. They arrested him, put a bulletproof vest on him for his own protection, and handed power to Ouattara. Months later, Gbagbo was shipped off to The Hague to await trial at the International Criminal Court; Outtara and his forces were never indicted.[19]

Depending on partisan affiliation, Ivoirians saw this as either neo-colonialism or a much-needed assault to support democracy by defeating a stubborn despot. The intervention itself was imperfect and set some unfortunate precedents. It also created some unintended ripple effects, sowing the seeds of important social divides that linger today. Still, it got the job done. Ouattara won the election and Ouattara took office. As a result, Côte d'Ivoire's experience can be used not as a paragon, but a flawed model for future action to enforce democratic verdicts.

I traveled to Abidjan shortly after the civil war had ended. Ouattara had recently taken power. There was an eerie calm, as the serenity of warm sunshine in the bustling capital was broken up with jarring reminders of what had just taken place. Government buildings were riddled with bullet holes. Every so often, a UN peacekeeping convoy would rumble through the streets, Bangladeshi soldiers at the helm of machine guns mounted on the backs of their armored vehicles. Their mandate was to support the fragile new government, which was largely composed of former rebels.

Ouattara's rebels cleaned up nicely. I met with an array of them. Many of the leaders of the Forces Nouvelles rebel coalition had become government ministers, occupying the very buildings that their troops had been shooting at months earlier. Others were living well but had not yet been "placed", waiting to see what President Ouattara had in store for their professional careers to reward them for loyalty through the years.

I wanted to understand how the international intervention had supported—or undermined—democracy in Côte d'Ivoire. Several political types encouraged me to meet with Kokhav Koné Abou Bakary Sidick, a self-proclaimed man of many talents, whose business card reads: "Geographer. Historian. Theologian. Doctor. Professor. Researcher. Writer." Like the initial phone conversation with General Ramakavélo in Madagascar, this one was not easy to forget. We arranged to meet in an area called Plateau Dokui, which is about as precise as setting a meeting in Washington DC to be held "somewhere in Georgetown" or "around King's Cross" in London.

"Yes, I'd be happy to meet with you," he said. "Do you know where Plateau Dokui is?"

"Yes... roughly. Is there a specific café or restaurant you'd like to meet at in Plateau Dokui?"

"Are you white?"

"Um, yes, why?"

"Just go to Plateau Dokui. I'll find you."

Clad in a suit and tie and just on the outskirts of the working-class Abobo neighborhood, an area of Abidjan where foreigners seldom visited, I had to admit I did stick out. But it was still fairly awkward when I asked the taxi driver to let me out on the side of a random road. Sure enough, less than five minutes later, a young man excitedly ran toward me. "Monsieur Brian?" he asked. I nodded. "Follow me." He led me to Professor Koné Abou Bakary Sidick's office, a modest little space with an aging air conditioning unit groaning in the background as we spoke. He explained that:

> The root of the problem here is that since the birth of Côte d'Ivoire, presidents have been unwilling to accept a political adversary. And, because of graft and corruption, the world of politics is the only avenue to becoming rich in Africa. It's the case in Côte d'Ivoire too. You launch a rebellion, you might become rich.

In his view, Côte d'Ivoire's flimsy democratic foundation needed external support to survive.

> Our democracy is young. It is fragile. A single power-hungry man can destroy something that millions have built. So even though I do not like that our former colonizer came in with guns and bombs, it was necessary. It stopped the violence. It ensured that the election result—the voice of the people—would be respected. We have had enough bloodshed. We have not had enough democracy.

Unsurprisingly, the former rebels that now occupied positions of authority echoed this message. But for nearly half of the country—the half that backed Gbagbo—the French/UN intervention was an unmitigated disaster, an example of imperialist overreach where foreign powers had imposed their preference on Ivoirians by force. To them, this was like the 2006 elections in Palestine, but on some exceptionally militaristic steroids.

I reached out to a former member of Gbagbo's entourage, a professor who only agreed to meet with me on the strict condition that I not identify him by name. "I'll get killed in a reprisal attack," he claimed. The whole meeting had an air of uneasy paranoia to it, but given the post-war political climate, I couldn't say it was wholly unjustified. He told me to meet him at a school, a welcome dose of precision after my interview in Plateau Dokui. When I arrived, however, the school was abandoned and partly in rubble, a victim of neglect and disrepair or civil war shelling—I couldn't be totally sure which. Regardless, when someone picks an abandoned school for a rendezvous, red flags pop up. Minutes later, an SUV with tinted windows rolled to a slow stop, the passenger window slid downward, and the driver motioned to me to get in. This is the type of thing that trained journalists would be told never, ever to do. I am not a trained journalist.

It turned out to be a good decision. The professor and his wife were warm and welcoming. We sipped French cognac, something I found particularly ironic given the circumstances and the attitudes they held:

> This was an election stolen by the French. This wasn't democracy. It was [French President] Sarkozy's revenge against us because we tried to be independent. But they'll never let us be independent. When they couldn't get what they want from the people, they just took it by force. They'll use any pretext to put Outtara in power. And now we have to be in hiding, hiding in our own country.

This was a bit of hyperbole; the professor was not wanted for any crimes and there had been limited reprisal attacks against former

Gbagbo partisans in Côte d'Ivoire, particularly once Gbagbo was in custody in The Hague. But the professor's nervous, angry sentiments, born from a feeling of being shut out of the political sphere, highlights three mistakes made by the French-led UN intervention. We must learn from each.

First, while it was most convenient for French troops to lead the assault because they were already stationed there, any military action to help "enforce" democratic verdicts must be genuinely multi-national and, ideally, not exclusively Western. It's also a bad idea to have a former colonial power dominate the intervention. It doesn't look good, to say the least.

Second, while the UN Security Council should play a crucial role in assessing the prospects of success for a military intervention—particularly because some of the five permanent members may play a role, at least with logistical support—they should not have veto control over any potential interventions. If they do, then the scope of possible interventions will be severely limited and unfairly skewed. China's, Russia's, and the United States' vetoes in particular could ensure that democracy is never "enforced" in ally or client states of world powers. As a result, the Security Council (like the International Criminal Court) will suffer a heavy bias, only to be wielded as a weapon in African states, places that tend to have disproportionately low geostrategic interests for major world powers. This would be a disastrous reinforcement of the "neo-colonial" impression expressed by the professor—and he may have a point. While it's impossible to know for sure, I'm not convinced that a similarly swift response from the international community would have been forthcoming if the vote tally had been reversed, and the Independent Election Commission had declared victory for Gbagbo, and not the West's darling, Ouattara. Therefore, such interventions must be divorced from geopolitics, as much as is possible.

Third, and perhaps most importantly, any post-election, post-conflict intervention needs to be genuinely even-handed. There is substance to the claim that President Ouattara, his political entourage, and his former rebel forces, have been the beneficiaries of victors' justice. It is highly likely that both sides committed war crimes in the 2010–11 violence, but only one is being punished. Ouattara is in power; Gbagbo is in a jail cell. Such lopsided application of post-election reconciliation strategies cannot be replicated in future interventions if they are to succeed; otherwise, the election may only establish a temporary peace, one that could relapse into conflict at the next vote.

This type of military pro-democracy intervention should not be used unless there is genuine international consensus as to the legitimate election victor, nor should it be used if there is a reasonable risk of exacerbating rather than easing violence.

Thankfully, Côte d'Ivoire is a success story. In 2016, Abidjan is booming, not with bombs and shells, but with the sounds of construction and commerce. The 2011 intervention helped pave the way for a flawed, but ultimately peaceful, 2015 election. The country is back on track.

Whereas the 2006 Palestinian Authority elections showed how Western governments can overstep their legitimate influence in the domestic affairs of another country, the democracy enforcement intervention in Côte d'Ivoire showcases the ability of Western nations to help consolidate democracy. There were mistakes, certainly, but by and large a low-level civil war was contained and the democratic will of the Ivoirian people upheld. Therefore, the two contrasting examples demonstrate the perils of direct interference in elections themselves, but make clear that foreign actors can help create a framework that rewards those that play by the rules and punishes those that don't once the democratic verdict has been decided.

Wouldn't it be nice, though, if there were a way to entice stubborn despots to simply step down in the first place, before the bloodshed begins?

# 7

# GOLDEN HANDCUFFS

*Principle 5: Give despots a way out*

Before widespread fighting broke out in Côte d'Ivoire, President Obama reportedly called the embattled incumbent, Laurent Gbagbo, and offered him asylum in the United States. Obama even went one step further, promising that he would arrange a faculty position for Gbagbo as a visiting scholar at Boston University.[1] Gbagbo was a history professor before he entered politics, and the idea was simple: tempt him with a cushy job and a guarantee of safety so that he wouldn't drive his country into a bloody, costly, destabilizing conflict. On that occasion, it didn't work. Gbagbo decided to stay and fight, and while it didn't cost him his life, it did cost him his freedom. But he could just as easily have been a faculty member gallivanting around Boston in tweed, teaching African history to rich kids churned out of East Coast prep schools.

The failure to remove Gbagbo with an enticing job offer does not mean that such overtures are a bad idea. Western leaders hoping to make the world more democratic should extend a set of "golden handcuffs" to leaders, conditioned on their willingness to peacefully transfer power to a successor, ideally after an election.

What happens to a leader after they leave power depends a lot on where they ruled. Since 1989, not a single leader has been imprisoned, killed, or forced into exile in Western Europe, Japan, South Korea, the United States, Canada, New Zealand or Australia.[2] Not only that, but there is a clear path to riches; leave power, and go off and make your millions on the speaking circuit. Bill and Hillary Clinton, for example, earned $140 million giving speeches around the United States from 2007 to 2015 alone.[3] Leaving power didn't exactly doom their prospects for future prosperity.

For leaders in the rest of the world, the risks are different. Leaving office is perilous. In non-Western countries, 6.5 per cent of rulers leaving power since 1989 have found a new home in a jail cell, and 2 per cent have been killed. In Sub-Saharan Africa, the odds are even worse. Since the end of the Cold War, 23 per cent of deposed African rulers were forced into exile; around 8 per cent were jailed; and 5 per cent were killed.[4] Put differently, more than one in three Sub-Saharan leaders can expect not to be allowed to return home after leaving office, because they are killed, jailed, or banished from the country they formerly ruled.

Let's think about that. For an African leader, losing power is like playing Russian roulette with two loaded chambers and four empty ones. If they happen to pull the trigger on the first or second chamber in the barrel, they will either never go home, or lose their freedom, or even die. That credible risk creates a strong incentive for leaders to cling to power rather than taking any chances. Ruthless repression becomes rational. Election rigging seems like the most obvious thing in the world. Mitt Romney might have behaved a bit differently if losing the presidential election meant he could be dragged through the streets of Salt Lake City by an angry mob or sent to rot in a dangerous prison cell.

In short, unless a more enticing incentive comes along to break that line of thinking, we shouldn't be surprised that rulers like Robert Mugabe of Zimbabwe (in power since 1987) or José Eduardo dos Santos of Angola (in power since 1979) are willing to do just about anything to avoid stepping down. To avoid the risk of losing power, they badly overstay their welcome. Some 83 per cent of Zimbabweans and 85 per cent of Angolans have never even been alive to see a different leader in power; their despots are all they know of what politics entails. The same is true for more than half the population in eight other African countries.[5]

This hurts democracy in three ways. First, if presidents refuse to relinquish power, democracy obviously cannot take root. If the people can't fire their leader, the system cannot be democratic. Second, when 83 per cent of the population has only known an authoritarian ruler like Robert Mugabe, the succession process is less likely to be a seamless democratic success. After all, if eight out of ten people have never lived under a system of political pluralism or democratic accountability, the shift into that system requires a completely new form of political socialization. The negative legacy of overstaying despots may therefore be generational, lingering well after they leave office (or, as is more likely with Mugabe or dos Santos, they die). This has played out in disastrous ways in Libya, where today's chaos was made more likely by the fact that Gaddafi had been in power for forty-two years, strangling the political life of his country and ensuring that any post-Gaddafi period would be exceptionally volatile.

Third, recent scholarship has shown that countries that punish their leaders after they step down are more likely to succumb to a failed transition to democracy, a reversal of fortunes that ends right back at square one: with an authoritarian despot.[6] Dictators, despots, and counterfeit democrats often abuse their office, steal from public coffers, and violate human rights. They often deserve to be punished. But, although it pains me to say it (and this is the cue for liberal idealists to roll their eyes), sometimes, punishing a leader is the worse of two evils. Just as it may arguably be justified to shoot down a civilian airliner if it's about to crash into a stadium of 50,000 people, giving bad leaders a cushier-than-they-deserve treatment to entice them to relinquish power is often the less bad option, ensuring that a grim situation doesn't morph into a grisly one.

In perhaps a more apt analogy, awful rulers are akin to someone who has hijacked the nation's airplane. The people on board are all victims of the regime. Allowing the leader to land safely and go unpunished for the hijacking is a grave injustice to all of his or her victims, but one that spares the people in the nation's stadiums and skyscrapers. If not managed carefully, cutting a deal for the hijackers could also encourage future hijackings. But by contrast, staunch international and domestic pressure that makes the president or prime minister paranoid that they will lose office—with no safe way out—makes it more likely that the plane will crash into a populated area, killing thousands of others in the process.

Haiti, the tiny nation occupying the western portion of Hispaniola Island, has quite the habit of punishing its rulers after driving them out of office. Two-thirds of presidents that left office in the last 115 years have been exiled, jailed, or killed. In a particularly bloodthirsty period between 1908 and 1915, Haiti's departing leaders were, in order, "exiled, exiled, bombed and blown up, imprisoned, exiled, executed, exiled, and, particularly gruesome, 'dragged from the French legation by an angry mob and impaled on the iron fence surrounding the legation and torn to pieces.'"[7] Governing Haiti required a generously large life insurance policy—it still does. But in 1994, the United States broke up the cycle, cutting a deal that was unsavory—to put it mildly—but necessary to save Haiti from further bloodshed, conflict, and political turmoil.

In 1990, Haiti looked like it had turned a page on its violent, authoritarian past. One of the worst despots in the region, "Baby Doc" Duvalier, had been deposed, and fresh elections gave Haitians a new hope that they could pick leaders who would rule by consensus forged in consultation with public opinion, rather than death squads. The election itself was widely heralded as a reasonably good one, in spite of the logistical challenges that tend to plague election management in such undeveloped nations. Jean-Bertrand Aristide won convincingly, garnering the support of two out of three Haitian voters. Three out of four Haitians voted. Aristide championed the plight of the poor, and began ambitious reforms, claiming that his goal was to "transition [Haiti] from misery to poverty with dignity."[8] The popular voice of Haitians began to matter more and more, challenging the longstanding political dominance of military factions and wealthy elites. Aristide was no angel by any stretch of the imagination, but it seemed that democracy could at least conceivably start to take root.

Roots take time to grow, however, and Haiti's sapling democracy was cut down almost immediately. Aristide had only been in office for eight months when a coup d'état overthrew him. On 29 September 1991, soldiers fired on Aristide's house. He was rescued by an armored personnel carrier driven by loyal troops, and transported (accompanied by the French ambassador) to the National Palace. The next day, at 5:30pm, a second attack succeeded and soldiers captured Aristide inside the palace. They brought him before Lieutenant General Raoul Cédras, the chief coup plotter. With Aristide listening, they discussed whether to hang him on the spot, kill him later, or force him into exile. Through fierce negotiations with the Venezuelan, French, and American ambassadors, they reached the conclusion that Aristide's death would be an inconvenience to the new military junta, as it would attract too much foreign consternation. Aristide was put on a charter flight to Caracas to enter what would be a three-year period of exile.[9]

Raoul Cédras took power. There were rumblings and allegations that the CIA may have had a hand in the coup, but those claims have not been substantiated. At a minimum, the United States did play a role in Cédras' training, as he was a graduate of the Department of Defense's notorious School of the Americas training program. Once in power, Cédras went right back to the vicious playbook of Haitian political brutality. The new government established its dominance not with a new constitution but with blood. The night of the coup, hundreds of protesters gathered on the Champ de Mars, in front of the National Palace. As a column of soldiers drove past, the protesters cheered, assuming that these were the loyalists, coming to quash the renegade Cédras and his followers. Instead, the soldiers stopped, turned their machine guns on the crowd, and opened fire. Hundreds were murdered. In the following ten months, at least 1,021 extra-judicial executions took place; the true number may be as high as 3,000.[10]

During this same period, the United States began a slow shift against Cédras. Haiti was becoming more intertwined in the global drug trade, a scourge that the Bush administration had vowed to stamp out. Washington insiders began to worry privately that "support for the coup leaders in Haiti could invite coups elsewhere in the hemisphere and undermine Washington's neo-liberal agenda for that region."[11] This was an astute assessment, and a warning that has been forgotten. But as the Washington elite turned against Cédras, and as Bill Clinton replaced Bush, it became clear that something would need to be done about the man himself; like most despots, he feared what would come once he left office and therefore wasn't willing to simply give up power. There wasn't much of an appetite in Washington for a full-blown US invasion. It would invite serious risks, and given the immense and unpopular 1993 Black Hawk Down debacle in Mogadishu, Clinton's administration was eager to avoid another foreign policy disaster—if it could be avoided.

In a late-twentieth-century version of gunboat diplomacy, Clinton deployed massive warships and parked them just off Haiti's shoreline. The maneuver was aptly titled "Operation Uphold Democracy" for maximum propaganda effect. As talk of an American invasion permeated discussions in Port-au-Prince, Haiti also started rattling its sabers—admittedly much stranger sabers than the American gunboats: "We will fight and face the invader. Zombies in the first line and us behind them."[12] The junta also promised that American GIs would be attacked with HIV-infected syringes and repelled with voodoo spells emanating from a *houngan*, or voodoo priest (the acting president, who was a stooge for General Cédras, claimed to be one himself). They warned that if American troops deployed, they would also face being attacked by special plants that made skin peel off, unleashed by an army of 60,000 invisible zombies.[13]

On 8 September 1994, the invisible gloves came off. Two *houngans* and four *mambos* (female voodoo priests) drew magical curses on the sidewalk just outside the American embassy in the capital. Four days later, in Washington, a red-and-white-liveried Cessna 150 flew over America's capital. The pilot, a disturbed truck driver from Maryland who had almost certainly never heard of Cédras or *houngans*, made a U-turn around the Washington Monument, and flew straight toward President Clinton's bedroom. He crashed at the base of the presidential mansion.[14] The pilot was killed, but nobody else was injured. For superstitious Haitians in the junta, this was a clear sign: the voodoo spirits were on their side.

In spite of this belief in mysticism, President Clinton hoped that a peaceful resolution could be reached by appealing to Cédras' rationality. The White House sent a diplomatic delegation to Haiti to negotiate, including former president Jimmy Carter, Senator Sam Nunn, and General Colin Powell—a man who knew General Cédras personally from his time training in the United States.[15]

I don't like or relish what happened next, but it was probably the right move. Together, the US delegation offered Cédras a $1 million golden parachute to leave power. Bizarrely, Cédras insisted that part of the deal include a commitment from the United States to rent out three of his properties in Haiti, including his mother's villa. American taxpayers were on the hook essentially as diplomatic landlords, renting Cédras' home in Peguyville, a suburb of Port-au-Prince, at a cost of $4,000 a month.[16] Just before 3:00am on 13 October 1994, a United States military charter aircraft ferried General Cédras, his deputy, Brigadier General Philippe Biamby, and fourteen of their family members to Panama City to start a new life in exile. A second charter aircraft brought twenty-three further family members and associates to Miami, where they were given political asylum. That same day, the White House announced the release of $79 million in assets held in 600 military officers' bank accounts, which had been frozen as part of diplomatic pressure against the regime.[17]

These were not secret moves. They were executed out in the open, by a presidential administration eager to ensure a peaceful return to democracy rather than a prolonged military intervention and the destabilizing bloodshed sure to accompany it. Anthony Lake, President Clinton's national security adviser, told reporters: "There is no bribe here, there is nothing hidden here, there are no hidden inducements. I am not apologetic in the slightest here. This is a success."[18] Cédras set up shop in a palace in Panama City, then relocated to Contadora Island, a retreat that had ironically previously been used by the Iranian Shah—a man who also benefitted from a little American government help.[19]

It may sound bizarre to identify as a "success" a ruthless and vicious military regime and a bloody coup going unpunished, but Lake was correct. It was an injustice, but a diplomatic victory. Rather than a prolonged conflict, there was a reasonably smooth transition. President Aristide, the elected leader, returned to power to finish his term. Haiti still had immense problems and it did not become an exemplar of democracy, but it did make several important steps toward a democratic system. The 1995 elections were flawed, in some ways severely, but there was a peaceful transfer of power from Aristide to his successor, René Préval. Yes, it was still a counterfeit democracy, but the death squads went away—at least for a while—and the Haitian people had more of a meaningful voice in their government. Giving Cédras an exit option wasn't enough to give Haitians democracy, but it was enough to give them a window of opportunity to seize it for themselves. The fact that they did not effectively seize it does not negate the fact that the attempt was worthwhile.

The model of intervention in Haiti was nonetheless problematic, for several reasons. The financial incentives were likely too generous given Cédras' crimes; the United States' application of unilateral gunboat diplomacy set a dangerous precedent of introducing geopolitical considerations into such interventions (though it was at least bolstered by the veneer of multilateralism under a UN Security Council resolution); and the long history of American meddling in Haiti's affairs undermines the claim that this was a purely principled foreign policy operation. But for $1 million (and whatever the price of violating our Kantian sense of justice), Haiti was spared what was certain to be a bloody and economically devastating showdown or the needless prolongation of a terrible, bloody regime. With Cédras gone, the political situation improved markedly. It was, in my view, a bargain—even if I have to hold my nose while writing that. How many millions of people could have been spared from civil wars or foreign interventions in recent decades if the leader had been offered a way out?

Before I am accused of being an apologist for despots and thugs, however, I think there's room for something like the golden parachute extended to Cédras that doesn't commit a cardinal sin of diplomatic politics: incentivizing war crimes and human rights violations. It doesn't take a political genius to realize that what I am proposing—and what the United States did in Haiti—teeters on a very sharp razor's edge. If ruthless leaders around the world assume that they can commit any number of horrendous crimes and then just hop on an all-expenses-paid charter jet to a seaside villa with millions waiting for them in a Swiss bank account, the world will become an even more bloody and violent place than it already is. Ultimately, given my views on democracy, I believe that this calibration, of political amnesty intended to stave off conflict against the risk of incentivizing brutality, should be made on a consensus basis, forged by governments around the world, and not just in the West.

However, I can imagine a three-tiered system that would allow for more flexible transfers of power for the low- and mid-range despots, while maintaining International Criminal Court prosecutions for the worst of the worst. At the lowest level would be the approach taken with

Cédras, the golden parachute: hold your nose, sign the deal, and the leader gets away with it. It should be reserved for corrupt despots who (unlike Cédras) didn't viciously slaughter thousands. In Africa, the Mo Ibrahim Foundation already offers this approach, providing a $5 million "prize" for leaders that peacefully transfer power to a successor after losing an election or reaching the end of their constitutionally mandated term limit. (Unfortunately, the prize usually goes unclaimed.)

Above the golden parachute would be the mid-level approach—the one that should have been used for Cédras—or what I call "the golden handcuffs." Cédras was in a weak bargaining position and he was a legitimately bad guy; the United States should have guaranteed his safety, but forced him to agree to an asset forfeiture and a reasonably long period of house arrest: enough to make him feel punished but not enough to deter him from signing the deal.

Then, International Criminal Court prosecutions should still function as a major deterrent, but one reserved for war criminals, perpetrators of genocide, and others whose actions are so abhorrent that no level of utilitarian commitment can absolve the injustice of letting them go unpunished. These are the worst of the worst, and the "moral hazard" of letting them get away with their crimes is far more devastating than any failed transition could be, as it could spark copycats in presidential palaces around the globe.

In this vein, Laurent Gbagbo is an interesting case. The civil war that he helped spark resulted in the deaths of 3,000 Ivoirians, but fighters on both sides committed atrocities. Moreover, there seems to be only tenuous evidence that Gbagbo personally authorized the types of brutality that his soldiers executed, just as there is no "smoking gun" evidence that his counterpart, Alassane Ouattara, authorized the atrocities that his rebels committed. Gbabgo may be facing trial for war crimes, but it's worth debating where the threshold should be for ICC prosecution. Certainly, a fair global ranking of despots and dictators would not have Gbagbo anywhere near the top of the "bad guy" list. ICC prosecution should therefore be carefully weighed against the potential benefits of plucking a leader from power on a chartered flight to safety and security. Ultimately, it's a decision that should be made democratically by a community of nations, but a re-calibration does need to take place.

A three-tiered system would have another key advantage: the international community would have the opportunity to offer the golden parachute, the golden handcuffs, or a one-way ticket to The Hague at their discretion. This uncertainty is an advantage, because it would mean that despots would still fear the consequences of their actions, but diplomats would nonetheless retain the flexibility to prioritize stability for smaller and medium-sized fish in the international pond of counterfeit democrats. Just as with the Cédras deal, the security and safety guarantee should be predicated on a peaceful transfer of power with the aim of holding quick but credible elections.

Admittedly, the Haiti intervention was made possible, at least in part, by American gunboat diplomacy. It was a lot easier for Jimmy Carter and Colin Powell to play "good cop/bad cop" with warships virtually casting shadows on the Haitian coastline. The calculus for Cédras came into focus: take the golden parachute, or try your luck with a lead one. If this is to become the modus operandi for future guarantees of exile for embattled rulers who have overstayed their welcome, then the mechanism for using the threat of force should be multilateral, consensus-based, and granted the narrowest possible intervention to get the job done. If it's unrealistic to arrest the leader without starting a major international war, then this strategy is not one that's worth pursuing.[20] As with the strategy of "enforcing democracy" outlined in the previous chapter, this is one possible option that should be very much on the menu of possible interventions to help guide despots out of power and democrats into it. However, to ensure that such interventions do not transform into thinly veiled imperialist adventures, the scope of intervention must be tightly controlled and its legitimacy must be broadly agreed.

If the golden handcuffs are offered wisely, they can shackle irresponsible rulers rather than shackling their people with indefinite authoritarianism. The principle embedded in this unsavory utilitarianism can be reinforced by the other principles argued previously; if Western governments think about the long term, they will be less prone to chasing short-termist and ultimately counterproductive attempts to impose a sense of righteous justice, bringing the country down in the process. The key is changing the leader's political calculation, so that the safety and security of exile seems more enticing than the inevitable ruthlessness that must continue for them to remain in power.

However, as with the Rwandan genocide, or Slobodan Milošević's "ethnic cleansing," or Bashar al-Assad's reckless barrel bombing of civilian populations, eventually, horrible leaders arrive at a point of no return where a golden parachute wouldn't fly under the weight of their crimes. In those instances, as with voodoo priests in Haiti, there may be little room to use rational argument to convince them to step down. But in a world where leaving office is like playing Russian roulette for many of the world's leaders, voluntary and democratic transfers of power will not start to make rational sense until the costs of losing office are lowered considerably.

Twenty-seven current heads of state have been in power for more than fifteen years. Thirteen of them have been in power for at least twenty-five; they ruled when George H.W. Bush was president and the Soviet Union still existed. The winner in this dubious contest of despots overstaying their welcome is Paul Biya of Cameroon. He took power during the Vietnam War, when Queen was atop the charts with *Bohemian Rhapsody*, and has remained in charge for more than four decades—edging out Teodoro Obiang Nguema Mbasogo of Equatorial Guinea by just over four years. Some others are eager to break that record. In 2011, Yahya Jammeh, the president of The Gambia, that tiny sliver of land sandwiched within Senegal in West Africa, proclaimed: "If I have to rule this country for one billion years, I will."[21] It's a long road from his current tally of twenty-two years to a billion, but everyone loves a dreamer.

Many others, such as Joseph Kabila in the Democratic Republic of the Congo, have not been in power for as long but are currently angling to lift term limits to extend their time in office.[22] The DRC is on a risky precipice in the meantime. Kabila, and leaders like him, are prime candidates for a charter flight or a set of golden handcuffs. This approach could be used to ensure that those who lose elections or reach their constitutional term limits step down without a bloody fight.

What comes next? Once the golden parachute has been deployed, or the leader is wearing their golden handcuffs, what is to be done with everyone else linked to the deposed regime? When a dictator, despot, or counterfeit democrat falls, there remain hundreds, thousands, even tens of thousands of elite members who are "tainted" by their affiliation with the fallen leader. What is done with them has an incredibly important influence on whether or not a democracy is likely to survive. Surprisingly, more often than not, it's better to extend an olive branch to the remnants of dictatorship in order to salvage democracy.

# 8

## THE UNTHINKABLE OLIVE BRANCH

*Principle 6: Encourage new democracies to include the old regime during transitions*

In November 2013, I met with Lieutenant Colonel Mohammed Ahmed in Tunis. His posture and short-cropped salt-and-pepper hair gave away his army background. Yet he was not in uniform. This wasn't by choice; Ahmed had been stripped of his rank and kicked out of the Tunisian officer corps. In 1991, Tunisia's dictator, Zine El Abidine Ben Ali, had accused Ahmed and 200 other officers of conspiring to overthrow his regime and take power for themselves in an audacious coup d'état. They called it the Barraket Essahel affair, named after the town where the plotters allegedly hatched the scheme.

There was just one problem: the whole thing was made up. There was no plot. There was no coup. It was all a decoy, a pretext to allow the dictator to crack down on legitimate opposition within Tunisia. Ben Ali was worried about a coup being launched by either Islamists or ambitious, competent military officers. To kill two birds with one stone, he concocted the Barraket Essahel Affair to discredit both.

Even though the plot was faked, the suffering it unleashed on soldiers like Lt Col Ahmed was all too real. As I sat across the table from him and two fellow ex-officers who were also victims of this devious dictatorial conspiracy, he told me how the harrowing ordeal unfolded.

They picked us up and drove us to the Ministry of the Interior, the scariest building in Tunis. They say it's as deep as it is tall. They didn't tell us anything about why we were there. But we were brought into the basement and I was put in what they called the "roasted chicken" position, my body suspended from a metal rod for hours. They beat me. They hung me from my feet with my hands tied behind my back. They forced my face into a basin of urine and feces until I thought I would drown.[1]

Ahmed's torture lasted off and on for three weeks. At the end of it, he could no longer stand. He couldn't eat because his lips were so badly bruised and bloodied. Thoroughly battered, Ahmed was brought before one of Ben Ali's right-hand henchmen, Minister of the Interior Abdallah Kallel. Ahmed's insistence that he had not done anything wrong only earned him further beatings. Then, inexplicably, Kallel returned a week later and wished Ahmed a happy Eid al-Kabir—he was released, with no explanation. The timing was fitting, as Eid al-Kabir is a Muslim holiday recognizing Abraham's willingness to sacrifice himself in submission to a higher authority.

After his release, Ahmed's nightmare continued. He was stripped of his rank, pension, and uniform. The government intervened to make sure that Ahmed and his compatriots could not find work. They took away their passports. After such intense suffering, Ahmed understandably harbors a simmering hatred for the people responsible for his torture, and Ben Ali most of all. When Ben Ali was overthrown in the January 2011 Arab Spring uprising, Ahmed and his fellow victims could be forgiven for wanting to ensure that Ben Ali would never return. But what about everyone else in Ben Ali's regime? To wipe everyone from Ben Ali's political past out of Tunisia's political future, as happened in Iraq during the post-Saddam de-Ba'athification campaign, would mean purging anyone who had been involved in Tunisian politics since 1987.

"We need to exclude the former regime," Ahmed told me, "so that sturdy democratic structures can be put in place. Right now, the foundation for Tunisian democracy is fragile." It's easy to be seduced by this point of view. Ben Ali was a dictator. His entourage and those that worked in his system were shaped by it and supported the strongman, at least publicly. But this type of affiliation isn't the same as being tainted by partisanship in the West. Being a Democrat or Republican, Tory or Labour, involves much more choice. For anyone who was interested in a career in Tunisian politics between 1987 and 2011, becoming a cheerleader for a despot was the only game in town. The opposition was virtually non-existent for much of Ben Ali's reign.

As a result, in the wake of the dictator's downfall, members of the old regime found allies and advocates in unexpected places. There were moderate voices coming from people who should have been much more radically opposed to the old regime. But, somehow, Tunisians who had suffered horrifically under Ben Ali's yoke found forgiveness for his entourage and for those who had perpetuated his system of oppression. Tunisians were mature enough to realize that the system rotted from the head, but perhaps not from the body. They understood that purging the old guard completely would also mean purging Tunisia's hopes for future prosperity.

As the world's second largest producers of olive oil, Tunisians know a thing or two about olive branches. At a crucial moment, the Islamists who came to power after the Arab Spring rose above the political fray and did something truly remarkable: they extended one to former regime officials who had previously been complicit in persecuting, jailing, and torturing them.

On a sunny autumn day in late 2013, I hopped in a taxi to meet with Said Ferjani, an Islamist political leader in Tunis. That day remains one of the most vivid emotional juxtapositions I've experienced in my travels. On the way to meet with the eminent Ferjani, I was practicing my Arabic with the cab driver, who turned out to be a jovial 53-year-old divorcé named Bashir. When I told him I was American and that I was in Tunis to learn about the political situation, he lit up—but much more about the former comment then the latter. "Politics is boring. Ben Ali was bad. What we have now is bad. But you are American. Tell me," he said, lowering his voice, "do you know any young, crazy, blonde American girls I could add on Facebook?" I laughed and told him I would have to think about it. "Okay," he said conspiratorially, "but just remember, put the ones that speak Arabic—or at a minimum French— at the top of the list." I was still shaking my head and laughing as I exited the cab and walked up to meet Ferjani. I didn't know that it would be one of the most serious and memorable interviews of my life.

More than anyone I've encountered in Tunisia, Said Ferjani is a walking parable for why Tunisia's democracy has continued to grow while that of the other Arab Spring nations has withered and returned to the barren soils of dictatorship, conflict, or both. Ferjani grew up poor. He became a devout Muslim, even though Tunisia's politics at the time was unapologetically secular. He watched as President Habib Bourguiba sipped orange juice on TV during the fasting month of Ramadan, deliberately flaunting his disdain for Islamic customs. That moment of alienation spurred Ferjani to join a group of Islamic activists and intellectuals.[2] They dreamed of a different path for Tunisia, one that eschewed secularism and replaced it with the Prophet's teachings.

In 1987, when Bourguiba fell seriously ill, Ferjani plotted a coup attempt with several of his Islamist colleagues. But they were beaten to the punch. Just seventeen hours before they were planning to carry out the attack, Ben Ali took power instead in a putsch of his own. The Islamist plot was exposed. Yet unlike the Barraket Essahel Affair, this coup attempt was not a pretext or a fantasy.[3]

Ferjani and his co-conspirators were arrested. Like Ahmed, they were tortured. The beatings and abuse broke Ferjani's back, but not his will. He went into a coma for five days, but eventually recovered enough to be released. After leaving prison, Ferjani vowed to escape Tunisia and only return when a new regime was in power—a regime under which he could be himself and actively participate in the politics of his own country. He learnt to walk short distances, even though he was confined to a wheelchair, the lingering effects of torture. Ferjani had a friend drive him to the airport, borrowed his passport, and walked convincingly enough through the searing pain so as not to arouse suspicion at the passport control check or the gate. The plane took off, and he was free. Ferjani established a new life in Britain.[4]

Twenty-two years later, a vegetable vendor in the deprived region of Sidi Bouzid set himself on fire in protest against Ben Ali's authoritarian rule. The Arab Spring germinated out of those ashes, uprooting Ben Ali in the process. When Ben Ali fell in 2011, Ferjani returned after more than two decades in exile. He became a top official in the Ennahda party, an Islamist political venture aimed at bringing political Islam into Tunisia's mainstream, reversing decades of persecution. Ferjani had faced a long and challenging road to get to this point, so when I met him at his home in Tunis, I expected him to share Lt Col Ahmed's opinion: everyone tainted by Ben Ali must go, and never return. When I walked up to his door, and saw Ferjani's imposing figure, silvery hair, and an even more silver traditional Islamic beard, I assumed I was in for an earful about the need to exorcise Ben Ali's lingering presence from the current generation of Tunisian politics.

My assumptions couldn't have been further from the truth. When I entered his home, Ferjani's stern exterior transformed into a warm smile and an enthusiastic handshake. For a man who had been tortured, Ferjani was somehow positively jovial. It was contagious. It was hard not to smile back at him when he was laughing and telling me about his turbulent past, but things got more serious—and intriguing—as he turned toward Tunisia's future. Vengeance for past wrongs was the last thing on his mind. "For us," he told me, "the success of the democratic process is dearer than Ennahda itself; this is not negotiable. Patience is key in a transition. We are conscious of the fact that any mistakes now could make democracy reversible."

I've spoken to hundreds of people across the globe who, like Ferjani, know how to say the right thing when Western ears are listening. So, I have to admit that I was skeptical, at least at first. I pressed him. Rosy rhetoric was easy. Successful transitions are hard. Wasn't he eager to see a widespread purge, as some in his party were advocating? Didn't he want revenge for the injustices of the past?

In fact, Ferjani insisted the opposite. "We have to study the old regime. The old structures were homogenous and coherent. When you get rid of the head, the rest must remain intact." In other words, Ben Ali had to go, and perhaps some of his closest confidants, but nobody else. While some in his party (and more extreme Islamist parties) drafted and pushed a so-called "Immunization of the Revolution" law aimed at purging the old guard from Tunisian politics once and for all, Ferjani resisted. This was not because he harbored any hidden affections for those who had propped up a dictator responsible for persecuting and then torturing him and his fellow Islamists, but because he understood a difficult truth: new democracies need the expertise of old despotism in order to succeed.

And, making good on what turned out to be much more than empty words, Ferjani's party, Ennahda, did something that political scientists usually assume is impossible: they voluntarily gave up power. At a time of political crisis, Ennahda handed over the keys to the country to a group of technocrats.[5] This wasn't a ploy or a trick. It was Ferjani and his cohort making good on what he told me: that the success of the democratic process was more important than Ennahda itself. That self-less act may have saved Tunisia's fragile democracy.

However, Ennahda still had a critical voice in Tunisia's parliament, and some were still calling loudly for a total purge of Ben Ali's entourage—and anyone who could be tarred with that label. Yet when it finally came to the fateful vote on whether to exclude or include the remnants of the fallen dictatorship, Ennahda was savvy. It knew that while many of its members could not possibly vote in favor of inviting the unpopular vestiges of Ben Ali's regime back into Tunisia's political life, they could avoid voting altogether. When the tally came in, the situation was tense. 100 had voted for the bill, twenty-seven had voted against, but an astonishing forty-six MPs had abstained. A two-thirds majority was required for the law to pass, and so it failed—just.[6]

When transitions fail, everyone looks for the smoking gun. What went wrong? Could it have been avoided? This seemingly banal vote was the moment that saved Tunisia's democratic transition. But instead of a smoking gun, it was the steady hand of men like Ferjani that stopped Tunisia's political elite from pulling the all-too-tempting trigger. Why did this vote matter so much? Would it really have been so bad if the law had passed and anyone affiliated with Ben Ali had been cast aside to allow a new generation of committed democrats to take the reins alone?

The answer, quite simply, is yes. My doctorate focused on precisely this question: what happens when political elites are excluded from politics? The answer is harrowing. It increases the risk of future coups and civil wars considerably. Moreover, during transitions—what Ferjani called "the most painful and difficult process in the political life of any nation"—the fledgling political structures are fragile. Any self-inflicted wound can be fatal.

As a result, extending an olive branch to the remnants of a toppled dictatorship may be a critical step in reinforcing nascent democracy. This may seem counterintuitive, but it also seems to be correct. Libya and Iraq took a different approach and both quickly fell apart—in the wake of the Political Isolation Law in Libya, and the de-Ba'athification process in Iraq. There are three reasons for including the old guard, to stave off instability, conflict, and a return to authoritarianism.

First, after decades in power, people affiliated with the old regime are almost always the people who wield the most authority, influence, and money in the post-authoritarian state. Excluding them outright ensures that the most powerful people in a given society will have a strong incentive to undermine the new state. If you want to doom a transition, make sure that the richest, most powerful class in society wants it to fail because they are sure to be left out of it.

Second, the old guard may be authoritarian, but it is also often the only cadre of people that understands how to run the country. Ben Ali had been in power since 1987; Gaddafi since 1969; Saddam Hussein since 1979. As mentioned in the previous chapter, a sizeable proportion of African citizens have only experienced life under a single president. Shattering those longstanding regimes and then excluding the people who made the system function is a surefire recipe for chaos spawned by avoidable amateur mistakes. This is less of a problem in democracies because there are established opposition parties that have expertise and often have previously occupied positions within government. But in authoritarian states, that is not the case; being an opposition figure in Ben Ali's Tunisia or Gaddafi's Libya was not just a dangerous game, it was also one that provided no real experience of governing.

In Tunisia's transition, a constant critique of Ennahda, usually made by their political rivals, was that the Islamists didn't have a clue how to run things because most of their leaders had spent the Ben Ali years either in prison or in Paris and London living in exile. As Ferjani's experience attests, there is some truth to this. But Ennahda was mature enough to recognize this truth, and reached out to those with expertise, rather than shunning them and attempting to force them into exile or jail too. It turned out that many members of the old guard had harbored serious reservations about Ben Ali and his authoritarian system; when they were liberated from his top-down leadership, they made clear that they too wanted a democratic Tunisia to succeed. They worked to support it. The old regime's expertise continues to help Tunisia navigate the choppy waters of transition.

Third, including old guard politicians in future elections defuses volatility and disarms ex-authoritarian candidates without turning them into political martyrs. My research shows clear evidence that inclusive elections lower the risk of a coup or a civil war. Conversely, these two risks are roughly doubled when major political candidates are excluded from elections.[7] The reason for this is simple. People who used to occupy positions of authority are well equipped to rally support, particularly drawing on their links with military and ex-military figures of the toppled regime. Now, nobody would suggest that Ben Ali should have been allowed to stand for election after he was felled by a popular uprising; after all, his ability to rig elections and manipulate the system in his favor had been crucial to his longevity on Tunisia's throne. If invited back, his old playbook would be invaluable as he worked to re-assert himself. Beyond that highest level, though, most top officials, and everyone else, should be allowed to run for office. Not only is it more democratic, it's also more effective at neutralizing the old regime. When old guard candidates are included in a democratic transition, they often simply lose elections, and lose badly.

Less than a year before Tunisia's 2014 presidential elections, I met with Kamel Morjane, who served under Ben Ali as minister of defense from 2005–10 and minister of foreign affairs from 2010–11. Morjane was one of the men most closely linked to Ben Ali's later years in office. He was complicit in the dictatorship but certainly not an all-around bad guy: he worked for decades for the United Nations High Commissioner for Refugees, and lamented to me: "I almost was the pick for the UN High Commissioner, but I narrowly missed being nominated because of petty politics." So, instead of fighting for refugees, he became part of Ben Ali's ruling core.

I would certainly understand if people like Said Ferjani or Lt Col Ahmed wanted to ensure that Kamel Morjane never set foot in government again. Nonetheless, he was allowed to run for Tunisia's highest office. He formed his own political party, al-Moubadara, or "The Initiative." In the presidential campaign, Morjane ran hard and lost badly. He came in a distant sixth, earning just 41,000 votes—a measly 1.27 per cent of the total. Instead of making enemies of powerful men like Morjane, Tunisia's inclusive democracy allowed him to stand freely, and let the people decide—they rejected him. And that, ultimately, was a far savvier move than giving the former of minister of defense any shred of an incentive to turn to men with guns for help in undermining the new democratic Tunisia. Plus, nothing cuts an old guard politician down to size like 1.27 per cent of the vote.

Unlike Morjane, though, most old guard figures who wanted to re-enter politics under a new banner joined another party, Nidaa Tounes, or Tunisia's Call. Yet the party was not simply a revamped version of the former regime; it was a hodge-podge of Ben Ali's toppled entourage mixed with ex-communists, socialists, secular liberals, exiles, and intellectuals. They were unified primarily by their opposition to political Islam, but not much more. Nébil Karoui, a key member of the Nidaa Tounes leadership, told me when we met in London recently:

> Nidaa Tounes was never designed to be a party, really, it was more of a Noah's Ark. We just threw all the species into the same boat. We've had our disagreements, because we had tigers alongside gazelles and they were sometimes tempted to try eating each other, but overall, it has still worked.

Indeed, the creation of Nidaa Tounes represented a major boon to Tunisia's political future. Some extremists within the Islamist ranks predicted that this would be the party to usher in a return to authoritarianism "through the back door," but that has not materialized—at least not yet. Instead, in the wake of elections that Nidaa Tounes won handily, the party reached out to the Islamists and made an agreement to govern by consensus in coalition.[8]

This spirit of cooperation earned Tunisian civil society the Nobel Peace Prize in 2015. It was truly well deserved. But Tunisian democracy could still be uprooted, even as it grows slowly but steadily. Tunisia is in a bad neighborhood, surrounded by a collapsing Libya on one side and a despotic Algeria on the other. The transition to democracy has been so successful that extremists have flooded out of Tunisia, which is one reason why the country has provided the largest number of foreign fighters to ISIS in Syria; it will be yet another challenge for Tunisia to work out how to deal with them if, or more likely when, they try to return in their thousands. Within Tunisia itself, two 2015 terrorist attacks against Western tourists, one in the Bardo Museum in Tunis and the other on the popular picturesque beaches of Sousse, have destroyed the tourism sector and therefore crippled the economy.[9] The Tunis coastline, which used to be dotted with hulking cruise ships, is now an uninterrupted sea of shimmering blue and white—peaceful and picturesque, but not lucrative. Job growth is projected to be worse in 2016 than it was in 2015, and worse in 2017 than in 2016. If the economy fails, democracy could too.

So on a cold, blustery day in February 2016, I met with Ferjani again to discuss Tunisia's uncertain future, this time in London. We met outside Baker Street Tube station, his silver hair obscured by a brand new newsboy cap, the tag freshly lifted off the plaid wool. "I bought this one just now," he explained. "I am no longer used to this weather," he added with a sheepish smile. His twenty-two years of rainy exile were over—but it had been a long and painful road. As we walked over to a Pizza Express opposite the station for a quiet (and warmer) place to chat, I still couldn't fully wrap my mind around what he had told me three years earlier: that he was ready to work with people who had, at a very minimum, been complicit in his torture. I asked him to tell me now, five years after the Arab Spring, how he was confronting his past and reconciling it with his consensus-based vision for Tunisia's future. I suggested that it must be difficult to put the past completely behind him.

"Look," he said, pausing to think about how to phrase his answer, "in my left leg I have paralysis still sometimes. When I sleep, if I turn over in the night, I wake up from the excruciating pain. One of my vertebrae is still badly damaged. My wife and children were harassed constantly. Anyone who talked to me, anyone who knows me, they were made to suffer just to get to me. I still feel guilty about that."

Ferjani paused again, his voice breaking as it trailed off. He resumed, haltingly. "Once I was in exile, I wrote a letter to the UN High Commissioner for Refugees, asking for help being reunited with my family. I remember the letter like I wrote it yesterday. The title I gave it was 'When death has become a wish,' because I had suffered so much and the situation seemed so hopeless that I was ready to welcome death."

As Ferjani spoke, I had been scribbling feverishly, wanting to be sure of capturing every word. Suddenly, he was silent. I looked up. His hands were covering his face. He was crying, but shielding his tears from me. Those dining at the tables around us looked up from their pizza, totally unaware of why this imposing figure had broken down in their midst. Wiping away his tears as he looked back up at me after a moment, he regained his fierce sense of purpose. "I never let anyone see me do that," he said, "because I don't ever want anyone from the old regime or from any authoritarian state around the world thinking that they can break people like me. They can't."

Ferjani meant it. Even after everything he has been through, he rejects vengeance.

> Ben Ali misused power against me because he couldn't accept anyone that wanted something different for Tunisia. I vowed to never do the same if I ever had power. I leave it to the hereafter to make their judgment; the best thing is to leave it to the most just of all: God. For now, I differentiate between the old regime and the people that were in it. They are not the same, and I reject the view that there is some black and white, that we are good guys and they are bad guys. It is more complicated than that.

Ferjani is right; the world of politics is a lot more complicated than a black-and-white world of good and bad. Ferjani himself, of course, in spite of my portrayal here, has flaws. But the consistent embodiment of compromise and consensus, in someone who has every reason to shun both, is a truly remarkable feature of Tunisia's transition, and it is a parable for the lone success story—thus far—of the Arab Spring. Somehow, against all odds, Tunisian democracy plods forward, old and new working together.

So far, Tunisia has chosen to extend an olive branch to members of the former regime. That was a wise and important choice. But other countries may not show the restraint necessary to follow suit. For every Tunisia, there are several Iraqs and Libyas, where the cycle of vengeance consumes democratic change. This should be a key lesson of Tunisia's success and one therefore embedded in Western foreign policy. Diplomatic pressure, consistently, subtly, and intelligently applied, can help ensure that other nations take the Tunisian high road and extend an olive branch to the felled branches of the old regime. Only then, together, can truly lasting democracy take root.

When Ferjani and I finished talking, I paid the bill, got up, and shook his hand. On the way out the door, I asked him where he was heading next, on his final day in London visiting friends and family before returning back to Tunis. "Edgware Road," he answered, "I've got an X-ray for my knee again and they're going to check out my vertebrae and hopefully check if it has deteriorated since my last visit." With that, we parted ways, as he set off to heal wounds inflicted by a despot in 1987 so that he could return to build democracy in 2016.

9

# FOOL'S ERRANDS

*Principle 7: Don't waste money. Target reformers instead.*

In January 2010, six months into a tumultuous period of post-election protests in Iran, Voice of America announced that it had developed a tailor-made, state-of-the-art new iPhone app to help the Iranian people raise their collective digital voices against the oppressive regime. With the new app, it was argued, Iranian "citizen journalists" could directly upload their photos and videos to a server so that abuses could be easily documented and beamed around the world. It was a well-intentioned idea.

There were several problems. First, due to sanctions championed by the United States itself, it was illegal for Apple to sell its iPhones in Iran. Second, the App Store—necessary to buy and download apps—therefore didn't exist in Iran. Third, at the time, the only mobile carrier of iPhones worldwide was AT&T—which didn't operate in Iran. Even if an Iranian "citizen journalist" had managed to smuggle an iPhone into the country and unlock it for use on alternative data networks, there were none in Iran at the time that would have supported iPhone data transmission. So, the app could still be useful, but only if the user had an active Wi-Fi connection. But at that point, the savvy citizen journalist who had smuggled an iPhone into Iran, unlocked the phone, and found an alternative source from which to download it, could just use a laptop or a desktop computer to upload the images.[1]

It was therefore difficult to imagine how the app provided anything of value even to the most determined citizen journalist in Iran's failed Green Revolution protest movement. Voice of America never publicly disclosed how much it paid the app's developer, Intridea, to develop the product, but it was almost certainly a sizeable sum. It was a poetic and poignant mistake, illustrating broader failures of democracy promotion: one wing of geopolitically driven democracy promotion (sanctions against Iran) ensured that the effort from another (an iPhone app) simply wasn't feasible. But the two did not coordinate, and so the funding was disbursed to no effect.

This obviously misguided effort was a drop in democracy promotion's bucket of wasted money. Of course, I do not believe that promoting democracy is not worthwhile; in fact, I believe that Western governments would be well served if they expanded funding in support of democracy around the globe. But the way that money is targeted and the programs that it funds need to change in two important ways.

First, assessments of cost effectiveness need to gravitate away from the mentality of "moving the money" without meaningful results.[2] It doesn't much matter that 200 parliamentarians attend a luncheon training session on the rule of law if the regime can simply steamroll parliament and override the rule of law. Nobody would suggest that it would be a worthwhile expenditure to run a multi-million-dollar training workshop on political party development in North Korea. All the training North Korea's elites need comes through their ears: instructions from the top officials and Kim Jong-un himself. On the other hand, such training programs can be extremely useful in places where political elites are open to democratic principles.

Therefore, which countries receive assistance is a particularly important question. Recent scholarship by Jennifer Gandhi of Emory University and others has demonstrated that some savvy dictators use their parliaments as a means to expand their grip on power, rather than as a meaningful check on the regime's will.[3] Western support for those parliaments can, at times, unintentionally play into the hands of an authoritarian elite. At other times, though, the programs are a misguided use of funds from the start.

In October 2014, for example, USAID announced $216 million in funding for a five-year venture aimed at empowering Afghan women, by ensuring that they will be included in the next generation of Afghanistan's political elite. Additionally, the project aimed to garner an additional $200 million in funding from supportive Western governments, for a total expenditure of $416 million.[4] This is an extremely important goal and one that I wholeheartedly support. The world would be a much better place if more women were involved in politics, from Afghanistan to Zimbabwe. But, according to John F. Sopko, Special Inspector General for Afghanistan Reconstruction, it is likely that "Afghan women engaged in the program may be left without any tangible benefit upon completion."[5] Afghanistan's First Lady, Rula Ghani, echoed his concerns in even more scathing language: "I do hope that we are not going to fall again into the game of contracting and sub-contracting and the routine of workshops and training sessions generating a lot of certificates on paper and little else."[6]

Unfortunately, those fears seem to be justified. Even if they were not—even if the program were implemented perfectly and the women involved benefited—there is a reasonable question to ask: is the spending cost-effective? Is it good value? Well, as of 2014, the World Bank estimated that the per capita GDP of Afghanistan was $634.[7] The joint USAID program is slated to cost $416 million to help "empower" 75,000 women. In other words, Western taxpayers will be spending about $5,545 per woman in the program, equivalent to almost nine years of wages for the average Afghan. Moreover, with just 75,000 women targeted, the program will, at best, reach one in every two hundred Afghan women, or 0.5 per cent of the female population. The program has an absolutely admirable goal. I believe in the long, slow process of democratization by education as much as I believe in empowering women—and other disempowered groups—to become more involved in politics. But given the global scarcity of democracy promotion resources, the program was simply misguided, because of its feasibility, not its laudable intentions.

Moreover, when the inspector general began asking questions about this specific program's funding, the answers he got back were troubling. In a letter sent to USAID, he lamented that:

> despite multiple requests, USAID could not provide the audit team a list of all the agency's projects, programs, and initiatives intended to support Afghan women, or how much the agency spent on each effort. USAID was

also unable to provide data demonstrating a causal relationship or correlation between the agency's efforts to support Afghan women and improvements in Afghan women's lives.[8]

The main contractors used by the program were Chemonics, Development Alternatives Inc., and Tetra Tech. All three are for-profit contractors.

Women certainly deserve to be empowered in Afghanistan, where the human rights situation for women is indeed dire and worthy of significant Western attention and consternation. But the real problem is two-fold; first, Afghanistan is facing a serious insurgency from Taliban forces that are taking over significant swathes of territory in the country. If that advance continues, women will suffer far more than men— and not just in terms of political rights—regardless of their empowerment training. Second, the current government is not democratic. So even if the program does successfully empower 0.5 per cent of the next generation of women to be involved in politics, they will become involved in a system that is fundamentally rigged. Is that the best use of $416 million? What are we thinking?

A second change in approach also needs to occur: Western governments must roll back low-level democracy promotion efforts that pour funding into regimes driven by an overt hostility to democratic reform. I have outlined how the "Saudi Arabia Effect" compels Western governments to support strategically important despots rather than working to undermine them by promoting genuine democracy. Yet in some cases, Western governments disburse considerable resources aimed at sowing the seeds of democratic change in places that are lost causes for low-level democracy promotion programs. Countries like Saudi Arabia, North Korea or Turkmenistan might become democratic in the long term, but the catalyst is unlikely to come from Western training programs for civil society.

While I believe that Western governments should consistently promote democracy as a long-term geostrategic interest, above and beyond competing short-term interests, I also recognize that it is unlikely to happen anytime soon. So, at a minimum, for countries like Saudi Arabia that are considered security imperatives where democracy is put on the diplomatic backburner, I would at least recommend not wasting money on half-hearted training programs aimed at democratic reform in a fundamentally undemocratic system. Those resources could be better spent in countries that actually have an appetite for reform.

Uzbekistan offers a compelling illustration of this problem. Western governments are engaged in Quixotic democracy promotion there, tilting at authoritarian windmills rather than investing strategically in democracy where there are more realistic prospects for change. Until his death on 2 September 2016, the twenty-five-year president of Uzbekistan, Islam Karimov, was one of the world's most ruthless dictators. Some 10–12,000 so-called "dissidents" have been jailed, but they are clearly political prisoners.[9] The litany of human rights abuses perpetrated by Karimov's regime reads like a horror story of history, featuring barbaric practices that ended elsewhere hundreds of years or even a millennium ago. With startling parallels to slavery in the American South, right down to the same commodity, thousands of university students—and even small children—are conscripted to pick cotton each year.[10] In 2003, an inquest by Western governments into the deaths of two detainees who had died in custody revealed that they had been boiled alive. When the disfigured bodies were returned to the families of the victims, the families found that the victims' fingernails had been ripped off before they were boiled.[11] There are thousands of documented cases from Karimov's secretive regime that showcase a systematic pattern of state-sponsored torture and abuse that seems straight out of a medieval tragedy rather than a modern political system. Some practices would even be amusing for their strange novelty if the stakes weren't so high for the people involved. In one particularly bizarre case, an inmate's prison sentence was extended because he had committed the grave offense of "incorrectly peeling carrots" in the prison kitchen.[12]

Against this backdrop, the idea of democracy taking root while Karimov was in power-or, indeed, soon after his death-is clearly an absurd farce. As Freedom House notes, "Uzbekistan's constitution enshrines the freedom of speech, religion, assembly, and participation in politics."[13] Yet in practice, none of these freedoms exist and the police state eagerly silences anyone attempting to exercise such rights. The parliament is a rubber-stamp for the regime's will; the judiciary is a tool of the state that is often used to silence its opponents; corruption is rampant, as Uzbekistan's rulers routinely partner with organized crime.

Corruption is even part of family life in the ruling regime. Take Karimov's own daughter, Gulnara Karimova. She dabbled as a jewelry designer; as a diplomat representing Uzbekistan at the United Nations, based out of a $20 million villa in Geneva; and as a self-proclaimed political scientist (before her father banned political science completely in Uzbekistan, in September 2015).[14] But that wasn't enough, so Karimova set out to become an international pop star. She recorded with legendary Spanish star Julio Iglesias, convinced Sting to perform a controversial concert in Uzbekistan in 2009, and aimed to make her own ascent up the international music charts. She opted for the stage name of GooGoosha, allegedly because it was her father's pet name for his beloved daughter. Her first major music video, for a song called *Unutma Meni*, or "Don't Forget Me", features a surreal computer-generated dreamscape involving an expensive baby blue sports car flying through the air toward a mythic golden city—a wonderfully apt reflection of her opulent lifestyle, floating high above the oppressed people of Uzbekistan.

In 2014, that dream lifestyle came crashing down. GooGoosha was accused of taking $1 billion in bribes, largely from Scandinavian and Russian telecommunications giants, in return for guaranteeing access to the Uzbek market. She required telecoms businesses to give her a 26 per cent stake in their investment in exchange for preferential treatment.[15] When the story broke, President Karimov broke ties with his daughter over the embarrassing scandal and confined her to house arrest, since which time nothing has been heard of her. In spite of her earlier musical pleas not to forget her, it seems quite likely that GooGoosha will be forgotten as she languishes away for bringing public disgrace to a secretively disgraceful regime. Leaked diplomatic cables refer to the famed GooGoosha as "the single most hated person in the country."[16]

This Shakespearean intrigue is indicative of a simple fact: democracy is as plentiful in Uzbekistan as oxygen is in space. On Freedom House's scale of 1 to 7 (7 being most authoritarian), the best score that Uzbekistan has managed on any indicator was a 6.75. It hasn't budged from its overall score of 6.93 for years, though it has steadily and gradually gotten worse since 2003, when it had a still dismal score of 6.46. In short, there is every indication that this is not only a horrific a regime, but one that is asphyxiating any remaining gasps of democracy over time.

In spite of all this, Western governments still spend tens of millions of dollars to "promote democracy" in Uzbekistan. The USAID webpage on "Democracy, Human Rights, and Governance" in Uzbekistan touts American democracy support funding that "strengthens organizations that champion women's issues, disabled rights, and the environment."[17] None of these efforts are likely to promote genuine democratic reform. After all, perhaps the best thing for disabled rights nationwide would be a regime that didn't leave people wheelchair-bound after being tortured by the government. Again, as with women's rights in Afghanistan, the plight of disabled people living in unsympathetic governments is not an issue that should be ignored—far from it. Giving a voice to the voiceless is a major aim of promoting democracy. But it is worth asking the question: why are we funding these around-the-edges human rights and governance reforms while still providing direct military and financial assistance to a regime that boils people alive?[18] Couldn't that money be better spent elsewhere?

One possible rationale for niche spending comes from the democracy promoters themselves, who sometimes feel trapped by a system that tends to allocate funding based on "feel good" programs that may provide marginal benefits to the communities involved but fail to make serious inroads toward democratic reform—at least not for decades. They target deserving communities, but aim to help specific groups rather than reforming the system more generally. One country director of a major international NGO that works on democracy promotion in the Middle East told me:

> Each year when you're making grant proposals, you have to figure out which way the winds are blowing in the donor countries. Which programs will get the most support this year? Last year it was disability rights. The year before that it was youth outreach. The year before that was inclusion of women. And once you figure it out, NGOs tend to make their grant proposals accordingly.[19]

This approach is problematic, not only because it can't see the democratic forest for the trees, but also because it creates a disjointed strategy that shifts its focus year to year, rather than committing to meaningful long-term engagement. As Thomas Carothers, one of the world's most respected experts on democracy promotion, recently told me, "It's impossible to overstate the influence of short-term thinking in the field. Anything looking two years into the future is considered 'long-term.'"[20]

Others argue that Western governments need to work actively in places like Uzbekistan because Western (and specifically American) funding in Uzbekistan works to expand the presence of NGOs within the country. As the American government claims, "USAID's civic advocacy program trains and supports more active NGOs in their efforts to influence policymaking at the national level."[21] However, the few NGOs that still exist in Uzbekistan are simply apologist stooges for the regime, and the notion that anyone other than Islam Karimov has had any say in influencing "policymaking at the national level" since independence in 1991 is a joke.

Whether it's in Afghanistan or Uzbekistan or elsewhere around the world, it's easy to find programs that seem wasteful. What is more difficult, however, is figuring out how to spend the money more appropriately and cost-effectively. At the heart of that debate is where to spend the money. There are 196 countries in the world today. The United States provides about $3–5 billion each year for promoting democracy, usually around a quarter of what is spent globally. These are not fixed funding levels; they ebb and flow. But hard tradeoffs do need to be made. In my view, spreading the funding thinly and treating all countries as equal prospects for democratic reform is misguided. By contrast, targeted funding to countries that have an appetite for democratic reform can make all the difference during a critical transition period.

On this front, Tunisia is often touted as the closest thing there is to a paragon in the field, as Western organizations like the International Republican Institute and the National Democratic Institute provided crucial training to candidates, elected officials, and civil society organizations—helping them gain the technical expertise necessary to guide a transition and avoid the pitfalls that derail young democracies all too often.[22] It helped having men like Said Ferjani and his moderate, consensus-building counterparts in rival parties, but their efforts were pushed forward by foreign support. It would be an enormous boon to democracy in the Middle East if Tunisia thrives, setting a model that can be replicated for other states in the region to follow.

Similarly fruitful efforts have been replicated around the globe in countries with a genuine appetite for democratic change. A milestone 2007 study published in *World Politics* found that democracy assistance funding from Western governments did indeed have a strong and positive impact on making recipient countries more democratic.[23] But the difference between somewhere like Uzbekistan and somewhere like Ghana—one of the better performing African democracies—is that the Ghanaian political system is receptive to reform. Both the ruling government and the political opposition are willing to enlist foreign sponsors to help iron out the wrinkles in the nation's democratic transition and consolidation.

For example, the Canadian government spent $2.5 million to help support the Electoral Commission's "Training of Candidates and Polling Agents" project. The project successfully provided technical expertise to twenty presidential candidates, their running mates, their campaign managers, and more than a thousand parliamentary candidates around the country. The program also reached 220,000 poll staff, the people on the frontline ensuring the election's integrity at the local level. The European Union spent $2.5 million to help print sufficient ballot papers; earlier elections marred by a shortage of ballot papers had been met by unrest as voters (understandably) reacted to being disenfranchised for such an avoidable reason. It was a comparatively tiny expenditure, but one that made a tangible difference. Finally, the Dutch government helped organize presidential debates, while encouraging the major candidates to strike a civil tone; they did, and the political climate calmed down considerably from earlier hints of vitriol.[24]

Together, foreign efforts to entrench Ghanaian democracy paid off; the 2008 election was not perfect, but it was a model for how other African countries could make significant improvements to their electoral systems. Since 2008, Ghana has had a peaceful transition from a president who died in office and a successful albeit imperfect presidential election in 2012, and is currently on track to replicate that success in a 2016 vote. Moreover, since 2008, the Ghanaian economy has grown at a breakneck pace, averaging roughly 8 per cent growth from 2008–16, with a high of 14 per cent in 2011.[25] Of course, there are myriad reasons for Ghana's comparative success in its transition toward genuine democracy, but it is the type of country that is worthy of further support.

In Chapter 5, I argued that high-level and low-level democracy promotion needs to be coordinated so that diplomatic rhetoric and high-level pressure matches strategies on the ground. Countries like Tunisia, Ghana, Georgia, and Bolivia are all imperfect democracies that face considerable challenges. This is a pivotal time for each of them, and they will benefit from—and eagerly embrace—foreign support from all echelons. They need both diplomats on their side (who also hold their feet to the democratic fire), and training staff and technical expertise. Between the two, they can transform a democratic transition into a consolidated democratic pedestal to build upon. In these places, individual programs have a reasonable chance of making a difference. Money spent there is a good democratic investment. It's a different game in Uzbekistan, North Korea, Saudi Arabia, Turkmenistan, and a slew of other countries where programming for disenfranchised communities is more like rearranging the deck chairs on the Titanic; empowering disabled people in Tashkent cannot stop them from being oppressed, because the entire nation is under the yoke of a ruthless authoritarian despot.

There are therefore two possible solutions that could work for low-level democracy promotion in dictatorial countries that seem like lost causes. First, Western governments could stick to a grant-based approach by directly funding local civil society organizations rather than international NGOs that waste considerable amounts of funding setting up offices and providing housing, security protection, and other amenities to foreign staff. This is the approach used by the United States National Endowment for Democracy and it could be continued in places like Uzbekistan.[26]

Alternatively, the United States could simply divert democracy and governance funding from places with no demonstrated willingness to reform. This is a difficult choice, because the West should not simply leave oppressed Uzbeks or Turkmen to fend for themselves. But it is questionable whether low-level democracy promotion is a worthwhile expenditure when President Karimov's successor is most likely to be ousted, or to institute democratic reform themselves, if the West uses high-level tools to pressure the regime. When funding push comes to budgetary shove in democracy promotion allocations, it may—at times—make sense to prioritize the Ghanas and Tunisias of the world over the Uzbekistans.

I could be completely wrong about all of this. And the reason for that, as Thomas Carothers explained to me recently, is that:

> Our democracy assistance programs were set up twenty or thirty years ago and have been surprisingly static. There has never been a comprehen-

sive bottom-up review. The State Department, for example, doesn't have a very well thought out policy review process to figure out what works best and what doesn't work at all.[27]

This, in short, is why programs like the doomed iPhone app in Iran, or the $416 million scheme that provided "no tangible benefit" to Afghan women, get funded in the first place. We are simply not entirely sure what works when it comes to on-the-ground democracy promotion, an example of what former US secretary of defense Donald Rumsfeld would call a "known unknown." That obviously needs to be fixed, and a systematic review of spending should be enacted by the United States and the European Union to ensure that every dollar spent is spent well (while being careful not to micromanage with an excess of bureaucratic hoops for organizations to jump through). USAID is already moving in that direction, thankfully. But regardless of the findings of any specific funding review, it's safe to say that Western governments need to be more careful about how they spend scarce resources to promote democracy across the world—and to be sure that they target those resources to places where funding has a reasonable chance of catalyzing meaningful democratic change. Otherwise, some of the West's programs amount to a fool's errand, bringing expensive and marginal programming to countries where, at least for the short- and medium-term, democracy is doomed to fail.

In the meantime, we can take heart in the fact that the recently lifted sanctions against Iran mean that Iranians can now easily access the iPhone app store, allowing them not only to download the next iteration of Voice of America software, but also any of the latest hits that GooGoosha is able to upload from her time spent in house arrest.

10

# THE CARROT

*Principle 8: Use economic incentives to encourage democratization and discourage despotism*

In late 2015, I visited the infamous Corner House in Riga, Latvia. The history of Latvia is closely intertwined with this single chilling structure, an Art Deco building that was KGB headquarters since before World War II, when the Soviet intelligence services didn't yet go by that name. In 1940, as Soviet invaders began to overrun Latvia, General Ludvigs Bolšteins sat at his desk on the fifth floor of the Corner House. He wrote a simple note:

> To my superiors:
> We, the Latvians, built ourselves a brand new house—our country.
> Now, an alien power wants to force us to tear it down ourselves.
> In this I cannot take part.[1]

Then, General Bolšteins put his revolver to his temple and pulled the trigger; he was found slumped at his desk. Bolšteins' warnings were prescient; by 1941, the USSR had either murdered or deported 15,000 Latvians, massacring them or sending them to forced labor camps in Siberia. In a single purge, Latvia's political, economic, and cultural elite ceased to exist.[2]

The Nazis then took control of Latvia from 1941 until 1944. In order to maximize local opposition to the Soviets, the Nazi regime opened the Corner House to the public. What visitors discovered was horrific. The dungeons in the basement were kept above 30 degrees Celsius (86 degrees Fahrenheit); the cells were constantly flooded with bright lights to inhibit sleep; and prisoners were randomly selected for execution to keep everyone afraid that their turn could be next.[3]

When the Soviet Union re-conquered Latvia in the final campaign of World War II, the Corner House returned to business as usual. The floors were painted red to conceal bloodstains. To get prisoners to talk, they were sometimes hoisted onto hooks in the courtyard and left suspended off the ground. When that didn't work and execution was chosen instead, KGB officers ran noisy car engines outside the doors of the Corner House each morning—partly to obscure the sound of gunshots from neighboring residents and partly so that the vehicles were ready to transport the bodies quickly out of sight.[4] On the exterior facade of the Corner House, a nondescript postbox was installed. Family members of the prisoners could enquire after their relatives— were they still alive? And conspiratorial Latvians could slip in accusatory notes, giving the KGB information about a possible dissident or sowing suspicion against a personal enemy.

Knuts Skujenieks was one prisoner who was lucky enough to escape with his life. After he was discovered writing Latvian nationalist poetry, his thick notebooks were confiscated and he was imprisoned. He spent six months as a prisoner in the Corner House before being shipped off to a forced labor camp in the Ural Mountains for the following six years. His story is fairly representative of Latvians who were blacklisted and arrested during the Soviet occupation of Latvia—at least the ones who made it out.[5]

Visiting the Corner House is a jarring experience. The haunting authoritarian past permeating the decaying walls of the former KGB headquarters is so distinctly at odds with modern Latvia. Riga today is a beautiful city, with a thriving democracy, a booming economy, and flourishing culture—home to the next generation following in the footsteps of Knuts Skujenieks, as activist artists are now celebrated and encouraged, rather than detained and deported. In the span of just twelve years, Latvia went from life under the Soviet yoke to life as a full-fledged member of the European Union. In 2014, Riga was Europe's Capital of Culture, an about-face from a time when writing poetry was enough to earn a one-way ticket to Siberia.

This stunning and sudden transformation was replicated elsewhere in Central and Eastern Europe. But one of the major drivers of democratization in places like Latvia was the European Union's extraordinarily successful program of political conditionality for accession. Put simply, the policy that only democracies could join the European Union enticed bordering states to become democracies. In Latvia, there was already a strong drive for democracy right after the dissolution of the Soviet Union. The European Union's insistence on maintaining and consolidating democracy ensured that Latvian politicians never took their eye off the prize; they knew that any backsliding away from democracy would jeopardize their application to tap into the immense benefits of being formally part of Europe. That is a strong carrot to offer a country like Latvia. There is broad agreement among scholars that this policy has been an unparalleled success—perhaps the most successful democratization program in modern history. In this chapter, I argue that the model should be expanded. Multilateral economic incentives can be a major force for democratization—if they are conceived and implemented carefully.

Latvia's transition to democracy was comparatively smooth. For other European countries that had rockier transitions after the end of the Cold War, the accession criteria focused political leaders to rally behind a common purpose. Petty squabbles gave way to compromise for the sake of democracy. As with any political transition, there were stops and starts in places like Estonia, Bulgaria, and Romania as they vied for membership, but by and large the pattern was the same: the economic carrot was sufficient to ensure that a punitive stick was not necessary.

In 1992, Latvia's per capita GDP stood at $1,854, about $5 per day per person. For comparison, Botswana's per capita GDP at the time was $1,000 higher than Latvia's. By 2003, the eve of Latvia's induction into the European Union, things had improved, but not by much—to just $4,890 per year, or $13 per day. Today, after just over a decade as part of the European Union, the per capita GDP in Latvia is $15,375, $42 a day, higher than Russia, Argentina, Brazil, Turkey, and Mexico, and more than double Botswana's.[6] It didn't take a genius during the 1990s to realize that joining the European Union had major economic benefits for Central and Eastern Europe, which is why virtually every prospective member state got its democratic ducks in a row as it was being considered. Today, every country in the European Union is a consolidated democracy—something that hardly seemed possible for countries that were cleaved from the collapsing Soviet Union at the end of the Cold War.

Yet just as Latvia is emblematic of the EU's dramatic pull, its capital, Riga, was also home to an interaction that shows the limitations of Europe's stick for countries that veer away from democracy. In May 2015, a relatively minor EU summit was held in Riga. At the canned and scripted photo-op, the president of the European Commission, Jean-Claude Juncker, was smiling a canned, scripted smile as cameras clicked away by the dozens. Then, in a surprisingly unscripted moment, the bespectacled, gray-haired president turned to his colleagues and said: "The dictator is coming." On cue, Hungary's president, Viktor Orbán—who has been accused of dangerous authoritarian tendencies as he rolls back democracy in Hungary—arrived on the scene. He walked up to Juncker to shake his hand, but Juncker held up his hand in an awkward salute, slapped Orbán's hand, smiled, said "Hello Dictator," and then slapped Orbán's face (sort of) playfully.[7] The whole uncomfortable incident was a telling window onto the frustrating limits of the EU's ability to corral wayward leaders within the Union back toward democracy once they are tempted by authoritarianism. Beyond the slap, there's not much more.

Orbán's Hungary is worrying. But at first glance, Hungary's accession to the European Union seemed promising. As with Latvia, the economy expanded considerably in just over a decade, from a pre-accession GDP per capita of $8,365 in 2003 to just under $14,000.[8] Hungary seemed on track, matching its economic progress with a democratic upswing as political institutions continued to solidify around liberal democratic principles. Yet in 2010, the rightwing populist Fidesz Party took power, with Orbán at the helm of a supermajority in parliament. The supermajority was forged with just over half of all votes cast, but it nonetheless resulted in Fidesz capturing 68 per cent of the seats up for grabs. Clearing the two-thirds supermajority threshold was hugely consequential because it put Fidesz out of reach from dissent as it turned to the momentous task of enshrining democratic principles in a brand new constitution.

Constitutions are not like run-of-the-mill laws; rather than shaping what is legal and illegal, constitutions shape the rules of the game for writing all future laws. They define the parameters of political action for years, if not decades or even centuries, to come. In that sense, they are the documents most dependent on political consensus. Without consensus, constitutions are doomed to fail and it's usually just a matter of time before contested constitutions incite destabilizing political strife.

Yet Orbán and his party chose to shut out the opposition and plow ahead with drafting the constitution entirely on their own. In one particularly out-of-touch moment, József Szájer—one of Orbán's close friends—boasted in a blog post that he was enjoying writing the entire constitution himself, on his personal iPad: "Steve Jobs will surely be happy when he gets word that Hungary's new constitution is being written on an iPad, actually my iPad." And then, without further reflection on the fact that some people might find it deeply troubling that a single politician from the ruling party could personally draft the whole constitution, Szájer went on to sing his iPad's praises: "The best is I don't have to wait for minutes to turn it on, like with a normal laptop. I can open it anywhere and can take advantage of every minute. It's a miracle! ... Thanx (sic) Steve Jobs!"[9] This bizarre post was published on 1 March 2011, just a day before Steve Jobs unveiled the thinner, faster iPad 2. Yet another miracle from Cupertino, California, this time enlisted to erode democracy in Budapest faster than would have been possible with a laptop.

For the opposition, the new constitution was anything but a miracle. They boycotted the drafting process and the vote approving it. But they were powerless to stop it. Since then, Fidesz has weakened media independence, cowed the judiciary, and passed skewed electoral "reform" aimed at maintaining its political dominance even if the votes don't warrant it. Former American ambassador Eleni Kounalakis has related the following: while she was reminding Orbán of democratic principles—and prodding him to stop undermining them—he burst out: "All this talk about democracy is bullshit!"[10] A democrat, Orbán is not, but he is in charge of a country that is firmly ensconced in the European Union.

That's the trouble. While Latvia, Hungary, Estonia, and many others were induced to democratize in pursuit of Europe's economic carrots, there has been no stick to punish those who would rollback democracy once they joined the club. That needs to change, certainly, but it also raises two key provocative questions: can the European Union's ability to transform countries like Latvia from dictatorship to democracy with economic incentives be replicated elsewhere? And can we learn from and correct the European Union's failure to punish countries like Hungary that are guilty of democratic backsliding?

Many see the European Union as an outlier. It was formed by a group of democracies, giving the body remarkable cohesion when it rallied around democratic criteria for membership. Moreover, prospective members were all on Europe's doorstep, an important boon for democratization; scholars have found that there is a sort of democratic diffusion effect, as countries in a democratic "neighborhood" are more likely to democratize than nations surrounded by dictators, despots, and counterfeit democrats.[11]

These factors are critical aspects of why Europe was able to use its economic carrot to such effect. A hundred years ago, any approach to creating international organizations to bind members more closely— be it in politics or economics—usually had to be regional, for logistical reasons. But in a globalized, hyper-connected world, the European Union's ability to use economic incentives to spread democracy can be replicated elsewhere without the need for contiguous borders.

Specifically, Western governments should consider creating a free trade zone called, for instance, the League of Democracies, an international organization that only offers membership to consolidated democracies. This is not a new idea; it has been trumpeted in the United States by major players—including senators and intellectuals—on both right and left.[12] But those proposals typically envision not a commercial but a strong political alliance, one that could be used to supplant the United Nations, or, as cynics would have it, to give a legitimizing rubber stamp to American policy on the global stage. It's not a good idea. Intertwining politics between countries as diverse as Brazil, India, South Korea, and the United States is sure to be messy and divisive. As a result, I do not support that vision, but I do support creating a democratic trade zone. Keeping politics out of it as far as possible could reduce the inevitable impulse of Western governments to politicize the club and only open it to allies, rather than using democratic government as the sole condition of membership.

Economic partnerships are strong incentives for national policy-making, and not just in Europe. If you don't believe me, just ask the governments of Chile, Malaysia, Peru, or Vietnam, as they scramble to adapt in order to secure their membership in the Trans-Pacific Partnership, a controversial Pacific Rim free trade zone that is currently in its birthing stages. Whether you favor or oppose the proposal, parts of the free trade zone (stretching from Nunavut, Canada to Hobart, Tasmania, for example) are separated by more than 10,000 miles—nearly four times the span of the European Union. Moreover, unlike the EU, which is connected by overland transport options, most of the Trans-Pacific Partnership members can only trade with one another via air or shipping routes. The Trans-Pacific Partnership proves that globalization has made international free trade zones possible and desirable even when gargantuan distances separate the member states. If bordering the Pacific Ocean is a good enough linking factor to bind together prospective members of that proposed partnership, why not bind together the world's democracies with stronger trading links and other economic incentives?

Here's how it would work. Rather than the current convoluted process of determining free trade zones with a disjointed and inconsistent morass of diplomatic jockeying, membership in the League of Democracies would be meritocratic and removed from the whims of individual member nations—even powerful ones like the United States. There are already many, many organizations that score individual countries on their democratic qualities; founding members of the League from across the world (and not just Western Europe or the United States) could agree upon existing indices or come up with robust, technocratic assessments of democratic quality. What matters most is that membership not be politicized, but instead guaranteed to genuine democracies and closed to non-democracies. This would be the (very) hard part. Yet, like Odysseus strapping himself to the mast of his ship because he didn't trust himself while it passed the Sirens, this process would ensure that individual member states tempted to give into a despot's siren song could not invite them into the League during a moment of diplomatic weakness.

Most importantly, perhaps, the League of Democracies would provide a powerful and static incentive for prospective members to reform their political systems. From the perspective of a despot, democratization is a risky move. As Chapter 7 illustrated, a number of autocrats fear being killed, jailed, or exiled if they open the political floodgates to democratic competition. And, as I outlined in Chapter 5, some regimes face unexpectedly harsh diplomatic treatment one moment, only to receive unexpectedly warm treatment the next. This inconsistency undermines the enticement of democratization. From the perspective of those in power, the transition to democracy currently offers concrete and serious risks, but only shaky and indeterminate rewards.

The League of Democracies would drastically shift that calculation: with a clear reward waiting, two new pressures would push despots to open their political systems as they drift ever closer toward that tantalizing economic carrot. First, business would be on board with democracy. Whether in Turkmenistan, Bolivia, or even a solid democracy such as Japan, business interests exert an important force on politics. By making clear that further democratic reform will result in new (and potentially major) economic trade routes, business can be enlisted as democracy's ally.

Second, despots themselves may be tempted to experiment with democratic reforms in order to retain political popularity. It is a myth that people like Islam Karimov and Alexander Lukashenko are indifferent toward their people; they may not care deeply for their wellbeing and they may not care to hear their political voices, but they do worry consistently about the risks of becoming deeply unpopular with their own citizenry. For the same reason that Thailand's military junta chose to give away free haircuts after it took power (in a strange attempt to win over the public), despots facing a clear slate of economic enticements to democratize may view this as an avenue to assuage public criticism. Certainly, not everyone who rules with an iron fist will trade it in for the velvet glove, but some will—and, as was the case in Latvia, it could be a major driver of reform across the globe.

Of course, it is a long road from despotism to consolidated democracy. For those making progress on that journey, a second tier of the League could be created—again, with clear, consistent, and de-politicized membership criteria. This would be akin to the stepping-stones used during the scrutiny process prior to EU accession: some benefits, but nothing like the real rewards that come as a full member state. As with my "golden handcuffs" proposal (see Chapter 7), this idea is one mere blueprint for change, but makes clear that it's not only possible, but a huge missed opportunity to make democracy something that countries can use to cash in; by making democracy financially beneficial, a whole host of problems associated with stalled democratic transitions could disappear, while other nations might even be brought out from the dictatorial cold.

This is not the current approach. The European Union has "association agreements" in the Middle East & North Africa region with Tunisia (signed by Ben Ali's regime), Morocco and Jordan (kingdoms), Egypt (military dictatorship), and Algeria (a hybrid authoritarian regime, somewhere between dictatorship and democracy). The United States has free trade agreements with a variety of countries from across the spectrum, from Canada and Mexico (democracies) to Singapore (authoritarian-lite) and Bahrain (dictatorial monarchy), with many shades in between.[13] It is a haphazard approach that is inefficient and fails to make use of trade policy as an effective tool to catalyze political reform.

Now, I'm not so naïve as to believe that this proposal is problem-free. There are major wrinkles that would need to be sorted out; the birthing pains of any free trade agreement involves some compromise, sacrifice, and vigorous debate in pursuit of an agreement that leaves all nations better off. Hard choices would need to be made. The logistics are tricky. Nonetheless, the current slapdash approach to trade policy does little to achieve the political transformations that Western governments generally hope to see in the world. That is a wasted opportunity.

Opponents of this idea will certainly worry, and legitimately so, about a possible foreign policy straitjacket that limits diplomatic flexibility. It's a risk. But it's also worth bearing in mind that a League of Democracies would not force Western nations to cut off trade links with non-democratic states. It would simply guarantee a coherence to trade policy, all while creating a race toward democracy, as nations compete against one another to be democratic enough to join and reap the rewards.

Moreover, it is also true that such a League may have a limited effect on countries that are already economically self-sufficient, such as Qatar or Brunei. However, these are not likely targets for democratization anyway. Rather, a democracy-based free trade zone would be a powerful force for countries that are trapped between democracy and dictatorship—tipping the scales in favor of the former while making the latter seem even more unappealing.

The League would also be a clear boon to countries that are trying to do the right thing but are suffering the growing pains of a democratic transition. Tunisia, for example, needs economic help. The combination of terrorist attacks bleeding across the border from Libya, the subsequent loss of tourism, and the lingering effects of decades of crony capitalist dictatorship, has left the country's economy badly battered. Right now, Tunisians like Said Ferjani are doing the right things. But they need more than a Nobel Prize to stay the course and continue selling the virtues of democracy to their people; after all, as I acknowledged in Chapter 1, people tend to prefer a growing economy under authoritarianism to a collapsing or stagnating one in a democratic system. The longer a democratic transition looks like Benin, the more likely it is to fail as people clamber to be Singapore instead. An outside force could help, making democracy and growth a self-fulfilling prophecy.

A League of Democracies would be an extremely powerful bloc. If you add up the likely members—the European Union, the United States, the United Kingdom, India, Brazil, Canada, Australia, Japan, New Zealand, Indonesia, Argentina, South Korea, and Mexico, to name a few—you get roughly $55 trillion in GDP. That's more than three times the size of the European Union or the United States. Cumulatively, it accounts for roughly 7 out of every 10 dollars in the world economy. It's a big carrot.

Critically, the more influential the carrot, the less necessary a stick becomes. That's an important maxim, because, as outlined in Chapter 4, democracy by war hasn't exactly worked recently. But it's also important in the economic realm, because the major economic "stick"—sanctions—has proven woefully inadequate at compelling reluctant elites to democratize.

Ever since the Athenians contributed to the outbreak of the Peloponnesian War 2,400 years ago by imposing an early form of sanctions on Megara, the use of sanctions as a diplomatic tool has had a checkered history at best.[14] Scholars and policymakers both agree that sanctions are never a "good" policy; they are simply sometimes the least bad option.

Sanctions were imposed on Iraq from 6 August 1990, four days after Saddam Hussein invaded Kuwait, sparking Operation Desert Storm. They remained largely in full force until 2003, when Saddam Hussein was toppled by the US-led military intervention. As a result of the sanctions, which included severe restrictions on all trade, including medicine and food, the Iraqi government established a program for its citizens that provided 1,000 calories per day, about 40 per cent of their daily nutritional requirements. Nearly two out of three Iraqis relied on this program. Malnourishment soared for children. Water and sewage systems collapsed, and doctors were unable to cope with even basic maladies that had previously been easily treatable. The biting economic cost of the sanctions siphoned huge amounts of cash away from Iraq's comparatively robust school system. The plight of women worsened, as families that had previously enrolled their daughters in school pulled them out to help at home. Yet still, Saddam ruled. And even though democratization was not the primary goal of sanctions against Iraq, there is wide agreement that the sanctions were a humanitarian disaster with limited, if any, political upside.[15]

On the other hand, sanctions against apartheid-era South Africa probably had little effect on digging the regime's grave, but at least did have an important "psychological" effect, according to Phil Levy of Yale University.[16] In this sense, sanctions can be important signals to regimes as to just how isolated they are on the international stage. But careful diplomacy can achieve that same signaling, using surgical precision rather than taking a meat cleaver to the target regime's body politic with economic sanctions.

Learning from these biting unintended consequences, some "smart sanctions" have been developed—including economic instruments that exclude food and medical supplies from the blacklist.[17] These can still produce unintended consequences because they are difficult to tailor effectively, but they may offer a better approach. In other instances, widespread sanctions are avoided altogether. "Targeted sanctions" are currently in vogue. They aim to punish the elite while sparing the population. For example, in Zimbabwe, Western governments targeted President Robert Mugabe and his entourage with travel bans and asset freezes.[18] These have been stunningly inconsequential, and have possibly even entrenched the 92-year-old's wrinkled grip on power; Mugabe has cleverly blamed Zimbabwe's economic woes on the perceived neo-imperialist bullying represented by the sanctions, successfully deflecting blame from where it should be: on his mismanagement of the economy.[19] With a bit of political jiu-jitsu, the sanctions, sent to Mugabe as an economic attack, have been transformed into an unintended gift.

The lesson is that sanctions that truly bite may have a shot at changing the status quo, but only with tremendous collateral damage and the risk that public opinion in the targeted country will turn irreversibly against the Western governments making their economy—and sometimes their children—bleed. In most cases, the spilled blood is in vain. On the other hand, sanctions that only target the elite are unlikely to work, and may even entrench the regime further.

Even the biggest proponent of the sanctions "stick" would likely acknowledge that they should be used only when carrots have been exhausted. Since trade is not being employed to even close to its full potential as an economic incentive to lure despots into democracy, it's hard to argue that the approach of diplomatic overtures has ever truly been exhausted. We should try to craft a bigger carrot, and the League of Democracies would do precisely that.

Finally, there is a hidden but crucial benefit that would accompany the formation of such an economic partnership. Member states—from Indonesia to Chile to the United States—would have to agree upon criteria that could be used to evaluate democratic governance. For the first time, there would be an official, agreed-upon classification of democracies beyond scholarly datasets and esoteric NGO reports. The second tier of countries would require a uniform judgment as to which countries were actively democratizing, rather than stagnating between the extremes. Imagine how different it would be if countries were competing against each other to be more democratic, in hot pursuit of a lucrative label.

Knowing whether a country deserves the "democracy" label or not is more important than you might think, because democracy is more than just a word. The term is currently bandied about far too often to describe countries that host sham elections without any system that could warrant being called a democracy. This over-use has been helped along by the sort of democratic "grade inflation" described in Chapter 5. The problem is that people then begin to associate "democracy" with governments that are not at all democratic. This has seriously damaging long-term effects for the prospects of democracy. If citizens believe that they are living in a democracy when they are, in fact, living in a counterfeit version of it, they are far more likely to reject democratization as a concept. They will, over time, become more willing to embrace the false prophets of military rule or authoritarian strongmen who, more often than not, promise everything but deliver nothing.

For example, with a few key exceptions, Africa is a patchwork quilt of counterfeit democracies with some nasty despots thrown in the mix. Most African countries hold contested elections, but few are meaningfully free or fair. The rule of law is weak. Yet when tens of thousands of Africans were surveyed and asked whether they were satisfied with democracy in their country, just 965 out of more than 50,000 respondents replied: "this country is not a democracy."[20] Instead, most accepted the premise that they lived in a democratic country but that it was not necessarily a good system. More than four out of ten respondents said that they were "Not at all satisfied" or "Not very satisfied" with democracy. If you add in those who replied that they were only "Fairly satisfied" with democracy, those with, at best, a tepid view of democracy comprise more than three-quarters of respondents across the continent. Electoral grade inflation and low expectations have adjusted the bar ever lower.

Of course, this is not because democracy is failing Africa, but because most of Africa is not actually democratic. As a result, it's no surprise that skepticism is the overwhelming response to Western initiatives aiming to help reinforce democracy south of the Sahara. It doesn't need to be reinforced; it still needs to be created. The longer that counterfeit democracies are able to pass convincingly as the real thing, the longer it will take to dispel the false notion that democracy cannot deliver results.

The League of Democracies is an idea that is long overdue. Now, with more diverse democracies than ever before scattered across the globe, the organization would not easily be dismissed as a simple stooge of Western interests or a re-constituted wing of Western imperialism. Instead, it would provide a solid and enduring incentive for countries to choose to chase democracy rather than being told or pressured to do so. It could end the current backsliding and stagnation of global democracy and possibly acting as a springboard for a "Fourth Wave" of democracy. But even if that's a gross overstatement, it certainly could prove transformative for several cases, while providing a guiding direction to global trade policy that produces a more just, safe, and democratic world.

In Latvia, it's incredible to see the Corner House, a vestige of a terribly dark authoritarian past, now nothing more than a museum—a distant memory of a long-gone tyranny. Yet Latvia's trajectory in the wake of the Soviet Union's collapse was not pre-ordained. Democracies are made, not automatically born phoenix-like from the ashes of despots. They are built by fallible people. Given that the majority of countries around the globe are stuck in some form of hybrid counterfeit democracy, it's clear that transitions are all too easily diverted.

As Latvia's path toward the European Union showed, economic carrots provide a powerful means to keep countries on track. Importantly, such tools can be used to draw reluctant nations into the fold of democracy voluntarily—a far more effective form of transition than one externally applied with force, the threat of force, or the economic stick of devastating sanctions. Tying economic rewards to democracy would not only create a self-fulfilling prophecy that democracies create growth, but would also prompt business interests to pressure the regime from within. For existing democracies, the League of Democracies would open new trading partnerships, providing key emerging markets for Western goods. When countries like Hungary stray from democracy, they could simply be kicked out of the League. After all, unlike the European Union, there would be no explicit political integration or common currencies to cope with. It's a win-win scenario, even if the prospects of this idea becoming reality—at least in the short term—remain, sadly, dim.

In the meantime, though, there are new glimmers of hope that may help prod unwilling despots to embrace democratic reform. Many of those glimmers of light, interestingly enough, are being reflected off the shiny metal of new technology, the most promising new weapon in the global battle for democracy.

## 11

## THE NEW BATTLEGROUND

*Principle 9: Harness the power of information technology to outfox and undermine despots, but recognize its limits*

On 23 August 2014, Dr. Bilgin Ciftci, an official at Turkey's Public Health Institution, logged onto his Facebook account—just as about a billion people do every day. And, like many of them, Ciftci saw an amusing meme. Rather than simply "liking" it and moving on, he posted it on his own page, sharing it with his Facebook friends. It was a perfectly banal act. Hundreds of people around the globe have done exactly the same thing in the time you spent reading this paragraph.

Ciftci's meme, however, was politically sensitive. The image he had shared showed three photos of Turkish president Recep Tayyip Erdoğan making exaggerated facial expressions, compared side-by-side with remarkably similar expressions on the face of Gollum, the wretched *Lord of the Rings* character. In the first picture, both Erdoğan and Gollum look surprised; in the second, they are laughing; and in the third, one is eagerly devouring a raw fish, while the other happily gnaws on a chicken leg. It was a funny image, but its consequences have not been amusing for Ciftci.

Someone reported him. Turkish authorities swiftly opened an investigation to get to the bottom of the doctor's incendiary meme sharing. By October, the Public Health Institution, likely worried about crossing Erdoğan's regime, fired Ciftci. In December, he was hauled in front of a judge for violating Article 299 of the Turkish penal code, which holds that anyone who insults the president may face up to four years behind bars.[1] It appears that Erdoğan has thin skin; Turkey files five times more requests to remove content from Twitter than any other country, and more than 100 alleged violators of Article 299 were indicted between late 2014 and early 2015 alone.[2]

In December 2015, Ciftci got his moment in court. His defense team tried to argue that public officials should be more open to criticism, scrutiny, and satire than the average Turkish citizen. But the judge was not receptive. Instead, he focused on another part of the defense's argument: that comparing Erdoğan to Gollum was not an insult, as the bug-eyed, slimy creature, corrupted and torn apart by greed and his unending lust to regain his lost "precious," the one ring of power, was in fact intended to be a sympathetic victim and an unlikely hero who unwittingly saved the world from surefire destruction.

The judge, bewildered at being forced to weigh in on a literary figure, sheepishly admitted that he had not watched all of the *Lord of the Rings* films, nor had he read J.R.R. Tolkien's masterpiece. As such, he used all the authority vested in him by the Turkish state to compel five "Gollum experts" to carefully study the creature and report back on whether or not the comparison could be accurately construed as an insult.

As the court adjourned, Peter Jackson, the director of the films, weighed in publicly in defense of Ciftci. He claimed that the images shared on Facebook were depicting Smeagol, the more sympathetic, Hobbit-like persona trapped inside Gollum's corrupted, villainous exterior: "Smeagol does not lie, deceive, or attempt to manipulate others. He is not evil, conniving, or malicious... Smeagol would never dream of wielding power over those weaker than himself. He is not a bully. In fact he's very loveable."[3] At the time of writing, those comments have been included in the case file, but no decision has yet been made. In the meantime, Ciftci's freedom hangs in the balance, tied to literary interpretation. It is truly theatre of the absurd, but high-profile cases like this one will chill future digital speech, as Turks think twice before re-posting a silly meme within their little sliver of cyberspace.

Turkey's rising Internet censorship and associated media crackdown are deeply troubling for democracy, and worsening. Turkey passed a law in February 2014 that allows the government to block any website within four hours of an order, without needing court authorization. And, most damaging, in July 2016 the regime responded to a failed coup attempt with a stunningly brutal purge of tens of thousands of civil servants, soliders, judges, and teachers. Comparatively, the Gollum story may seem like a silly distraction, but it represents an important and under-appreciated trend in the global battle for democracy.

Social media, information technology, and digital communications offer a huge and perhaps even unprecedented opportunity to level the playing field between the people and state power. Even with heroic efforts to the contrary, digital information flows are difficult to stop—and knowledge and social coordination can be extremely powerful when it comes to standing up to despots.

But the corresponding backlash by authoritarian rulers, who also have learned a thing or two about digital communication, is undermining naïve predictions made across the Western world in the wake of the Arab Spring. Everyone seemed to think that it was only a matter of time before Twitter revolutions began toppling despots left and right. It was a return to the notion, initially articulated by Francis Fukuyama, that we had reached the democratic endpoint, the "End of History"[4]—but this time the end would be announced in 140 characters or fewer. There was even a movement to nominate Twitter for the Nobel Peace Prize.[5] Yet as the grip of authoritarianism has tightened rather than loosened in the last decade, it has become clear that reports of despotism's death at the hands of Twitter and Facebook have been greatly exaggerated.

Social media, information technology, and digital communication are incredibly powerful tools that scare despots—and rightly so. But they are just tools. Throughout history, swords have been used to liberate and to oppress. And the new era of digital communication offers its fair share of double-edged swords. The key is to ensure that the blade strikes despots, not democrats.

Take Omar Afifi, for example. Afifi, a former Egyptian police officer who stood up to his superiors, fled Egypt in April 2008 and landed in New York "with nothing but $50 and a gold watch."[6] After being granted political asylum, Afifi settled in Falls Church, Virginia—inside the DC beltway and just a fifteen-minute drive from the Pentagon. During the Arab Spring and the social media-fueled Tahrir Square standoff between protesters and President Mubarak, Afifi shared insider tips about how police tactics would be used to crush the protests. He used Skype to stay in constant contact with those occupying the square. He used Google Maps to highlight potential routes that protesters should use if and when the eventual crackdown came.[7] There is no doubt that the digital revolution influenced the Egyptian Revolution.

However, just as Afifi played a part in establishing Egypt's brief experiment with democracy, he also played a part in its downfall. He may have had no love for Mubarak, but he had just as little for Mohammed Morsi, the man who replaced him as Egypt's leader. When anti-Morsi demonstrations began in 2012, Afifi again used social media to try to tip the scales: "Incapacitate them by smashing their knee bones first." On an equally grisly note, he instructed his Facebook followers to "Make a road bump with a broken palm tree to stop the buses going into Cairo, and drench the road around it with gas and diesel. When the bus slows down for the bump, set it all ablaze so it will burn down with all the passengers inside … God bless."[89]

Afifi's story illustrates an important but often overlooked truth about social media: it is neither intrinsically good nor intrinsically evil. Its impact on democracy depends on who is using it and to what effect. Frantic tweeting won't automatically bring down an autocrat. There is no doubt that new technology has the potential to level the playing field, lowering despots from their pedestals and placing them under the scrutiny of those down below. But despots can use those same tools, to divide, to misinform, and to crack down on those who oppose them.

In Thailand, for example, after the military junta took power in 2014, it attempted to co-opt public opinion using digital media in a novel way. Rather than Facebook Messenger, the Japanese messaging app LINE is the primary means of digital communication in the military-ruled kingdom. Given that Thailand is know as the Land of Smiles, it was appropriate that the junta's first major public incursion into social media came with the announcement that the government was spending 7 million baht (just under $200,000) to introduce twelve smiling digital stickers for the app, free of charge. Each sticker, released just in time for New Year's, depicted one of the "twelve values" taught by Thailand's military despot, Prayuth Chan-ocha. These included: "Loyalty to the Nation, the Religion, and the Monarchy";

"Discipline, respect for law, and obedience to the older citizens"; and, my personal favorite, "Correct understanding of democracy with the King as Head of State."[10] This last was particularly ironic coming from a military ruler who had come to power in a coup, no less because the video launching the twelve values provoked a brief public relations firestorm by including a scene of schoolchildren praising Adolf Hitler.[11] For the young Thais that I asked about the stickers, they represented a tone-deaf attempt by out-of-touch generals to win them over. But the military regime's attempt to use new media platforms to disseminate propaganda, even if it was done to little effect, is a striking development.

Sometimes, social media and web-based platforms don't even require state intervention to be effective antidotes to democratization. Thitinan Pongsudhirak, one of the world's foremost experts on Thai politics, notes that social media can polarize societies in two important ways. First, social media can become an echo chamber, as people only choose to digitally interact with like-minded individuals.[12] When that happens, ideas are amplified and made more extreme over time as criticism is silenced, not by force, but by self-selection. (This is not unique to Thailand; most people have a pool of Facebook friends who reinforce their existing political views rather than openly challenging them). Second, humans seem to have a knack for being nasty to each other, but particularly so when nastiness is typed rather than spoken. The higher degree of separation, distance, and, sometimes, anonymity that accompanies digital interactions allows vitriol to rise to levels that would be unthinkable in non-digital public spaces. In these two ways, social divides that can benefit the ruling elite may be deeply ingrained in national discourse, even without a junta buying stickers or coming up with other flimsy ploys.

Thailand's government isn't taking any chances, though. A Thai man now faces up to thirty-seven years in prison for a social media post that lampooned the revered King Bhumibol's dog, Tongdaeng. The dog, which died in December 2015, was used by the monarchy to showcase the desirable values of loyalty and obedience, a lesson that was apparently lost on Thanakorn Siripaiboon, who made the satirical post.[13] This event, and the infamous Gollum trial that preceded it in Turkey, are comical sideshows for a Western audience, but they can effectively silence critics and destroy lives. Nonetheless, it is worth asking whether they do the regime more harm than good, drawing international consternation and condemnation of a previously under-the-radar issue. In short, such instances are not the shrewdest attempts to tame the role of digital communications.

Other despots, however, are much more savvy, derailing democracy as they shut down or co-opt digital communication effectively. In Uganda's rigged 2016 presidential election, for example, the government unilaterally shut down all social media in the country during the voting, claiming that doing so was in the interest of combating unfounded rumors.[14] But in reality, it was almost certainly intended to stop digitally connected voters from sharing easily documented instances of voter fraud. Some reports still got out, including one striking image of a voter casting a ballot into an uncovered basket while a soldier watched which box he ticked, gun at the ready.

Other attempts to co-opt digital media for the benefit of the regime are more complicated, a tug-of-war between pro-democracy activists and the defensive regime. In 2009, the so-called Green Revolution (that wasn't) swept across Tehran. Writers in the West seized on the hashtag #IranElection, tweeting themselves into a frenzy that this was the first "Twitter Revolution."[15] The only problem was that the hashtag was, of course, in English, and dominated by English-speaking users outside of Tehran.[16] That is not to say that they did not have an impact; one Twitter user in particular, known only as OxfordGirl, provided the best Western window into the unfolding events. But she was in Oxford, not Tehran. She claimed in a *Guardian* profile (oozing with admiration for her new-fangled digital revolutionary persona) that she kept in constant contact with people on the ground in Tehran via her cell phone.[17] But Iranian authorities were simply switching off all mobile phone networks in the city anytime a protest broke out.[18] It is unlikely that her tweets from the City of Dreaming Spires played a decisive role in the Iranian protests (or their failure). Mostly, it was Americans and other Westerners tweeting amongst themselves. The regime, on the other hand, used Twitter to great effect.

In December 2009, during the Green Movement protests, a pro-regime website published a series of photos, with the faces of certain undesirables circled in red. Using Internet-based crowdsourcing, at least forty people were arrested, showing that despotic regimes can use the web to request popular involvement, rather than fearing it or trying to shut it down. Then, the regime disseminated a video online that had possibly been altered, showing Green Movement protesters burning the image of Ayatollah Khomeini, a clear attempt to divide the opposition against itself. This move demonstrated the regime's ability to use social media for misinformation campaigns to great effect.

Furthermore, Iranians living abroad received anonymous messages on social media warning them that if they posted about the protests online, their families might be harmed. Such a tactic would have been unthinkable in past decades; it's hard to imagine the Iranian government sending out similar messages on official letterhead. Facebook has provided an easy way for government thugs to intimidate opponents abroad, using their digital presence as a weak pressure point and pushing it aggressively. For those considering posting on social media or blogs in Iran, the Iranian police chief, General Ismail Ahmadi Moghaddam, warned that digital dissidents "have committed a worse crime than those who come to the streets."[19]

Those high-level threats were reinforced via text messages. The intelligence ministry did not mince its words nor hide its identity when it sent text messages to a wide swath of Iranians:

> Dear citizen, according to received information, you have been influenced by the destabilizing propaganda which the media affiliated with foreign countries have been disseminating. In case of any illegal action and contact with the foreign media, you will be charged as a criminal consistent with the Islamic Punishment Act and dealt with by the Judiciary.[20]

Tacked onto this intimidation were savvy and sophisticated attempts to sow doubt within the ranks of the opposition. While the exact details are difficult to discern with absolute accuracy, it seems that the Iranian government planted on the Internet, and then facilitated the spread of, the tragic tale of an Iranian activist, Saeedah Pouraghayi. Pouraghayi had allegedly shouted "Allahu Akbar" on her rooftop, in protest against the regime, only to be subsequently raped and murdered by regime supporters. Her story went viral. But the whole thing turned out to be a hoax; after becoming the poster-child of Iran's digital protests, Pouraghayi showed up on state TV to show that she was very much alive and the whole tale was untrue. By co-opting the opposition to unknowingly spread misinformation, the regime undermined legitimate claims of state brutality and rape and more broadly cast doubts on the veracity of opposition claims against President Mahmoud Ahmadinejad.[21]

Ultimately, the prevailing and seductive Western narrative on Iran's failed 2009 revolution is badly mistaken. This was not a revolution that thrived on Twitter and Facebook. At best, digital communication provided a modest boost to a largely disorganized movement. At worst, the regime outfoxed the protesters, using new platforms to enhance their repression, freeze protest, and undermine the legitimacy of the regime's fiercest opponents through intimidation and misinformation. Social media is not automatically a tool for democracy. It's just a new battleground. Based on the last decade, it seems that the democrats are losing the battle.

I'm confident, though, that they will win the digital war. The so-called Umbrella Movement that grew into large-scale protests in Hong Kong in late 2014 provides cause for such optimism. Protesters used digital communication effectively, organizing protests, sit-ins, and other acts of resistance by rallying online. As in the Arab Spring, virtual communication was a key mechanism of the movement. But China's government fought back with intense digital counterattacks. Several of the most popular pro-democracy websites in Hong Kong came under unprecedented DDoS (Distributed Denial-of-Service) attacks, a digital assault that overwhelms the digital server with extreme volumes of junk web traffic.[22] In one instance, a single website reported being inundated with 500 gigabytes of traffic per second, the equivalent of downloading more than 390,000 full-length films per hour.[23] These attacks succeeded in outpacing the sites' bandwidth capacity, and they were knocked offline—stopping pro-democracy activists from spreading information through them. The Chinese government complemented these cyber attacks with insidious "50-cent" commenters. These low-paid stooges of the regime were compensated for flooding comment boards, blogs, anywhere that users could post, with pro-government propaganda attacking the Umbrella Movement.[24] And, just for good measure, they followed the tried and tested approach: blame the protests on a plot by the American government.

These underhanded tactics succeeded in the short term. The Umbrella Movement eventually fizzled. But the tens of thousands of protesters jamming the city's main arteries changed the political narrative, spreading ideas that cannot be censored even if some websites can be—for a time. Nine months after the protests ended, the Hong Kong Legislative Council vetoed the proposed constitutional amendment that sparked the protest movement in the first place: a plan that would have allowed Hong Kong's residents to vote on their leader, but only from a slate of three candidates handpicked by Beijing. The proposal had seemed sure to pass before young students occupied Hong Kong's streets. After the protests, it failed by a margin of twenty-eight votes against to eight in favor.[25]

As a result, Hong Kong's government is left with its antiquated colonial-era system of allowing 1,200 business and political elites to pick the city's chief executive. That system is, understandably, deeply unpopular, and the ruling elites in Hong Kong cannot simply rest on their laurels and hope that the simmering unrest will disappear. It won't.

In February 2016, protests during the Lunar New Year turned violent in the working-class neighborhood of Mong Kok as protesters clashed with riot police.[26] The grievances were the same. These acts of defiance are becoming more commonplace and they are having a ripple effect that is sure to grow. Two weeks later, in late February, a key pro-democracy candidate, Alvin Yeung, defeated the pro-Beijing candidate, Holden Chow in a legislative council by-election,[27] seen as a bellwether for Hong Kong's politics. It is starting to seem more and more as though the students weathered the political storm of the Umbrella Movement much better than Beijing. Authoritarianism won the battle in late 2014; but the long-term horizon looks brighter for democracy as a result.

Hong Kong is not, of course, the same as the whole of China. Even if Hong Kong's protesters succeed in securing their right to elect their leadership and participate more meaningfully in policymaking, it is only a small slice of China, and one that retains unique special privileges. Only one in every 200 Chinese citizens live in Hong Kong. But that should actually be cause for optimism, because it shows a clear missing piece of the debate over new technology and its impact on democracy: local participation and oversight. There's a saying that all politics is local. If that's true, then politics is likely to become considerably more democratic as digital technologies continue to permeate modern life, from the skyscrapers of Hong Kong to villages in Togo. National politicians are less likely to push back against or crack down on local democratic movements than national protests, and the power of apps to influence local politics is far greater, because it is less entrenched and less politicized than national politics. Shrewd reformers have found an opening.

In existing democracies, such as India, digital projects have also helped to consolidate democracy by undermining its enemies, such as public corruption. For example, the website I Paid a Bribe allows users to anonymously report having to pay a bribe for basic government services like birth and death certificates, passports, train reservations, or interactions with the police.[28] Since its inception, more than 75,000 reports have been filed, including thousands of citizens lauding honest officers and reporting instances of not having to pay a bribe. Because the reports are anonymous, citizens feel confident enough to share authentic information, providing reform-minded government leaders with geo-targeted information of where corruption is running rampant and where it is comparatively subdued. In Karnataka State, for example, digital reports helped identify twenty corrupt officers in the motor vehicle department. But that was not enough for Bhaskar Rao, the transport commissioner. He transformed the system to ensure that all licenses could be applied for and purchased online, precluding any possibility of bribery in the system. Taking things to an unprecedented level of transparency and accountability, he also installed sensors and video monitoring equipment for driving tests. Previously, these tests were notoriously subject to bribe taking, a double menace because it involved both bureaucratic corruption and bad drivers improperly being allowed on the roads. With the sensors, it was impossible for the examiner to feign being on the fence as to whether they would pass the driver, in hope of eliciting a bribe; instead, there was an objective measure of whether the car was within the appropriate lines during parallel parking assessment, for example.[29]

Coming full circle, digital technology not only empowered the reformist transport commissioner to identify the corruption problem and its culprits, but allowed him to ensure that corruption became logistically impossible. Yet Rao's trendsetting approach could not tackle high-level corruption. In a poetic underscoring of this fact, a man with the same name, Bhaskar Rao, was disgraced after corruption charges came to light during his time, ironically, as the *lokayuta*, or anti-corruption ombudsman, for the same state.[30] If only there were some technology that could do for extortion what Rao did for driving tests.

The marriage of technical advances with the political willpower of people like Commissioner Rao is crucial to stamping out corruption, which is critically important for the survival of democracy. As eminent democracy scholar Larry Diamond of Stanford University recently put it, "It is hard to find an instance of the breakdown of democracy in which corruption did not play a leading or at least prominent role."[31] That starts with local corruption, and digital technology is a new and important weapon in fighting it. Since launching in India, I Paid a Bribe has set up sister sites in fifteen other countries, including states as diverse as Colombia, Guyana, Hungary, Ukraine, Zimbabwe, and Morocco.

Beyond exposing corruption, web-based initiatives are also helping to shine a light on the inner workings of arcane and opaque government decision-making. For example, the Nigerian website BudgIT provides digestible information about government budgets. Moreover, it also offers a project tracking feature, which allows citizens to upload photos of government projects that have been paid for, holding politicians accountable to spend government money as they should rather than lining their own pockets. In all its simple glory, BudgIT lets Nigerians know when the local emperor has no clothes—when millions have been allocated for a school but all that exists is a hole in the ground.[32] The project recently expanded to Ghana and Sierra Leone, and could serve as a model well beyond West Africa.

In Mexico, Mejora Tu Escuela allows parents to become involved in the oversight of their local schools. The platform provides detailed comparative information about how each local school stacks up, allowing parents more information that can be used to pressure local officials to be more responsive to their concerns—with hard data to back it up.[33] If knowledge is power, then Mexican parents are more empowered today than they were in the digital dark ages. Local participation in such government services can form the critical bedrock for bottom-up democratic change. Apps are also making a difference in advanced democracies. FixMyStreet in the United Kingdom, for example, allows citizens to flag potholes, uncollected waste, broken streetlights, and other banal government failures.[34]

These digital tools exist, then, in consolidated democracies (India, the UK), nearly consolidated democracies (Mexico), and counterfeit democracies (Nigeria). But even in the most closed societies, digital communications can shine a light on government failures. In late 2009, floods inundated the Saudi Arabian city of Jeddah. The government response was badly bungled. More than 100 people died needlessly. Citizens turned to Facebook to document the flooding and express anger at their government in an unprecedented display of opposition to the ruling family. In response, King Abdullah promised "never again" and vowed to improve public services and flood preparations. But in early 2011, the city flooded again and the response was just as badly managed. Raw sewage mixed with rainwater as it flowed in the streets. Holding even less back, one brazen Facebook user posted an image of the "Saudi" flag, altered from the fierce national symbol of two sabers crossed over a palm tree to show two mops crossed, somewhat less menacingly, over a stack of buckets. It went viral, and Saudis used digital platforms to demand more from their government at the local level.[35]

These examples of local-level democracy, from Bangalore and Jeddah to Birmingham, may seem trivial, particularly when compared to the lofty battles against despots in palaces highlighted previously. But for most people, this is what democracy is for: to improve the experience of day-to-day life and allow them a meaningful say in the decisions that affect them most directly. Journalists, politicians, diplomats, and political scientists find these low-level topics so much less "sexy" than national policymaking, so anything local inevitably receives minimal attention. But for most of the planet's occupants, the battles that they care about most intimately are fought over local problems and local solutions, not showdowns between democrats and despots at the presidential palace.

Government responsiveness at the local level adds up to something that is bigger than the sum of its parts. In aggregate, it can help create citizen expectations of participatory, responsive government while stamping out corruption, graft, and mismanagement. People who get used to this are unlikely to indefinitely accept something completely different at the national level. In short, forcing good governance at the local level is likely to trickle up to the national level. And on the local political battleground, digital communication is being used to win both the battle and the war.

As a result, over time, we should expect to see local democracy become more vibrant while despots become increasingly vulnerable to pressure from below. The digital democracy revolutions may not have happened yet, but they still could come—even if they are forged over years and years, from village to village, rather than in the span of a few spectacular tweets. This would arguably be better than a series of explosive revolutions spawned online anyway. Transitions to democracy can be messy, volatile, and destabilizing. Anyone who says otherwise is a naïve idealist. Therefore, for those places that may not experience a rapid breakdown of authoritarianism, digital communications technology could help prod leaders—particularly counterfeit democrats— toward reform.

Even with these bright local beacons of hope, it's premature to give up on the national-level digital fight just yet. The ground is shifting under despots from Equatorial Guinea to North Korea in new and unpredictable ways, and the West can help speed up their reforms or, if they are resistant to change, their demise. Computerized statistical analysis, digital election integrity, and online polling each hold tremendous promise in dealing a blow to reluctant despots.

One of the wonderful things about computers is that they can sometimes tell if we're too human for our own good. Empirical research shows that if you ask someone to write down a series of "random" three-digit numbers, the end result is anything but. People rarely pick numbers that end in 0, 5, or are written in ascending order (such as 123). Conversely, other types of numbers are overrepresented: numbers that end in odd digits like 7 or 3, and numbers that are in descending order like 987.

That matters when it comes to election results in places that have a systematic problem with vote tallies simply being fabricated. If statisticians are given sufficient data points (such as all the vote tallies from every precinct in the country), they are able to develop a certain degree of confidence in making a judgment as to whether the election was tampered with or not. Even if election officials get lazy and simply start tallying everything with 0s and 5s, a non-random distribution of final digits is telling and highly indicative of election tampering. A 2012 study used this method to highlight stolen elections in Nigeria with considerable accuracy and confidence in their results, a new tool for democracy that is facilitated by technology—both in the transparency and collection of data and in its statistical analysis for massive datasets.[36] The West should simply not tolerate election results that do not involve full precinct-level tallies; nobody should be able to hide behind figures that are aggregated at the regional or even national level. As use of this technology becomes a global norm, making up vote numbers will become either a thing of the past or an easily exposed embarrassment.

Yet such statistical methods are complicated. Simpler solutions exist. For example, when I served as an election monitor in Madagascar, I was heartened to see that the ballot boxes were secured with bar-coded and individually numbered zip ties. A poll worker can scan the zip tie at the beginning of the day and again at the end of the day. If anyone has tampered with the ballot box and replaced the zip tie, the numbers and barcodes won't match up. Of course, this doesn't stop people from stuffing ballot boxes if poll workers are complicit in the rigging, but, with digital technology and the ever-falling price of simple software, it's a cheap and powerful antidote to at least some electoral fraud. Finally, online polling offers a potentially new frontier for dispelling the official myth that 99.9 per cent of the population loves a given despot. Again, knowledge is power, and knowing whether the people actually despise their leader is powerful intelligence for those who oppose the regime.

Polling has already shifted considerably over time. Ever since the infamous mistake of oversampling wealthy *Literary Digest* readers that ended in the embarrassingly wrong prediction that Alf Landon would roll FDR in a landslide election, pollsters have become increasingly savvy at accounting for bias in their samples. But in the last several years, targeting a representative swath of the population has become difficult. Polls in the 1990s were conducted almost exclusively through landline telephones. Then, as more and more people dropped landlines in favor of mobile phones, pollsters adapted and tried to ensure that an appropriate percentage of their respondents were mobile phone users.[37] These approaches were deemed vastly superior to online polling, which tended to have huge problems with selection bias—primarily because it oversampled young people who made up a disproportionately large share of Internet users but a disproportionately small share of the electorate. That problem is diminishing, slowly but surely, as Internet usage becomes more equally distributed demographically over time. This is an important development, because it offers a new, potent means of gauging the mood of the people under authoritarian rule.

Most despots operate in an environment where polling is either banned or simply does not exist. Unlike in the West, where voters have a 24/7 stream of the latest snapshot into the race, voters living in dictatorships and counterfeit democracies rarely have access to reliable information about who is likely to win or lose. That can be a problem on two levels.

First, the absence of polling means that the election takes place with an avoidable unknown—how closely the vote tally matched expectations. Any major divergence can be strong grounds for more thorough investigations by independent electoral commissions and international observers beyond the scrutiny on polling day itself.

Second, polling helps temper expectations. As unfortunate as it is, there are despots who are genuinely popular and would go on to win hypothetically free and fair elections—even if their elections are usually neither. Yet in those instances, the opposition often believes the contrary. When the election returns are announced, any mismatch between the lofty but unfounded expectations of the opposition and the ultimate electoral verdict can be hugely destabilizing, sparking riots and widespread violence. With accurate polling, such violence can at least be made less likely.

Online polling offers possible solutions to both problems, primarily because it can be conducted outside the nation's borders. So long as the Internet is not shut down completely or the website blocked outright, the international community could develop an agreed method of conducting pre-election digital polling that does not suffer the common pitfalls of skewed poll results. There is, of course, no magic elixir that can make polls accurate, but I'm hopeful that a group of nations working together might come up with a reasonable way to accurately measure popular opinion using digital tools.

Doing so multilaterally is hugely important, as despots will almost certainly dismiss any polling conducted by a Western firm as a biased American propaganda ploy. Such accusations will ring hollow if the poll is backed by a wide array of nations. Again, the key is international norms. The more uniform standards are agreed, the easier it is to name and shame those who violate them. That may not be enough to sway entrenched dictators in Uzbekistan or North Korea, but it could do wonders for those hundred or so nations trapped between dictatorship and democracy, whose leaders are trying desperately to masquerade as the latter.

Moreover, digital polling offers an important advantage: people are more honest with computers than with people. The so-called Bradley effect[38] showcased this in American politics: human-to-human telephone polling requires adjustments to account for the fact that voters overstate their preferences for African-American candidates so as to avoid being seen as racist.[39] In the context of despotism, there is an enormous risk that human-based polls will have voters simply toeing the line and indicating support for the ruling party regardless of their opinion. Internet polls help mitigate that problem, even if it remains a challenge.

These potential applications of technology make clear that despots fighting the spread of ideas are like a cracking dam: they can aggressively fill in the cracks, but eventually one will prove too deep and the flow will come rushing through. The West can and should help this happen, not by fomenting Twitter revolutions as they mistakenly aimed to do in Cuba with ZunZuneo (see Chapter 2), but by letting citizens in their own countries empower themselves with information technology. The free flow of information is more likely to be effective than Western plots anyway.

Uganda's efforts to shut down social media on election day did not stop voters from realizing that the election was rigged. Hong Kong's Umbrella Movement protesters couldn't access certain websites for a short while, but the movement still drastically changed hearts and minds. And in Turkey, Dr Bilgin Ciftci may rot in a jail cell for sharing a Gollum meme. Eventually, the despots who stubbornly resist reform and shut down expansive information flows will become more and more like Gollum themselves: isolated, paranoid, and clinging to the elusive promise of ultimate power as they ensure their own destruction.

## 12

## CITY ON A SWAMP

*Principle 10: Lead by example*

In the West African nation of Burkina Faso, trouble is brewing before
an upcoming presidential election, slated to take place in late 2016.
Tensions throughout the campaign have been running high. The opposition candidate, Ousmane Aboubacar, has stoked those tensions with a
protectionist message against integration into the global economy,
embracing xenophobic rhetoric against immigrant communities and
migrant workers (particularly from Togo to the south) who, he claims,
are stealing Burkinabé jobs. As a result, his rallies have frequently
devolved into ethnic clashes, as protesters from disproportionately
impoverished ethnic minority communities have been bloodied and
beaten by Aboubacar's supporters.

Moreover, Aboubacar has raised red flags with Western observers
and divided Burkinabé public opinion by offhandedly suggesting draco-
nian counterterrorism tactics to deal with the rising threat of Islamic
extremism in West Africa, including from Boko Haram and al-Qaeda in
the Islamic Maghreb. Indeed, international experts have agreed that
several of his proposals seem to be in violation of the Geneva
Convention, which Burkina Faso ratified in 1955. Those comments
have caused some extremists—including religious extremists—within
his movement to question his credentials to lead. At the time of writ-

ing, several prominent analysts have spoken out, worrying that the opposition movement could tear itself apart and devolve into catastrophic and potentially violent infighting.

The ruling party is hoping to capitalize on that divided opposition. For the first time in Burkina Faso's history, the ruling party elite—which holds disproportionate influence over the landlocked country's politics—has coalesced behind a female consensus candidate, Maïmouna Fadilatou. She is well regarded in international circles but has been criticized extensively as being part of a dynastic system that allows certain tribes and families to dominate the Burkinabé political scene. Two decades ago, her family was pushed from power by a rival political dynasty, and some say this will be their comeback. Nonetheless, international observers are cautiously optimistic about Fadilatou's candidacy, as fewer than one in five elected officials in this former colony are women. Indeed, for more than half of the time since obtaining independence from its colonial administrators, Burkina Faso has had no female representation in the political sphere. Observers insist that Fadilatou's optimistic chances in the upcoming vote may therefore signal a watershed moment in the divided West African nation.

However, Western officials have also expressed concern that the election could be unfairly manipulated by powerful donors, particularly given the shadowy election financing system, which is subject to minimal regulation as the rivals battle to secure power in Ouagadougou. Whether the funding sways the electorate or not, international observers worry that a close election could reignite slowly healing wounds between the two factions, as Burkina Faso tries to move on from a damaging contest nearly two decades ago, when an unelected court overruled voters, handing victory to a candidate who had received half a million fewer votes than his opponent. Democracy in Burkina Faso is clearly being threatened by this potentially explosive campaign.

Except, of course, that none of this is about Burkina Faso. It's about the United States in 2016.

Try re-reading the above section, but substitute Donald Trump for Ousmane Aboubacar; Hillary Clinton for Maïmouna Fadilatou; the United States for Burkina Faso; immigrants from Mexico for immigrants from Togo; and Washington DC for Ouagadougou. (The Burkinabé names are made up. Burkina Faso recently had elections in late 2015 after a military coup).

In this chapter, I argue that the overly myopic geopolitical view of "The West" vs. "The Rest" is particularly flawed today, given the short-comings of Western democracies. This is not to say that Western democracies are not democratic—they most certainly are. Western governments, like the United States, stand strong as citadels of and for democracy that other nations can emulate. But it's still important to stress that some aspects of democracy promotion would be better facilitated if Western democracies took criticism of their own flaws and procedural anomalies more seriously. The attitude that "we are perfect, and you must learn from us" is counterproductive and often insulting. In democracy promotion as in life, it's easier to lecture others on their failings and press them to do better when they cannot turn your criticisms against you; telling someone to quit smoking from a gray haze of your own is not the most effective strategy. The credibility of Western democracy promotion therefore turns on whether or not Western nations can lead by example. Nobody wants to mimic a broken system. Today, too many components of Western democracy are underperforming.

In 1988, Ronald Reagan gave his farewell address from the Oval Office. In closing, he invoked one of his favorite lines of imagery, likening the United States to a "shining city on a hill," a beacon that the rest of the world can always look up to see for inspiration.[1] Writing in 1630, John Winthrop, an early Pilgrim settler to the United States, popularized the line. But its original source is the Bible—Matthew 5:13: "You are the light of the world. A city set on a hill cannot be hidden." Reagan signed off from the presidency by eloquently elaborating on that same reference, saying:

> After 200 years, two centuries, she still stands strong and true on the granite ridge, and her glow has held steady no matter what storm. And she's still a beacon, still a magnet for all who must have freedom, for all the pilgrims from all the lost places who are hurtling through the darkness, toward home.[2]

It's beautiful imagery, a powerful metaphor, and one that is unfortunately becoming less apt. Parts of American democracy seem to be breaking off from the "granite ridge" and sinking into a dank, undemocratic swamp rather than perching tranquilly atop a shining hill.

As a bloc, Western governments represent most of the world's major bastions of democracy. They are not the only ones, of course, but they are the longstanding rock that governments around the world have turned to as they formed their own democratic foundations. However, nearly two decades into the twenty-first century, the crisis of democracy is not just a global one; it's also a Western one. Western democracies are struggling. Some of their practices are undemocratic and deeply flawed. This "hypocrisy" of promoting democracy abroad while simultaneously failing to address democratic challenges at home rings hollow.

In the European Union, the Eurozone crisis has prompted accusations of a serious "democracy deficit."[3] Technocrats have a disproportionate role that is insulated from democratic pressures. Turnout for European Parliament elections is notoriously low, and there is a "disconnect" between voters and their representatives that is more pronounced with European institutions than any similar phenomenon at the national level. Indeed, 12 million more Brits voted for Big Brother, a major reality television program in the UK, than voted in their country's 1999 European Parliament elections.[4] However, turnout for such elections is not markedly different from stubbornly low turnout in congressional midterm elections in the United States (just 36.4 per cent of eligible voters in 2014, the lowest level since 1942).[5] This cannot absolve the European Parliament of its failure to hold elections that are sterling examples of democratic process. But it can highlight the fact that there are troubling trends throughout Western democracies that speak to a series of related concerns: voter apathy, structural procedural deficiencies, and gridlock in the face of increasingly urgent global challenges. Simply put, most people in Western countries are not confident that their democracy is performing as well as it should be. The rise of Donald Trump is a culmination of these fault lines in Western democracies; he is a candidate who could only be spawned by an electorate driven to anger by overwhelming dissatisfaction with the ability of democratic politics to deliver what it promises: consensus and concrete results, rather than partisan bickering and gridlock.

Democracy in the United States has recently been performing badly on several fronts, and most of them are due to three major pitfalls: gerrymandering, ensuing gridlock, and out-of-control campaign spending. Each of these, in turn, erodes international admiration of the

American model of democracy, and further undermines Western efforts to promote democracy while dragging the proverbial city further down the hill toward the swamp.

The lesson, however, is not to stop promoting democracy. Instead, the lesson is to work to fix democracy at home while promoting several possible democratic models—not just the American one—abroad. After all, amidst the wide array of global diversity in cultures, political systems, and historical trajectories, the real world is not a place where "one size fits all" approaches thrive. American democracy is not the only form of democracy and it should not be presented as such—particularly given the problems that are plaguing American democracy today.

Imagine a system of government where incumbents are re-elected more than nine times out of ten, where sitting members of the legislature tend to win in landslides—by an average of 36 per cent greater vote share than their nearest competitor. In this same system, some systematic procedural flaws end up producing surprising outcomes; at times, more than half the voters might vote for one party, only to see seven out of ten representatives elected for the other side.

Unfortunately, it doesn't take much imagination, because again, this is the case today in the United States. In a quarter of all congressional races, the incumbent wins with a margin of more than 50 per cent of the vote—something like 75 per cent to 25 per cent, or wider.[6] Such elections are not remotely competitive, and the opposition candidate is simply put up as a sacrificial lamb hoping to garner more name recognition as they walk sheepishly to their inevitable electoral slaughter. In 2012, John Boehner, the Republican Speaker of the House, won re-election with Kim Jong-un-style margins, receiving 99.2 per cent of all votes. How can this be? After all, the United States is widely regarded as a divided country, wherein a presidential contest is considered a landslide if the electorate is split 55/45, rather than a more usual 52/48 type of split. Why are the margins so drastically different when it comes to electing Congress?

One of the most important answers, of course, is gerrymandered districts—an enormously consequential challenge to American democracy, yet one that very few people care about. The term "gerrymander" comes from a political cartoon drawn in 1812 to parody Massachusetts Governor Elbridge Gerry's re-drawn senate districts. The cartoon depicts one of the bizarrely shaped districts as the contorted form of a fork-tongued salamander, standing menacingly over the other, more traditionally shaped districts. The term "Gerry-mander" was born, and in the following two centuries, it has been used to great effect (in the United States and elsewhere) to divide the electorate and distort the will of voters by arranging districts into strategically beneficial chunks. In most states, the process of drawing districts is deeply politicized; more often than not, state legislatures get to decide, which is akin to the electoral foxes guarding the henhouse districts.

The practice would be laughable if its consequences weren't so disastrous. Democrats and Republicans are both guilty. In the Illinois 4th, for example, the district looks like a pair of earmuffs turned on their side, a thin line connecting the two ear warmers.[7] A less charitable interpretation would be that it seems like a severely distracted child has colored in parts of the electoral map at random, or spilled a bottle of ink somewhere on the map just west of Chicago. But it's anything but random. Others have dubbed the Illinois 4th "Latin Earmuffs", because each side of the earmuffs links up two completely distinct blocs of Latino voters. It's absurd in its cynical simplicity. The lines were drawn based on race and partisanship but little else. Really, there seems to be no other way to interpret it; the areas linked together have nothing else in common. At one point, the district is stitched together by a sliver of highway a few dozen meters wide. That's it. Google it. You'll be shocked. As a result, 71 per cent of the district is Latino by design. Unsurprisingly, a Latino congressman, Luis Gutiérrez, represents the district. His margins of victory match the absurdity of his district's shape. In 2014, Gutiérrez won with 78 per cent of the vote, compared with 22 per cent for his Republican opponent. As a result of favorable district lines, he has easily stayed in office since 1993, re-elected every two years like clockwork.

There are three main ways to gerrymander, which political scientists refer to as "stacking, cracking, and packing."[89] The Illinois 4th congressional district is a case of "packing," wherein an overwhelmingly Democrat-leaning minority population (in this case Chicago-area Latinos) are lumped into a single district so as to ensure that they did not influence the outcome of surrounding seats. The idea is to give that Democrat-leaning community one seat in a landslide victory, rather than allowing a fairer distribution, which would make other surrounding districts competitive. As a result of the packing in the Illinois 4th, the nearby Illinois 6th Congressional district is not competitive either, guaranteeing a safe Republican seat in a form of engineered electoral tit-for-tat. And, because most of the Latinos in the area are crammed into the 4th, 85 per cent of the 6th district is white. So is their Congressman, Republican Representative Peter Roskam, who has also been in Congress since 1993. In 2014, Roskam carried the district by a margin of 67 per cent. If the districts were drawn as a square or even something that resembled a coherent blob, the elections would regularly be competitive. Instead, they are always safe-bet landslides, foregone conclusions before the ballots are even printed.

Such gerrymandered districts are a problem for three main reasons. First, they produce undemocratic outcomes, drawing lines strategically to dampen the voices of some voters while amplifying the voices of others. This can result in some truly bizarre election results, as was the case in North Carolina in 2012. More than half of the state's voters cast their ballot for a Democrat, by a narrow margin of 51 per cent to 49 per cent. But, because of gerrymandered districts, Republicans won nine of the state's thirteen seats, or 70 per cent of the total.[10] More than half of the votes received less than a third of the seats. It's undemocratic, plain and simple. Countries like Zimbabwe have learned from it, gerrymandering their own districts using the lessons of "successful" gerrymandering in the United States.[11]

Second, drawing districts in order to create "safe" seats has huge knock-on effects that damage the core of democracy: constructive dialogue and consensus building. In the 2014 elections, thirty-four of the fifty states did not have a single competitive congressional election. In other words, in only sixteen states was there any sense of suspense heading into election day about who might win, and even within those states, only a handful of districts were competitive. Only twenty-six congressional races (out of 435) were decided by a margin of 5 per cent or less.[12] Out of 79 million votes cast, fewer than 5 million were cast in competitive districts. And in 2012, only nineteen Republicans were elected in districts that President Obama won in the concurrent presidential election; this represented a sharp decline from even a few election cycles earlier—in 1992, seventy-nine Republican congressmen were elected in districts carried by President Clinton. In the United States Congress, the political middle has become almost undetectably small.

No wonder voter turnout was lower in 2014 than it had ever been since 1942. But beyond voter apathy, uncompetitive districting destroys moderates and is a major boon to extremists who eschew cross-party dialogue and avoid working with the opposing party. After all, there is no need for responsiveness, humility, or bipartisanship when 95 per cent of a district is solidly Republican or Democrat. Instead, there are rewards for elected officials who choose ideology and partisan deadlock over progress and compromise.

This leads to the third consequence of gerrymandering, and the second major failure of American democracy: gridlock. As safe seats drive polarization, polarization drives gridlock. People in Washington often aren't willing to compromise, lest they be exposed as a capitulating weakling on the 24-hour cable news television shows that pander to fringe wings of the electorate. Moreover, they have no incentives to compromise, because for most representatives, a solid majority of their home district shares the same worldview. Congressional districts have become partisan echo chambers.

This dynamic goes a long way in explaining why 96 per cent of the incumbent members of Congress were re-elected in 2014, even though between 9 and 15 per cent of respondents tend to say that they approve of Congress as a whole. In a particularly striking 2013 poll, respondents indicated that they liked both traffic jams and cockroaches more than they liked Congress.[13] But the poll did have some bright spots for Congress, which narrowly edged out playground bullies in popularity and held a commanding lead over Ebola (although, admittedly, a quarter of all respondents did say they liked Ebola more). Regardless of popularity, though, congressional representatives who originate from homogenous and overwhelmingly supportive districts have every incentive to be confrontational and no incentive to stand down when it comes to partisan gridlock. The result is unnecessary brinksmanship.

The point was proven with an atrocious display on 1 October 2013, when the United States government shut down as a result of partisan bickering over funding President Obama's health care law. The standoff lasted for sixteen counterproductive days even though more than eight out of ten Americans disapproved of the shutdown and a similar proportion agreed that it "damaged the United States' image in the world."[14] This coincided with an incredibly reckless form of gridlock as the United States flirted with default on its massive government debt—the Republican Party's conservative Tea Party faction held the entire nation's credit rating hostage in a bid to force budgetary concessions. The showdown, which amounted to nothing, resulted in the United States' normally sterling credit rating being downgraded. It was an incredibly stupid self-inflicted wound at a time when the country needed all the help it could get to crawl out of the financial doldrums ushered in by the 2008–9 financial crisis.

Those doldrums, however, didn't diminish the flood of money that poured into campaign coffers across the United States in the wake of the landmark 2010 Supreme Court decision in *Citizens United v. Federal Election Commission*. In that case, the Supreme Court effectively ruled that corporate donations on behalf of political causes (rather than to candidates directly) are akin to a form of free speech. This opened the floodgates further by spawning so-called Super PACs (political action committees), through which corporate interests or rich individuals could funnel unlimited amounts of money to back their favored issue or candidate. After this court ruling, the dam burst; in the 2012 elections, donors channeled $7 billion into the race, the same amount as the annual GDP of countries like Niger, Rwanda, or Kyrgyzstan.[15] The 2016 elections are expected to be far more costly. But even though the sum is enormous, that's not the real problem. Rather, it's the fact that the money is skewing politics by allowing groups with funds a disproportionate influence, making a mockery of the one person, one vote principle that is the "granite ridge" to which democracy should be anchored.

Take the wild and unpredictable 2016 presidential campaign, for example. In just the first six months of 2015, a key period for candidates to prove that they can elicit financial support from donors, a *New York Times* analysis demonstrated that just 158 families accounted for more than half of the value of all political donations nationwide during that period. Each of those families gave at least $250,000, with the Texan fracking magnates of the Wilks family topping out the list with donations totaling $15 million. That sum is peanuts, though, compared with the nearly $900 million pledged by the Koch Brothers and their political affiliates. As *The New York Times* points out, "the group of donors is overwhelmingly 'white, rich, older and male in a nation that is being remade by the young, by women, and by black and brown voters.'"[16] In other words, as demographics shift, American politics seems stuck in a distant past because of disproportionate clout for those with fat wallets.

The combination of outlandish sums of money being spent to win elections and the similarly extreme amounts being thrown at elected officials through lobbying efforts[17] is damaging the quality of American democracy. A striking Princeton University study from 2014 found an alarming result: "The preferences of the average American appear to have only a miniscule, near-zero, statistically non-significant impact upon public policy."[18] Translated from political science-speak to conversational English, that means that popular opinion doesn't really seem to affect which laws pass and which ones do not. If the voices of the people don't matter as much as we might hope, money still speaks loudly in contemporary American politics. When a majority of Americans oppose something but powerful moneyed interest groups support it, the average Americans almost always lose.

Take the issue of gun regulation, for example. It's abundantly clear that the United States has a problem with gun violence. In the wake of the Sandy Hook Elementary School massacre, which left twenty children dead just before the Christmas holidays in 2012, 92 per cent of Americans indicated that they supported a legal change to ensure that all gun sales were conducted with background checks, including those that currently avoid those checks through a legal loophole.[19] Yet when the bill went before Congress, it failed in a 54 to 46 vote. There was no doubt: the National Rifle Association had once again gotten its way.

I saw these tactics firsthand. Before I started a career trying to understand international politics, I worked as an intern on Capitol Hill for US Senator Mark Dayton and later as his deputy campaign manger and policy director during his successful bid to become governor of Minnesota. Mark (for he insists that all his staff call him by his first name) was and is a Democrat with a moderate record on gun control—a crucial viewpoint to get elected in Minnesota, a state home to many avid hunters. His generally pro-gun stance was one I disagreed with, but it taught me a valuable lesson. The National Rifle Association, one of the most powerful lobbying groups in America, had previously awarded him their highest "A" rating when he campaigned for the US Senate.[20] Then, in 2005, Senator Dayton voted to ban bullets that were made to pierce heavy-duty body armor, a feature of ammunition that is hugely helpful if you want to kill police officers, but not quite so necessary if you're shooting at an unarmored deer. Overnight, the NRA changed Senator Dayton's rating from an "A" to an "F" and began funding his opponents. This is how reason dies in politics. As a pro-gun Democrat, he was everything the NRA should have hoped for across the aisle. Instead, they put him in their crosshairs.

On the other hand, Mark was born rich and he is (in my admittedly biased view) a tenacious, dedicated, and tirelessly hard-working politician. This combination allowed him to overcome the NRA, run for governor, and win. He inherited millions from his father, a department store scion who instilled in his children the importance of giving back to a community that had given their family so much. Even though I found Mark substantially more comfortable sitting in a plaid shirt in a rundown café of the rural and rusting northern Minnesota Iron Range, he was nonetheless part of the socioeconomic elite. As a result, to the chagrin of his fundraising team, Mark didn't spend his campaign days calling donors and eliciting their support. "I do most of my fundraising while I'm shaving in the mirror in the morning," he would regularly joke with us.

This feature of Mark's campaign was welcome news to me, as staff in flagging American electoral campaigns can sometimes be left in limbo as to whether their paycheck will arrive after an eighty-hour work week. Such financial independence can also confer political independence in an era where the average American overwhelmingly believes that elected representatives can be bought and sold. With politicians stubbornly unresponsive to the will of the masses on several issues while bowing to well-financed organizations, it's no wonder that some people find it appealing when Donald Trump insists (rightly or wrongly) that his wealth makes him politically independent. The surprisingly resilient appeal of Trump should be reason enough for us to pause and wonder if the campaign finance system should, finally, be fixed.

Thankfully, with the right political will, gerrymandering, ensuing gridlock, and campaign finance problems could be solved. The solutions are not difficult. California, for example, which has hardly been an exemplar of good governance, has nonetheless largely fixed its gerrymandering problem.[21] An independent commission, rather than a partisan political body, now draws district lines. Iowa has also reformed its system. Over time, those districts are likely to become more moderate and increasingly based on consensus. The model is easy to replicate and proof already exists that it works. But it requires Republicans and Democrats to put aside their personal short-term interests for the long-term interests of the nation, and that has become an increasingly hard sell in 2016, when the deficit of trust and respect between the two parties may be at an all-time nadir. However, if reform can somehow be achieved more widely, gridlock would become an irregular occurrence rather than a routine feature of Washington's political landscape.

Campaign finance re-regulation can solve out-of-control campaign spending. If the Supreme Court opened a judicial Pandora's box and can't or won't close it, it may be up to the American people to stuff it all back in, with a constitutional amendment invalidating the notion that unlimited corporate donations are a form of political free speech. Most democracies don't have this problem, so there's no reason to believe that campaign finance reform would bring the political sky falling down.

At least in the short-term, though, the problems that plague American democracy are not going anywhere. What does this mean? Is it time to sound the death knell of American democracy and throw in the towel with promoting democracy around the globe too? Far from it. American democracy is still a well-designed system that has produced enduring stability and steady growth through turbulent times. But it is important to acknowledge and openly address the fact that the American model is not the only viable one out there, and that other nations may not be insane to look at it with some sense of distaste. After all, I'm not sure what I would think as a reformer in Papua New Guinea being told to gravitate toward the shining "city on a hill" when the man perched atop that hill is sometimes an angry, tomato-faced Donald Trump, proclaiming that his main foreign policy adviser is "myself, number one, because I have a very good brain and I've said a lot of things."[22]

To their credit, democracy promotion organizations have made use of some genuinely good brains in recent years. They have made strides since the early 1990s but are still limited by a myopic homegrown view of what democracy is and is not. Previously, there was a major sense of bias coming from the individual organizations. USAID hawked the American model, while the British development agencies would try to sell Westminster-style democracy instead, and so on. That mistake has diminished but not disappeared. The best technical assistance offers a democracy smorgasbord, showcasing the best parts of several systems in the hope that local decision-makers can pick and choose off the available menu and come up with a dish that suits their culture and politics.[23]

This is an important step, but it could be further augmented by genuinely introspective evaluations of Western democracy by the same standards that Western governments apply elsewhere around the globe. As Thomas Carothers pointed out in an early 2016 article, "it was a useful step forward when Freedom House, a non-profit dedicated to political rights and civil liberties, issued for the first time in 2008 a probing report on the state of freedom in America to complement its usual focus on the state of freedom 'out there'."[24] Moreover, German foundations like the Friedrich Ebert Foundation and the Konrad Adenauer Foundation routinely apply their evaluations to German democracy. These may seem like symbolic gestures, but they can help at home while simultaneously eviscerating the critique from abroad that democracy promotion is a uniquely imperialist exercise of do what I say, not what I do.

On the other hand, some attempts to situate American democracy in a global context have gone too far. A recent report from the Electoral Integrity Project, an ambitious and important multinational scholarly research program, ranked American election quality as on a par with Colombia, but below Rwanda, Mongolia, and South Africa.[25] That is too much; elections in Rwanda are largely uncompetitive, and opposing the president can get you killed—even by assassins if you're living abroad (see Chapter 5). There is a middle ground between such hyperbole that claims American democracy is as bad as an authoritarian strongman's rule to the other end of the spectrum, which pretends that American democracy is still a sparkling city on a hill. The truth lies in between, and that truth needs to be confronted in order to spread democracy more effectively while undermining the impulse to pursue a competing authoritarian model.

When I was in Zambia in late 2012, I met with several former advisers of Frederick Chiluba, the former president. One of the most controversial moves of his presidency arose in the early 2000s, when Chiluba announced his intention to repeal term limits and stand for a third five-year term, which was expressly prohibited under Zambia's constitution. Significant opposition from civil society and rival politicians—along with the international community sounding the alarm bells—stymied the proposal.[26] But when I asked them about it, with perhaps a hint of consternation in my biased Western voice, several had the same retort ready to go: "You have the Bushes, the Kennedys, and maybe even the Clintons. Yes, we wanted the term limits gone. But are we so different?"[27] They had a point, even though I explained to them that modern term limits were ironclad in the United States, and that each Bush had been elected in a popular vote. It was unthinkable to imagine George W. Bush trying to get rid of term limits to stay in power in the same way that African despots were increasingly doing across the continent. "Yes, but Bush didn't win the most votes, did he?" several unhelpfully chimed in. Touché.

Most democracy promotion officials could fill a notebook with these types of retorts. They are getting harder to just laugh off. Western nations still play host to most of the best democracies in the world. But several of them, including their superpower leader, have ample reason to look inward while projecting the virtues of democracy outward. They need to lead by example. This is particularly true because alternative—and undemocratic—models are emerging, challenging the ideological dominance of the notion that democracy is the most desirable form of government, or at least, as Churchill put it, the worst form except for all the others. The confluence of recent events has seen China and Russia rise and reassert themselves on the global stage at the same time as Western democracy is facing unprecedented challenges, from the surge in right-wing populism to the Eurozone crisis. As a result, this is a critically important time for Western governments to rise to the challenge. Otherwise, nations stalled between dictatorship and democracy will look east rather than west, casting the American eagle into the swamp and placing the Chinese dragon and the Russian bear atop a dark authoritarian hill instead.

# 13

## THE BEAR AND THE DRAGON

The ten principles outlined above all show a way for the West to reinvent its flawed approach to advancing democracy across the globe. While the West acts too often as the despot's accomplice—sometimes inadvertently and other times as an accepted tradeoff carried by competing economic and security interests—Russia and China prop up authoritarian regimes unblinkingly. They're often frustratingly good at it too. The success of the preceding ten principles therefore relies on an overarching ability to dampen the anti-democratic influence of those two major world powers, de-clawing the bear and extinguishing the dragon's fire. Otherwise, they'll continue to inhibit democracy on continents near and far. Western governments are not accomplices to Russia or China, which are geopolitical enemies of most Western governments. But understanding their anti-democratic influence is crucial to any strategy that aims to reverse the losses in democracy over the last decade.

There are two challenges that need to be addressed when it comes to Russia and China's impact on global democracy. First, both countries provide an alternative model to liberal democracy. The more that China and Russia succeed, the more regimes searching for a rising place in the world will be tempted to replicate those undemocratic systems. This is much more credible in the case of China, which has managed to lift hundreds of millions of people out of poverty while still ruling with an iron fist. Russia's success has been more tepid internally, but its aggressive foreign policy adventures have nonetheless earned it many admirers. Both China and Russia attempt to actively project the value of their models to potentially friendly states around the world.

Second, in a more direct effect, Russia and China prop up friendly despotic regimes wherever they can. Both countries are opportunists. China's regime can fly much further afield, with plenty of domestic economic might providing ample lift to their foreign policy. On the other hand, Russia's direct lumbering influence is limited mostly to Eastern Europe and the Middle East because of the size of its economy (few people realize that Italy's total GDP surpasses Russia's).[1] Its lackluster performance has only grown more fragile in the context of low global oil prices. In terms of anti-democratic influence, though, Russia punches well above its economic weight. Belarus provides an illustrative example of how Russian influence can create a democratic reversal.

In 1991, Stanislav Shushkevich, an unlikely Belarusian politician, signed an agreement that signified the breakup of the Soviet Union. Shushkevich, who was born five years before World War II broke out, started his career as a nuclear physicist. Alongside that work, he taught Russian to earn some extra cash on the side. Unexpectedly, one of his pupils in Minsk was none other than Lee Harvey Oswald, the assassin who killed John F. Kennedy in 1963.[2] Yet it turned out that Shushkevich's contribution to Belarusian history would be much more than that bizarre tutoring footnote linking East to West.

Unlike many countries that fought hard for their independence, the collapsing Soviet empire dragged Belarus into statehood somewhat unwillingly.[3] There were serious birthing pains, as one would expect when one nation splinters into many. As one of the westernmost parts of the Soviet Union, Belarus played host to an enormous frontline arsenal, which included an array of nuclear weapons. A quarter of a million Soviet troops were based in Belarus, which was clearly an untenable proportion for a country of 10 million people.[4] Those Soviet holdovers had to be dealt with but there was no precedent to follow. What was to be done? Shushkevich, a scientist at heart who had only recently entered the political fray, was tasked with answering those difficult questions as the first Belarusian head of state. His first job was a daunting one: establish a sovereign democratic country from the ruins of the authoritarian Soviet Union.

Shushkevich succeeded. Belarus rapidly democratized. But after three years in power, Alexander Lukashenko, a charismatic authoritarian populist, accused Shushkevich of being corrupt. The evidence was flimsy, but the accusation helped Lukashenko win a commanding (and arguably free and fair) victory in the 1994 presidential elections.[5] If Shushkevich's first task as leader had been building a democratic state, Lukashenko wasted no time in dismantling it. As happens all too frequently without proper safeguards, democracy ensured its own undoing.

I met Shushkevich in December 2015 in his modest, bleak, rundown apartment block in Minsk as temperatures plunged well below freezing. The gray building was a perfect caricature of brutalist Soviet architecture. It was hard to believe that I was heading to the home of a former head of state as I rode the rusty iron cage elevator upward through an aging and cracked concrete shaft. Either the accusations about Shushkevich being corrupt were grossly untrue, or he had managed to lose a hell of a lot of cash in the intervening years.

When Shushkevich opened the door, I was even more surprised by the man than by the modest location. A distinguished, portly 81-year-old statesman stood before me in a shiny bright blue athletic tracksuit. An exercise bike that had surely been purchased in the 1980s was in the foyer of his cramped, cluttered apartment. He smiled and welcomed me: "Take your shoes off. Put on these slippers. Your feet will get cold."

As my interpreter translated what he had said, Shushkevich shoved a pair of impressively fluffy white slippers into my hands. Somewhat dumbfounded, I replaced my shoes with the slippers. With more appropriate footwear, he led me into his study and began to talk about how Belarusian democracy had been dismantled piece by piece during the mid-1990s, until there was nothing democratic left. In particular, Shushkevich lamented how his successor, Lukashenko, got away with it. "The 1994 election was genuine democracy," he explained. "Everything that came after it was not." And, he told me, it was all made possible with Russia's help.

At the same time that the rest of Eastern Europe was democratizing, Belarus made reintegration with Russia an official state policy goal. Lukashenko beat Shushkevich in the 1994 elections partly because of

Lukashenko's pro-Russian campaign, which emphasized nostalgia for the Soviet Union. As the West tried to push for a continued advance of Belarusian democracy, the pull of Russia was too great. In 1996, President Lukashenko signed an agreement with Russian President Boris Yeltsin that created a community between the two nations, which was later formally upgraded to the status of a political union.[6] While the proclaimed relationship was met with stops and starts as a result of political disagreements, it was exceptionally clear that the Kremlin still very much viewed Belarus as within its sphere of influence. The West watched, with a feeling of powerless fatalism, as the formerly promising transition to democracy transformed into an authoritarian puppet of Moscow.

By 2002, with President Putin in the Kremlin, Russia floated the idea of Belarus simply reintegrating into the Russian Federation as six new *oblasts* (administrative divisions). This never came to pass, but President Lukashenko repeatedly said that he felt that Belarus and Russia were nonetheless "like brothers," even if they retained formally separate institutions.[7] With Putin's regime pumping cash, military assistance, and subsidized natural gas into Belarus, no wonder he felt such a familial bond.

The West hoped to break up the family. In 2004, Congress, urged on by George W. Bush, isolated Lukashenko's regime by passing the Belarus Democracy Act. The Act placed sanctions on Belarus and called for them to remain in place until the regime reformed. As Western pressure on Belarus mounted, Russia repeatedly acted like a safety valve, diffusing pressure with ever-closer cooperation. In propping up Lukashenko, Putin ensured that any efforts to return to Belarusian democracy would fail.[8] Without Russian backing, Lukashenko would not have had nearly so much latitude to act brutally in the face of protests, or to crush dissent using the KGB. But with Putin waiting in the wings, Lukashenko knew that Western pressure had its limits. "He's a thug, but he was Russia's thug and that meant everything," Shushkevich told me. I thanked him, returned the slippers, and asked him how else he spends his time these days. "I'm off to the airport now. I'm presenting at a scientific conference." I asked him where it was. "Moscow," he replied. The family bond endures, even if there are growing sibling rivalries.

Just weeks after this meeting, the European Union withdrew its sanctions from Belarus in the hopes of prising Minsk from Moscow's grip.[9] To do so, the first step was to take a softer stance and hope that Europe could woo Lukashenko back. Even though relations between Belarus and the West are thawing (inappropriately in my view, because there has been no meaningful political reform), there is little reason to be optimistic about Belarus' prospects for democracy in the short or medium term. Unless Russia completely collapses amidst its current crisis with stubbornly low prices, Belarus has an important ally, and one that can certainly help undermine Western pressure against Minsk. It's not so much that Russia wants to spread authoritarianism for the sake of authoritarianism, but more that Russia is opportunistic and wants to be sure that Belarus stays in its camp rather than defecting to the democratic West. For the West, Russian support also changes the calculation in Belarus. If Western ambassadors push too hard, they fear that Lukashenko will be driven right back into a big old bear hug with Putin. The specter of Putin's recently proposed airbase in Belarus has drawn that fear into even sharper focus in Western capitals.

Explaining the democratic reversal of Belarus without reference to Russian foreign policy is impossible. Today, Belarus remains authoritarian partly because Russia continues to inhibit Western gambits to restart democracy. Russia's direct support for prospective authoritarian allies is by no means unique to Belarus. Across areas that it deems to be in its political neighborhood, from Eastern Europe to the Middle East, Russia continues to inhibit democratization with a foreign policy that provides sanctuary and assistance to governments that should (and often do) receive sanctions and admonition from Western governments.[10] Yet because the West doesn't act with consistency, the status quo is often even worse: Putin continues to get his way with an ally, while the West naïvely hopes that a softer stance will pay dividends. It rarely does. It is unlikely to be any different in Belarus in the coming years.

However, it would be a mistake to suggest that Russia acts in such a way because it opposes democracy above all other considerations. Instead, Putin is ruthlessly pragmatic. This has sometimes led the Kremlin to back the more democratic option abroad, so long as it suits Russian interests. For example, after the ruling authoritarian Moldovan Communist Party rejected a Russian proposal on how to deal with the breakaway region of Transnistria in 2005, Putin actively backed the much more strongly pro-democracy opposition.[11] Of course, this is an outlier. Russia overwhelmingly supports despots above democrats in global politics.

China is often less aggressive than Russia, but its effect on inhibiting democracy is, if anything, more potent than Russia's. What Russia did for Belarus in the mid-1990s, China is doing for Thailand today. Most recently, China has given Thailand political cover against Western pressure, particularly in the context of the May 2014 coup d'état that installed a military regime at the helm in Bangkok. Since 1932, Thailand has "democratized" with a "one slow step forward, two quick steps back" approach. The backward pace has recently accelerated, thanks to the rising influence of Beijing in Bangkok.

Understanding China's anti-democratic influence in Thailand requires some longer-term context. In the wake of the Asian financial crisis of the late 1990s, a new political star emerged in the "Land of Smiles": Thaksin Shinawatra, a police officer turned media mogul who would eventually rise to become the juggernaut in Thai politics. Since the late 1990s, Thailand has been roughly divided into two major political camps known by colorful monikers: the Red Shirts and the Yellow Shirts. While both sides have support from competing elite networks, Thaksin's Red Shirts have secured their electoral support primarily from Thailand's rural north. His supporters, rice farmers in particular, have latched onto Thaksin's populism and repeatedly voted for his party in droves, propelling his party to victory. The Yellow Shirts, by contrast, tend to be more of a conservative force, with their strongholds in Bangkok and in Thailand's south.[12]

Since 2000, Thaksin's party has won every election, but the Yellow Shirts (or the military) have wrestled power away from his network with crippling protests, coups d'état, or, most often, both. There were coups in 2006, 2008, and 2014.[13] In earlier coups, Western governments would react sternly, providing sufficient diplomatic pressure to force the army back into the barracks even if that would still mean giving power to an unelected civilian of the military's choosing. Today, however, China's soaring influence in the region has changed the West's calculation; the threat of the dragon waiting in the wings has made the eagle a bit more timid around its former roost.[14] The American government worries that pressing Thailand too much on governance issues will cause it to re-orient toward Beijing. To some extent, that fear is warranted.

On 22 May 2014, Thailand's military took power from an elected civilian government in yet another coup d'état (Thailand is the most coup-prone country on Earth, with nineteen successful and attempted coups since 1932).[15] In previous revolts, there had been a familiar script: military takes power; military returns power to new civilian regime friendly with the military; new civilian government writes new constitution; civilian government fails in the eyes of the military; military takes power again and the cycle repeats. The 2006 coup followed this script. To a lesser extent, so did a "judicial coup" in 2008, in which, the People's Alliance for Democracy (PAD) opposed the government of Samak Sundaravej. In a stranger-than-fiction twist, Samak was removed from power under the pretext of corruption, for receiving small payments for hosting a cooking show called "Tasting and Grumbling". The Thai PAD movement successfully toppled a government for making Pad Thai on television.[16] It was strange, but it fit into the mold of what political observers of Thailand had come to expect: civilians being removed from power. It was business as usual.

The 2014 coup was different. Rather than transferring governance to an anointed civilian, the 2014 military junta (calling itself the National Council for Peace and Order) decided to retain power for itself in order to achieve its main stated goal: "to bring back happiness."[17] In August 2016, the Thai junta successfully pressured voters into adopting a new authoritarian constitution via a controversial referendum—even though few voters actually knew what was in that constitution. It is unlikely that the NCPO will relinquish power before at least late 2017, marking more than three years of formal junta rule. Even then, the generals are attempting to ensure that they never have to fully give up their grip on real power, even if an elected government officially takes the reins. The timing of this strategic shift toward a more hands-on military regime, as China has risen to become a major world power, is no coincidence.

Thailand's struggle with democracy reflects several of the themes that I've previously highlighted, but it also shows how China can act as a spoiler at key moments in potential transitions to democracy. In December 2014, just seven months after the latest military coup had taken place, I found myself in what can only be described as Thailand's junta's café. The hard part was getting a Thai soldier guarding the Government House with a very large weapon to believe that I was in the right place and was not, in fact, a confused tourist. Once inside, I had coffee with Major General Werachon Sukondhapatipak, the junta's official government spokesman. In an effort to downplay the military character of the government, he had traded in his uniform for an immaculately pressed suit, looking more like a businessman than a high-ranking officer. After exchanging pleasantries, he explained to me why he thought the coup had taken place. His answer was grounded in the context of large anti-government protests that had been clogging Bangkok's streets for months before the army stepped in. At times, the protests had turned violent: "On 21 May, we decided we could not let the situation go on. On 22 May, I was in the room—it was clear everyone was acting only on their interest. We cannot let people continue to die on a daily basis. We cannot let deadlock continue."

So, the military stopped the deadlock in the streets with force. It deposed the government of Yingluck Shinawatra, the sister of former prime minister Thaksin Shinawatra, who had himself been deposed in a prior coup d'état and forced into exile. The justification for this latest coup, General Werachon argued, was to avoid further chaos. Explicitly invoking failed transitions to democracy elsewhere, he suggested that letting the situation play out without military intervention was a recipe for disaster. "So many people have let 'the people solve things themselves'—Ukraine, Syria, Iraq—and how many people have to die? If it was 200 years ago, maybe we'd let a civil war happen but with a modern economy, the risk was too high."

Once the coup happened, though, the risks were much higher for those who had previously been favorable to the toppled regime or who dared to criticize the new one. Democracy was snuffed out in a day, and so was dissent. Pravit Rojanaphruk, an Oxford-educated journalist who wrote for *The Nation* daily newspaper in Bangkok, was watching television on the night of the coup when he was surprised to see his name appear in the government's announcement of which people had been "summoned" to report directly to the junta immediately. "I was number six, the sixth 'undesirable,'" he told me in a Starbucks at Bangkok's luxurious Siam Paragon mall, "my fear was only slightly dampened by the pride that being sixth brought me."

Pravit was brought to a military camp in Ratchaburi Province to the west of Bangkok for a bit of Orwellian "attitude adjustment". The aim was, he told me, "part intimidation and part Stockholm Syndrome. We didn't have a choice in going, but once we were there, they treated us extremely well. We got to choose between steak and lobster for dinner each night. The wine was $100 a bottle. And we even played a friendly football match against our military captors." The underlying message behind this lavish seduction by imprisonment was crystal clear: "I was told not to tweet, nor to write anything critical of the military. They wanted some time to 'settle into ruling' without any criticism. They told me I was being watched closely but they said so with a smile." After a week in detention, Pravit was released, but not forgotten. There is always the specter of going back for further "attitude adjustment."

Others were not so fortunate in the wake of the coup. Dr Weng Tojirakarn, one of leaders of the so-called Red Shirts, had an ambivalent relation with the party's symbolic leader, Thaksin, but was an ardent supporter of its political program. Dr Weng has advocated for democracy for most of his adult life. He participated in the student-led pro-democracy uprising in Thailand in 1973 and subsequent student protests in 1976 that ended in a bloody university massacre. After the massacre, Dr Weng joined the outlawed dissident Communist Party of Thailand, fled Bangkok into the rural Thai jungle, and used his medical training to help heal guerrillas.[18] But by 2014, Dr Weng had been back in Bangkok for some time as a major figure in the pro-Thaksin movement. At the time of the coup, he was addressing a large crowd of supporters:

> At about 2pm, I was told that they had announced a coup. After three or five minutes, soldiers aimed an M16 and a pistol at my head. They seized the microphone from me and I told them I would go with them if they didn't shoot or open fire on my supporters. Then they arrested me. They put my wife—a 70-year-old lady—put her in a black hood and handcuffs. I was thrown into a tiny cell and fed rotten chicken but at least they boiled the chicken after it had rotted so I wouldn't get sick. After seven days, they released us and told us not to speak about politics or to go abroad. Our TV station always has the risk of getting shut down or taken off the air. It's happened three times already. We cannot express anger about them but they express hatred against us.

I spoke to Dr Weng in an unused studio of the Red Shirts' glitzy modern television station, its offices a slightly odd sight perched above a roller disco rink in a working-class shopping mall. The studio was still broadcasting, but only in meaningless platitudes about the Red Shirts' hope for a better future for all of Thailand. If anything critical were to be broadcast, the station would quickly be taken off the air.

Thais, not the Chinese, were responsible for the 2014 coup and the subsequent crackdown. But the coup and its aftermath are the types of events that should elicit biting chastisement from Western capitals, followed by hard-nosed diplomacy and immense political costs. The reality was far more muted. Western governments condemned the coup, but they were mostly empty words. Several Western ambassadors told me variations of the same trepidation: if we push the military regime too much, other Western governments will just gain at our expense, or worse, China will continue to encroach on our spheres of influence here. And, indeed, China was the main beneficiary of this classic foreign relations prisoner's dilemma. Western rhetoric against the coup was just rhetoric. Foreign direct investment increased in the wake of the coup—something that couldn't be more different from the international response to a geopolitically irrelevant country like Madagascar.

What accounts for the muffled Western diplomatic response to Thailand's 2014 coup? Thailand has a longstanding alliance with the United States, dating back 180 years but with intensified closeness during the Cold War.[19] Driving down Witthayu Road in Bangkok, the leafy grounds of the American embassy sprawl endlessly. It is, by some measures, the third largest American diplomatic mission in the world (it was the second biggest until the Iraq War; the embassy in Beijing is now second biggest). The vast embassy walls are adorned with painted murals documenting "180 years of friendship" between Thailand and the United States. That friendship grew dramatically with Thailand's strategic importance during the 1960s, as 25,000 troops were stationed in Thailand during key phases of the Vietnam War. At one point, using Thailand as a staging base, "the annual cost of the bombs dropped over North Vietnam and Laos exceeded the size of the Thai economy."[20] In return, Thailand benefited from the "Saudi Arabia Effect", as the West turned a blind eye to elite-level corruption and political abuse.

At the end of the Vietnam War, Thailand became less geopolitically important to the United States, but it remained a trusted partner and a valuable one in the Cold War context and after the collapse of the

Soviet Union. In a show of the continued value placed on bilateral relations between Thailand and the United States, the two governments cooperate in joint military training exercises, codenamed Cobra Gold.[21] The exercises have taken place every year since 1982, whether in tandem with a military junta or an elected civilian government.

When the Berlin Wall collapsed, however, Western governments pressed Thailand to democratize further. Thailand made progress toward that goal, a paragon of counterfeit democracy that, at times, flirted with a more consolidated form during repeated bouts of elections, but never quite got there. Even after the rise of Thaksin, an elected populist, extrajudicial killings, corruption, and bad governance persisted.[22] The West initially pressed Thailand more aggressively on these issues, exposing key human rights abuses and warning Thailand it needed to improve in order to stay in the good graces of the West.

But, over time, Western governments (and the United States in particular) have become increasingly timid in condemning Thailand's government. The strategic importance that Thailand lost at the close of the Vietnam War has resurged, as Western governments see the map of Southeast Asia increasingly in terms of a zero-sum game against China. Moreover, in the context of the early phase of the so-called War on Terror, Bangkok may have bought itself a longer diplomatic leash with the West by allegedly hosting a CIA "black ops" base codenamed Detention Site Green at Udon Thani in northeast Thailand, near the Cambodian border.[23] In 2003, the George W. Bush administration became even more willing to overlook Thailand's governance problems when the Thai government dispatched 400 troops to Karbala in Iraq to fight under Poland's command.[24] These gestures of longstanding goodwill, combined with the increasingly credible rhetorical threat of a Thai re-orientation toward China's deep pockets, have been sufficient to disarm the United States of key weapons in its diplomatic arsenal. Out of geostrategic concern, Washington has been relegated to words but not much else—even in the wake of blatantly undemocratic coups. Such foreign policy weakness made clear to China that there was a ripe opportunity to make diplomatic inroads against the United States in its own backyard.

To understand how that shift might be playing out, and how Thais saw themselves in the Southeast Asian geopolitical tug-of-war between the United States and China, I met with Abhisit Vejjajiva in Bangkok just before Christmas 2014. Abhisit became prime minister in 2008 after being placed in power by the "Pad Thai" coup. He is, in some ways, a hybrid of east and west himself. Abhisit spent his formative years at the elite Eton College boarding school just outside of London. Then, he progressed onto St John's College, Oxford, where he rubbed elbows with the future British elite, including current foreign secretary Boris Johnson. He is, therefore, someone who is sympathetic to Western governments. He understands the West's point of view far better than most Thais. But upon taking power in 2008, no British education could have prepared Abhisit for the complexities, disarray, and violence of Thai politics.

In the spring of 2010, his government found itself facing more than 100,000 protesters clogging the streets of Bangkok. The protesters were angered by a judicial decision to seize billions of dollars worth of assets from their symbolic leader, the exiled former prime minister Thaksin Shinawatra.[25] They demanded that Abhisit resign and call fresh elections. The situation began to spiral out of control in April and May, as hundred were injured in clashes between the security forces and the protesters themselves. The government accused the pro-Thaksin protesters of throwing grenades and inciting violence; the protesters accused the security forces of using excessive force and killing protesters. By early May, Abhisit was facing considerable internal pressure to disperse the protesters. Over the course of several days in mid-May, the military violently cracked down on the protests. While it is difficult to say exactly what happened—the government claims, somewhat implausibly, that protesters started shooting while dressed as soldiers—it is nonetheless clear that the government repression involved snipers and live rounds fired into crowds. By its bloody end, security forces had killed at least ninety people. Roughly 2,000 more were injured.[26]

Notably, the US State Department only issued a weak statement in the aftermath of these events, and reserved its harshest criticism not for its ally, the Thai government, but for the protesters: "We call on both sides to show restraint and to work to resolve differences through Thailand's democratic institutions ... However, we are deeply concerned that Red Shirt supporters have engaged in arson targeting the electricity infrastructure and media outlets and have attacked individual journalists."[27] This dry statement said nothing about soldiers firing on protesters, even though that is widely regarded as the source of the majority of deaths.

Over tea at the posh Sukhothai Hotel in Bangkok in late 2014, I asked Abhisit if such diplomatic restraint from the United States—after the recent coup in particular—could be attributed to worries about China. "Of course," he said, "Westerners are worried that Beijing's rise will correspond with Washington's fall here in Thailand. And they may be right to be worried, because the military government seems to be headed that way." When I pressed him for details on how that shift was happening, he pointed to a burgeoning November 2014 infrastructure deal for a 542-mile-long Sino-Thai rail link that would be part of a larger regional connection between Thailand and China. The venture was supposed to signal a stronger partnership between the two countries, each working to benefit the other. But when I met with him again in March 2016 and asked the same question, he laughed. "Have you seen the news today? They just announced that they aren't working together anymore. Instead, Thailand is just going to pay for it, hiring Chinese contractors, Chinese companies to build the whole rail network and we're footing the bill alone." China isn't working with Thailand as an equal partner but rather as a regional hegemon intent on asserting itself in Southeast Asia, with a bold "take it or leave it" approach. So far, Thailand seems willing to take it. This is a new frontier in Sino-Thai relations, and it remains to be seen how they will continue to develop when (or if) civilians return to power.[28]

Deals like this have at least one clear effect: they are the equivalent of a diplomatic shot across the bow from Thailand and China, warning the West not to press too hard for democracy. General Prayuth Chan-ocha, the junta's leader turned prime minister, has repeatedly warned the West against lecturing Thailand and pushing it to return to democracy rather than charting its own unique Thai path forward. New forms of cooperation between China and Thailand, like the rail deal, only further weaken the West's stomach for diplomatic pressure, worrying that further attempts to draw Thailand back into the democratic fold will only ensure that it defects to China more meaningfully and permanently. Dr Weng, the Red Shirt leader, is ethnically Chinese, as are many figures in the Thai elite. He put it bluntly: "Thailand's head is still with the United States, but our closer culture gives our heart to China."

At the opposite end of the political spectrum from Dr Weng, I suggested to Abhisit that perhaps Thailand had learned a key lesson from the Soviet-American showdown in the Cold War and was attempting to play the sides off against one another in the emerging Sino-American showdown—to be courted by both while aligning firmly with neither. He laughed, but stayed silent and didn't disagree. Most importantly, he lamented that the geopolitical dynamic was allowing the military rulers to overstay their welcome due to China's backing and tepid Western pressure. Thailand could become yet another country cursed by low Western expectations: "I worry not as a politician but as a Thai that the military will retain a powerful oversight role, even after they claim a return to democracy." With China's shadow hanging over Bangkok politics, Thailand's return to "democracy" is likely to be as a counterfeit democracy at best, at least for a while. The proposed new constitution effectively enshrines the military as the most important veto player in the political system, seemingly legitimizing and making official the demise of Thai democracy.

In the meantime, Thailand's political elite has been carefully watching US politics, trying to read the tea leaves for what might come next after Obama leaves the Oval Office. Over omelets at a quiet outdoor café in Bangkok seven months before America's 2016 election, I asked Thailand's former foreign minister, Kasit Piromya, how he saw the future of Thailand's relations with the West, and the United States particularly. He had previously served as Thailand's ambassador to the Soviet Union and also to Germany, Japan, and the United States, so he knows a thing or two about how to navigate geopolitical divides. "For us, the Trump phenomenon is like a Broadway performance. And I must say, we're enjoying watching," he said, laughing in between puffs on his Sunday morning cigar:

> But we need reassurances of the reliability of the United States. They are behaving like a jilted lover because the military government was stupid enough to turn toward Putin and China. That was our mistake. But we— the democratic forces of Thailand—we need help. In our stupidity, we have recently been acting as a vassal state to China, even though we pride ourselves on a thousand years of independence.

Nonetheless, Kasit told me of other initiatives that showcase some of the exemplary work that Western governments are doing in Thailand, the types of activities that should be celebrated and expanded:

> The Swiss and the Norwegian embassies have been setting up informal meetings for us to meet with the Red Shirts, our political adversaries, for the last three years. It's very helpful. I even half-jokingly suggested that maybe I should go and see Thaksin in exile; I want to have another glass of wine with him. I come from the diplomatic profession. I believe in talking with one another.

While Kasit praises some Western efforts, he has thus far been unimpressed with American diplomacy in Thailand. In particular, he is hoping that he will find a more robust partner for democracy in the next administration, even if it doesn't come wrapped in the gaudy glitz of a blowhard's Broadway performance:

> The perception of Obama here is that he wavers too much and is a minimalist. He tries to avoid threats. But how can you do that as the president of the United States? He, and eventually his successor, need to become more engaged actively in a positive manner...I am still waiting for the United States to work with the democratic forces of Thailand.

He paused, thinking, dragging on his cigar. I asked him why he thought China has been more effective in establishing closer relations with Thailand since the coup. "Oh, well, the military government and Beijing have much more in common—if the military stays in power, it'll make China more comfortable. They have like-mindedness. They speak the same political language of authoritarianism and—" he cut himself off, as a group of four young American backpacker girls with knotted dreadlocks at the table adjacent began singing "Happy Birthday" for someone in their traveling party. I started to ask a follow-up question, but the eminent statesman firmly held out his hand to silence me and joined in the singing. When the song concluded, he picked up again mid-sentence as if nothing had happened, "and China feels like we are giving them an opportunity to deal a blow, score points, against the United States."

The experiences of Thailand and Belarus both demonstrate a key lesson in the twenty-first-century battle for global democracy: China and Russia can actively inhibit democracy by providing a credible alternative to the West as a powerful foreign partner. That risk not only shores up the domestic power base of countries in their orbit, it also forces the West to tread carefully; pushing too hard could drive a potential ally into an alliance with a geopolitical enemy. Belarus and Thailand couldn't be more different, but their experiences have been similar insofar as they have had more latitude to roll back democracy thanks to diplomatic shielding from Russia and China respectively. For the moment, Belarus is tilting ever so slightly away from Russia, while Thailand tilts slightly toward China. It's difficult to say whether these trends will continue, but the pull of Russia and China is enough to deeply damage the prospect of genuine democracy in each. Belarus has shown no appetite for meaningful reform; Lukashenko remains a post-Soviet dinosaur. Thailand's new draft constitution proposes that a third of the Senate will be military appointees, enshrining a veto point for the generals to create a system of elections without democracy. Together, though, these examples showcase the direct effect that bilateral foreign relations can have on rolling back democracy at critical points in faltering transitions. China's reach in particular extends much further than its own backyard; governments like Sudan and Zimbabwe have received crucial boosts from their Sino relations, severely weakening Western pressure against those abhorrent regimes.[29] Russia has less reach but, where it is active, is no less menacing.

That's only one half of the problem. Aside from propping up despots and peeling authoritarian regimes away from Western influence, China and Russia may have an even bigger impact on global democracy through the indirect effects of the model they provide to struggling nations around the world. The more Russia and China succeed themselves, the more other governments will see their style of ruling as a path forward, in contrast to the vision offered by Western liberal democracy. This has become particularly threatening to the Western model in the wake of the financial crisis of 2008–9, because China's economy grew by 9 per cent in 2009, while the economy of countries like Japan contracted by more than 5 per cent.[30] And, until late 2008, "nearly every top Chinese official still lived by Deng Xiaoping's old advice to build China's strength while maintaining a low profile in international affairs."[31] Now, Beijing is promoting its pathway of economic, but not political, liberalization as the Beijing Consensus, a term specifically modeled to parrot and mock the liberal Washington Consensus. China's government is actively trying to export it.

As the strength of their models grows in the eyes of prospective adopters from Latin America to Sub-Saharan Africa, China and Russia are both using a multitude of tools to actively replicate similar governance around the globe. This is not to say that there is no genuine standalone allure to China's economic success or to the Kremlin's ability to wield disproportionate might on the global stage. But it is to say that any positive aspects of these two models are overshadowed by serious drawbacks and shortcomings. Beijing and Moscow are aware of these flaws. That's why most of China's and Russia's diplomatic methods for spreading their respective models rely on some form or propaganda or disinformation campaign.

If you switch on your television in just about any hotel room these days, you'll be able to watch propaganda straight out of the Kremlin on Russia Today, now re-branded just as RT to subtly obscure its funding source. The programming is specifically designed to parry Western accounts of global news, spinning each story as Putin would hope to see it covered. While its unclear the extent to which Putin and his allies control day-to-day programming, it is clear that there is no overarching semblance of journalistic independence. The Kremlin has paid more than $2 billion to fund RT since its inception in 2005.[32]

While RT claims to reach roughly 700 million viewers, this figure is one that simply represents its potential viewership where it is offered as part of cable packages. In reality, RT viewership comprises less than 0.1 per cent of Europe's television audience.[33] In the United States, RT doesn't even garner enough regular viewers to score in many of the cable ratings. Perhaps this is because its programming is often extreme and frequently false. RT incorrectly claimed that Ukraine was committing genocide against pro-Russian separatists. One RT special report suggested that the CIA had manufactured the Ebola virus and initiated the recent crisis; this echoed Soviet propaganda claims in the 1980s that the CIA was behind the AIDS virus and was using it to kill off African-Americans.[34] These absurd claims are one reason why RT's impact is limited. After all, its most popular YouTube videos include a 2010 clip of Vladimir Putin singing Fats Domino's hit song *Blueberry Hill* and a series of overly graphic videos of live births.[35] Nonetheless, RT's existence is sufficient to provide an alternative Russo-centric narrative as global events unfold, and that is meaningful. RT's disinformation has worked in the past and it will work again.

Take for example, the story of "Lisa," a 13-year-old German-Russian girl living in Berlin who briefly went missing from her home and claimed that she had been raped in early 2016. Ivan Blagoy, a journalist working for RT, alleged on air that the German authorities were involved in a cover-up and that Lisa had been gang raped by Syrian refugees. Russia's foreign ministry stoked the fire of those accusations on Twitter. The timing was not coincidental. German Chancellor Angela Merkel was under intense political fire for her decision to welcome droves of refugees, and RT's allegations set off waves of protests in Germany that threw Merkel's regime into disarray.[36]

Yet after just rudimentary detective work, it became abundantly clear that no refugees had been involved and that Lisa had made up the entire story; she had run away from home and spent some time at a 19-year-old friend's house. Was it dubious and worrying that a 19-year-old man spent the night with a 13-year-old girl? Absolutely. Was it worthy of spreading rumors at the diplomatic level and using media to incite Germans to take to the streets against Merkel? Hardly. But for RT, it was a diplomatic success. Many Germans likely do not know that Lisa later recanted her story, yet her tale was splashed across German headline news for days. Misinformation can be a potent weapon at critical moments (Kermit Roosevelt working to incite the CIA's 1953 coup in Iran would certainly agree). Fortunately this time, in Germany, the consequences were not severe, though they could have been.

Not to be outdone by Russia, the Chinese equivalent of RT, China Central Television, or CCTV, has been more effective and is less outlandish than its Russian counterpart. CCTV broadcasts in English, Arabic, French, Russian, and Spanish. It usually exports a softer version of propaganda than RT, which tends to reflect China's foreign policy, generally less muscular than Putin's saber-rattling, barrel-chested provocations. In the 2016 Lunar New Year celebrations, for example, CCTV broadcast a series of songs with titles like *Without the Communist Party, There Would Be No New China*.[37] It was propaganda, but it wasn't as insidious as the Lisa story. Even if CCTV's content is less provocative than RT's, however, China clearly sees it as a major foreign policy tool. CCTV has twelve bureaus in Latin America and is fanning out across Sub-Saharan Africa. CCTV's messaging also dovetails with a sophisticated approach known as the "borrowed boat" strategy, aimed at ensuring that China's narrative ends up being broadcast on existing media outlets in foreign markets too.[38]

CCTV's global goals are complemented by Confucius Institutes. These well-funded non-profit organizations focus on teaching Chinese language and culture in universities around the world. There is nothing wrong with them in practice, but they do underscore the way that China actively attempts to promote itself as an alternative to the West—which becomes insidious when the lesson is drawn beyond culture and language. In total, there are roughly 500 Confucius Institutes in 130 countries as diverse as Bahrain, Armenia, Tunisia, Sierra Leone, Azerbaijan, Romania, and New Zealand. In the United States alone, China has established 109 Confucius Institutes, from the Community College of Denver to San Diego State University.[39] To fund such a broad spread, China draws on a variety of sources, including a "propaganda-industry tax" that has taken in 3 per cent of all profits from publicly funded enterprises since 1992.[40] Opacity is understandably a hallmark of Beijing's budgeting for propaganda, but analysts have estimated the total costs of gambits like CCTV and the Confucius Institutes to be around $7–10 billion annually—far more than the United States spends on democracy promotion activities.[41]

For RT, CCTV, and Confucius Institutes to work effectively, though, Russia and China need to be seen favorably. That means they also need to muddy the waters of Western criticism that sows doubt amongst those who might be swayed against their respective models by reports of human rights violations, bad governance, weak rule of law, corruption, and all the abuses that are routine in both authoritarian states.

One of the interesting (and sometimes unfortunate) aspects of most political debates is that when two opposing views exist, both tend to receive coverage. This is often a great virtue of independent journalism and of democracy itself, giving voice to the minority. But, as with topics like climate change, it becomes a problem when there is one accepted view and one fringe view that nonetheless receives equal media attention. It gives rise to the impression that there is an even split in opinion when there is no such thing.

Exploiting this phenomenon, Russia and China have established a series of Government Organized Non-Governmental Organizations, or GONGOs. These organizations, which purport to be non-governmental, simply cloak government narratives in the more palatable shell of a pro-government think tank or an institute that brands itself as a human rights watchdog. In his fantastic book *The Dictator's Learning Curve*, Will Dobson documents how these GONGOs regularly release conflicting pro-government reports to undermine the consistency of messaging coming from Western NGOs that accurately highlight government abuses. Sometimes, it's easier for journalists to take the safe path by reporting disagreement and conflicting reports rather than "taking sides" and ignoring reports from a GONGO.[42] In other words, they can be effective.

Moreover, for genuine domestic NGOs that attempt to expose regime abuses, Russia and China have mastered ways of choking their ability to operate with seemingly unrelated crackdowns. For example, NGOs operating in Moscow routinely face being shuttered for building code infractions or allegedly unpaid water bills. Even when these claims are unfounded (as they almost always are), they usually take months to resolve, and the NGO is knocked out in the meantime— while the Kremlin can plausibly deny any politically motivated involvement. Both setting up GONGOs and shutting down legitimate NGOs are critical efforts in muting the effect of Western criticism against the Russian and Chinese modes of governance. Injecting doubt and contradictory statements into such information wars helps ensure that Western messaging about each government is diluted. Michael Weiss and Peter Pomerantsev have aptly dubbed this phenomenon "the menace of unreality."[43] In turn, governments that may flirt with the idea of mimicking Beijing or Moscow are more likely to become fully seduced. In this way, authoritarianism spreads more easily, as the two titans offer an alternative vision for development—and one that struggling governments may eagerly embrace. After all, there are a fair few despots who may find it alluring to silence dissent with an iron fist while still aggressively pursuing economic development. This is particularly true if following China's or Russia's lead allows them to remain corrupt and stave off genuine electoral challenges simultaneously.

Even among such despots, though, most have found it difficult to fully resist Western pressure to at least create a counterfeit democracy involving some form of (severely flawed) elections. When this happens, China and Russia are ready to lend a helping hand too. Welcome to the world of so-called "zombie" election monitors, sham election monitors claiming to be independent observers.[44] These groups publish lofty praise of clearly rigged elections in order to create a perception of disagreement when Western observers condemn electoral fraud.[45] These groups have ornate names like The Inter-Commission Working Group on International Cooperation and Public Diplomacy of the Public Chamber of Russia Elections and the Commonwealth of Independent States Observation Mission (CIS-EMO). Both gave full-throated endorsements of the rigged 2013 election in Azerbaijan—the one that featured results being published through an app the day before voting.

Zombie monitors' strategy has been successful enough to have spawned copycats around the world, as authoritarian regimes attempt to legitimize terrible elections in an "I'll scratch your back by praising your electoral fraud, if you scratch mine" arrangement. The groups doing the scratching—"observing" but never condemning—have obscure names like Observer Mission of the NGO Forum of the Organization of Black Sea Economic Cooperation (BSEC) and the Observation Mission of the Standing Conference of Political Parties of Latin America and the Caribbean (COPPPAL). These complement more powerful groups like the Shanghai Cooperation Organization, which has China and Russia as two of its six core members. China sent monitors to notoriously flawed elections in Zimbabwe and to Madagascar's 2013 elections, even though China doesn't hold national elections itself. With this obscure alphabet soup of zombie monitors, authoritarian regimes across the world use the models developed by Russia and China to challenge credible Western monitors' claims of electoral fraud. As I've highlighted previously, Western monitors have their flaws too, but these pale in comparison with the zombie monitors sent by the Kremlin.

Cumulatively, the Chinese dragon and the Russian bear are formidable foes in the quest to stop the stagnation and decline of global democracy. They are the true despot's accomplices, as despotic regimes themselves, actively seeking to prop up similarly authoritarian leaders. This is all part of the diplomatic game, and it's nothing new. Russia and China are unlikely to change anytime soon. And, for some issues, like the threat that a given country will defect to a Chinese or Russian sponsor while doubling down on authoritarian rule, there are no diplomatic panaceas. But the West can do more.

For example, NGOs can help ensure that they are not derailed by fake GONGO reports, by making it easier to track and compare funding sources for all legitimate NGOs operating around the world. Once financial transparency is universally declared and easily searchable, it would be easy to see when NGOs that claim to be independent are actually being funded by the government, eager to obscure their shadowy financial backers. Journalistic standards should insist on identifying GONGOs correctly whenever they are cited in news reports. Furthermore, the ten principles outlined in previous chapters are crucial to limiting the influence of China and Russia on the global stage. In particular, democracies banding together to form a League of Democracies would further isolate Beijing and Moscow and make the allure of China's or Russia's orbits comparatively less appealing. Even with those improvements, however, Russia and China are not going anywhere. Neither is likely to willingly embrace democracy at home anytime soon; each is too powerful to be pressured into political liberalization in the near future. But their influence must be better contained around the globe, as the West can ill afford to allow critically important geopolitical regions to become simple puppets of Chinese and Russian foreign policy. Without better coordination against the bear and the dragon, democracy, from Latin America to Sub-Saharan Africa, from Belarus to Thailand, will continue to be devoured or scorched.

# CONCLUSION

## THE RESURGENCE OF DEMOCRACY

Global democracy is in decline. As a result, the world is becoming less stable, less prosperous, and vastly more dangerous.

The West has always been, and continues to be, the best possible hope for promoting democracy around the world. The West has expended money, political capital, and even blood to defend democracy and give a voice to the voiceless. It has often been tremendously successful.

Since 2006, though, the West has failed to help advance democracy beyond its high water mark. Too often, Western foreign policy has encouraged authoritarianism, acting as an accomplice to despots rather than their adversary. Western governments have aided and abetted friendly autocratic governments even as they have stripped away democratic elements, abused human rights, crushed dissent, and cracked down on those that have a simple demand: to have a say in decisions that affect their lives greatly.

Worse, this trend is set to continue, because investing in democracy has fallen increasingly out of fashion in Western capitals, from Berlin to Washington. With failed transitions in Iraq, Afghanistan, Libya, and Ukraine all looming large, Western elites have been tempted by previously heretical thoughts. Why bother promoting democracy? Is it really worth it? Those questions, which used to be whispered in muffled blasphemous tones in Western capitals, are now openly debated. There are more and more people in the Western establishment who prize stability above freedom, at least when it comes to how they believe their governments should interact with the rest of the world. That sentiment was on stunningly blunt display during the 2016 American presidential campaign, as candidates lined up to sing the praises of monarchs like King Abdullah II of Jordan and other friendly despots around the world. Donald Trump even had nice things to say about Russia's despotic thug, Vladimir Putin. Such praise would have been unthinkable from a leading American presidential contender even just a few years ago.

Those who have lost their appetite for democracy promotion tend to fall into one of two camps. In the first camp, democracy promotion is seen as a needlessly moral consideration that is thoroughly out of place in the cutthroat landscape of international politics. In this view, foreign democracy does not matter. Democracy promotion is a waste of money, energy, and political capital. Countries should matter to the West only insofar as they work with us rather than against us in advancing Western strategic agendas. Unfortunately, the more that approach is used, the less "soft power" the West will have to get its way in global politics without using force. Over time, the West will find fewer and fewer countries willing to work collaboratively, as Western governments begin to be seen as even more duplicitous and callously self-interested actors in global diplomacy. Nonetheless, the voices of these Henry Kissinger disciples are rising, gaining steady influence in London, Paris, Brussels and Washington.

In the second camp are those who believe in the value of democracy promotion, but find it worthwhile only if it aligns with the short-term geostrategic interests of Western governments. When it does not, it should fall by the wayside, as other overriding interests are deemed more important. This is the current approach. It has led us to a prolonged period of democratic stagnation and decline, giving despots the upper hand. Twenty-five years ago, Francis Fukuyama mistakenly argued that the world was nearing "The End of History," wherein democracy would ultimately supplant despotism everywhere as the ideological dominance of democracy became uncontested. Instead, because of the West's halfhearted approach to democracy promotion, despots have a growing number of defenders, and the West is far too often on the wrong side of "history."

There is a third way forward: promote democracy consistently and more intelligently. As I've outlined, democracy promotion is complex, fraught with danger, and even potentially catastrophic if bungled. There are risks. But it would be riskier to double down on an approach that has failed to deliver results or, worse, to abandon democracy promotion altogether. Critics of democracy promotion justify their opposition to consistent democracy promotion with a variety of arguments. I'll admit that democracy is no panacea; it is a system that presents new opportunities that are rarely present in authoritarian states, but it is no guarantee of prosperity in itself. Yet, for each argument that suggests Western democracy promotion should be relegated to the history books, the logic is alluring, but flawed.

First, authoritarian regimes are sometimes portrayed as governments that are needed to deliver results, giving people the prosperity they want without involving citizens in decisions over how to get it. Proponents of this view point to several outliers, like Singapore, Rwanda, and even China, to showcase systems where a small, unaccountable group is able to govern in the interests of the many. This is not government of the people, or by the people, the argument goes, but it is for the people.

This is the myth of benign dictatorship. It is frequently put forth as an alternative model, but it is just a myth. The countries put on a pedestal to elevate this myth are major outliers, standing out from a much uglier field. Every dictatorship has a period where it seems benign, until it isn't. By then, it's too late. By definition, you can't fire despots, and as this book makes clear, lots of people are trying very hard to do so and failing. Ultimately, Winston Churchill's statement has stood the test of time and rings as true today as it did when he spoke it just after World War II. Democracy is the worst form of government in so many maddening, frustrating ways, except for all those other forms that have been tried.

For anyone who truly believes that Churchill was and is wrong, I would urge you to conduct a simple thought experiment. Imagine that before you are born, you can choose to be born in an authoritarian state or a democratic one. You don't know which country it will be— you only know the government type. There are some grim democracies and a few better performing authoritarian regimes. But can you honestly say you'd roll the dice and pick authoritarianism if you had to choose between the two?

Second, even if you would take the gamble, there's another problem. "Good" authoritarian states would be better as democracies. China, Singapore, and to a lesser extent Rwanda, all have strongly functioning political institutions. They exploit comparatively high levels of state capacity to get things done. As a result, there is no reason to believe that they could not do the same, only better, if they incorporated the strengths of democracy into their regimes. Admittedly, there are innate strengths of authoritarian rule, like rapid response during crises and the opportunity for long-term planning, but those advantages are deeply outweighed by the rewards of democracy. Rwandans would be better served if they were able to openly debate state policies, blocking the good ones, and harnessing the country's creativity to produce better ideas. It's similarly unclear why a carefully managed transition to democracy in countries like China or Singapore would be catastrophic rather than fruitful. The liberalization of China's economy was, after all, seen as a major risk that could invite unwanted volatility. Then it happened, and everything got better rather than worse. A similar pattern could emerge in other high-performing authoritarian states as they liberalize politically and become more democratic. This is particularly true if change happens without a dramatic revolution that takes a wrecking ball to the institutions and individuals of the old regime, but instead builds upon existing strengths.

However, there is some truth to the fact that transitions are hazardous. This anticipates the third critique commonly leveled against democracy promotion. Some argue that the dangers of transition are so great that the West should therefore deter rather than invite it. Such status quo diplomacy is flawed for two reasons. First, transitions may happen anyway, and when they do, the new regime is far less likely to be friendly to the fallen despot's former allies (if you don't believe me, see Iran's relations with the United States since 1979). This is precisely why a democratic Saudi Arabia could be so dangerous to Western interests after decades of support for the oppressive ruling family. It is also precisely why the West would be better weaning itself off that relationship sooner rather than later.

Second, transitions may invite short-term instability but successful transitions ensure long-term stability. This is true for both dictatorships and counterfeit democracies that could upgrade to the real thing.

Significant swaths of the population often have a strong propensity for violent opposition to the regime under the leadership of both despots and counterfeit democrats. To deal with those threats and stave off violence, dictators are better equipped: they can use an iron fist to crush insurrection before it breaks out into the open. Counterfeit democrats have the worst of both worlds: plenty of opposition but less of an ability to repress it before it becomes violent. For this reason, significant swaths of research—including my doctorate—have shown that countries "in the middle" are most prone to civil wars and other forms of political violence.

This is, however, not an endorsement of the pragmatic value of iron fists to crush violence. Iron rusts. When that happens, the ensuing transition is far likelier to be messy and exceptionally violent. The risk of regime collapse exploding into a global or regional conflagration can be much greater in the wake of longstanding authoritarianism. Syria's current quagmire tragically showcases this point. As a result, the only genuine form of stability comes with consolidated democracy, which tends to have fewer people who oppose the regime's survival but also a built-in mechanism to incorporate, rather than silence, dissent.

Finally, Fareed Zakaria, who has an admittedly brilliant mind for this topic, has advanced the idea that countries should only get into the driver's seat of democracy once they have developed sufficiently.[1] In this patronizing view, poor, weakly institutionalized countries are like young children and should not be allowed to take care of themselves. I view it differently. Poor countries are like young drivers just taking the wheel for the first time. Yes, they are statistically more likely to crash than their richer counterparts.[2] Perhaps they will be more likely to have a safe initial journey if they start driving when they are 30 years old instead. But you have to learn by doing. Delaying democratization may have some marginal benefits in a select few cases, but using those cases to dictate the general rule would be a mistake, akin to letting a few democratic car crashes ruin everyone else's opportunity for self-governance.

Additionally, as Robert Kagan correctly pointed out in his critique of Zakaria's argument, "Those countries that manage to escape poverty are just as likely to be democratic throughout their period of economic growth (Japan, Ireland) as they are to be dictatorial (Singapore,

Malaysia) or to undergo transition from dictatorship to democracy (Portugal, Spain, South Korea)."[3] In other words, to get rich, there's not necessarily an advantage to being authoritarian, so it makes sense to at least try and be democratic. Moreover, Zakaria's logic is most alluring because today's transitions are held to an absurdly short time frame before they are considered failures. Assessing the Arab Spring five years on in 2016 is akin to assessing Japan's democracy in 1950. Early setbacks do not doom democracy's long-term trajectory.

Finally, call me sentimental, but I can't stomach the idea that people in poor countries should suffer the double indignity of poverty coupled with having no voice involved in changing their lives for the better. Zakaria is correct to point out the perils of premature and overzealous transitions. These are legitimate concerns that cannot easily be dismissed. But he is wrong to suggest that this means we should accept authoritarianism as a necessary and perhaps even desirable feature of impoverished nations in the meantime.

Similarly, there is a surprisingly pervasive (and borderline racist) view that democracy is neither compatible with Asian values nor with Islam. It is absurd. Democracy is not a one-size-fits-all form of government. That is precisely its strength. To reiterate President Obama's words in Cairo back in 2009:

> all people yearn for certain things: the ability to speak your mind and have a say in how you are governed; confidence in the rule of law and the equal administration of justice; government that is transparent and doesn't steal from the people; the freedom to live as you choose.

Muslims don't like corrupt and unresponsive governments any more than Christian Belarusians, and Confucianism doesn't mean that despotic governments should be free from citizen accountability. Adaptations of other democratic prototypes may need to be adapted to fit the local context, but Taiwan, Japan, and to a slightly lesser extent the Philippines make clear that Asians value democracy. Myanmar's fledgling democratic experiment after decades of military rule could soon be added to that list. While Indonesia has slid closer to authoritarianism recently, it gives hope to the notion of Muslim democracy. Tunisia has added to it too, the first and most promising model for Arab Muslim democracy. If they continue to consolidate, such countries should be cherished and asked to join in democracy promotion elsewhere, as paradigmatic examples of democracy's intrinsic ability to adapt to local context. Fundamentally, it's a mistake to measure democratic potential against the status quo landscape. Seeing the democratic wasteland that largely constitutes the Middle East and inferring that it could never be democratic is like seeing Europe in the Dark Ages and assuming it would always be impoverished and backward. Successful democracy requires people to make the concept their own; it might take a while, but it can be done.

Beyond Zakaria's influential critique, many opposed to democracy promotion suggest that it is an agenda advanced by ideologues with little reference to the pragmatism that pervades most people's daily existence. They are correct to point out that debates can become too theoretical. The average person certainly cares more about the struggles of daily life than about abstract concerns of governance. After all, who cares if your local governor was elected if you don't have a job? To an extent, that's a valid and underappreciated criticism of the scholarly debate over democracy. Foreign policy discussions about democracy promotion can become the intellectual plaything of political elites and academics. It's easy to let ideology or a fetishization of democracy overshadow the pragmatism that pervades most people's daily existence.

Nonetheless, the conclusion that we should not promote democracy is incorrect. Democracy's core attributes do affect daily life considerably. The aspirations of billions of people hinge upon this seemingly academic debate. Democracy, in its essence, has fundamental advantages over dictatorship. Consolidated democracies spawn more economic opportunity, enjoy better physical security, and are bastions of greater justice. They have less corruption, which is a scourge that lowers growth and takes money out of the pockets of hundreds of millions daily. They provide a marketplace of ideas which helps weed out bad ideas and gives rise to good ones. If bad ideas squeak through the system or the electorate swings too far one way at any given moment, there are built-in ways to correct those self-inflicted wounds without them becoming fatal. Importantly, they also have a mechanism to resolve political disputes without violence. Yes, democracies don't always perform up to their potential. These positive attributes are not uniformly apt for all democratic states. Some perform better than others; as I said in Chapter 1, not everyone can be Norway. But the potential of democracies to deliver prosperity is far greater than that of even the most well-managed and seemingly benign authoritarian states. To follow the alternative logic would require believing that the West should not promote democracy anywhere, simply because not all countries will consolidate and democratize as quickly or as well as the most exemplary existing democracies did.

Finally, in these debates, we need to stop pretending that counterfeit democracies are democracies at all. We're often led to believe that developing nations only have a choice between mimicking high-performing strongmen, as in Rwanda or Singapore, and becoming a divided and turbulent democracy such as Kenya. I have lost count of how many times I have heard this argument. There's just one major problem: Kenya is not a democracy, even though it is sometimes considered one. In an influential index used by political scientists to measure democracy, Kenya ranked above Belgium in 2014.[4] Any Kenya specialist will be the first to laugh at the notion that Kenya is more democratic than Belgium.

Getting these labels correct is crucial. Some may (perhaps rightly) disagree with my characterization of specific countries that I've discussed. Disagreement is important, so long as a consensus is then forged that insists on a high bar. If people view Kenya or Pakistan as deserving the same label as Japan and Sweden or even India, then the value of the term democracy is watered down. The people of Equatorial Guinea may view democracy less favorably if they associate the term with Madagascar or Guyana rather than Chile, Denmark, or Mauritius. Those latter three nations are spread across three regions. They have disparate wealth. Each has a different form of democracy. Yet all are worthy of the label. Proponents of democracy must therefore be the greatest defenders of the term and set a high bar for it. The words we use matter.

In this book, I have outlined a way forward to make sure that more countries are worthy of that precious label: democracy. The West needs to learn from its mistakes in order to unleash a resurgence of democracy and end the current trend. The principles above offer a blueprint for how to get started. Think long-term. Don't try to impose democracy with wars launched from the West. Coordinate diplomacy at the highest diplomatic echelons with democracy promotion efforts on the ground. Let other countries hold elections free from Western manipulation. Give dictators a way out to pave the way for transitions. Include the old regime in transitions. Target democracy promotion funding to where it is most likely to work. Use economic carrots and multilateral coordination to encourage democratization while shrinking the options available to despots. Use digital technology to expose authoritarian abuses rather than letting it be used as a weapon against democratic reformers. And finally, lead by example, so that the West looks like a much more alluring model to follow than China and Russia.

Even though I am realistic that, at best, a few of these principles could slowly trickle into Western foreign policy, I am nonetheless optimistic for the future of global democracy. In my quest to understand why democracy is in decline globally and what can be done to fix it, I traveled 102,822 miles to completely disparate parts of the planet. Some of the countries I lived in could hardly be more different. They nonetheless shared one unifying theme: in every corner of the world, there are people out there fighting hard on the frontlines of a global battle for democracy. Throughout my travels, I found the depressingly cynical machinations of dictators and despots matched at every twist and turn by the less powerful but equally determined democratic reformers. Whether it's politicians like Said Ferjani in Tunisia who are willing to put the nation before personal vengeance, journalists like Pravit Rojanaphruk in Thailand who are willing to speak truth to power even after "attitude adjustment", or the thousands of students in Hong Kong's Umbrella Movement who risk everything for their dream of political freedoms, democracy has its advocates, its fighters, and its defenders everywhere. They are buried more deeply in some places than others, but they can always be found if you look closely enough (or, as necessary under some authoritarian regimes, whisper quietly enough).

Following a decade and a half of stunning victories after the end of the Cold War, the advance of democracy has stalled and slipped backward. Despots who were on their heels have now dug themselves in, finding an accomplice in the West, which is grudgingly facilitating their authoritarian crimes. Their victims are the billions of people who routinely have their life ambitions held back by a government that mutes their voice and rules them without any meaningful choice. However, as long as the West acts as the despot's accomplice rather than its adversary, genuine global stability, strong economic growth, and justice will also be victims of these unfortunate crimes. Western governments need to change their strategy, holding dictators, despots, and counterfeit democrats accountable rather than rushing to their defense.

In my hundreds of interviews, it started to seem worryingly routine to hear horror stories of abuse and torture, of beatings and brutality. In places like Madagascar, where the average person lives on just over $1 per day, I simply got used to seeing crippling poverty when I wasn't interviewing politicians in their opulent homes or offices. I began to recognize that familiar pause in conversation, the hesitation of people's voices breaking as they told me about being tortured. It became normal to speak to both sides, sometimes in the same day, despots and democrats. The way I view these experiences, however, hinges so much on how I see each nation's prospects for democracy. In Belarus, sitting across from Mikolai Statkevich who had just been released from more than four years of prison and psychological torture and who was beaten nearly to death for the "crime" of calling for democracy, I could only feel a deep sadness. Alexander Lukashenko, the dictator who ordered Statkevich's beating, abduction and jailing by thugs, was going to get away with it. The West may not be guilty of oppressing Statkevich, but by becoming friendlier with Belarus in 2016 after a long and distinct lack of reform, shortsighted Western governments are driving Lukashenko's getaway car. Statkevich will never get those four and a half years of his life back. His body may never fully heal. And still, Lukashenko will remain in power, because he has powerful friends and reluctantly forgiving suitors, now including Western governments. It's hard to feel optimistic after those types of meetings.

I felt the same way with one the kindest people I met on my travels, one of Madagascar's best journalists, Alain Iloniaina. When I arrived on the island for the first time in 2012 without a single contact, Alain generously opened up his network to me within ten minutes of meeting me, allowing me to better understand the plight of his country. In 2013, however, the editor of Alain's newspaper decided to run for president. He required all of his journalists to support him in their writings. Alain refused out of principle and lost his job, a particularly courageous decision given the fact that he had young children at the time and money was tight. Over breakfast in December 2013, while I was serving as an election monitor, I told Alain how much I admired his decision. But I also told him, sadly, that nobody in the West would care. I was right. Nobody in the media covered his resignation. In spite of his last journalistic stand, Madagascar is still a terribly run country that too many in the West falsely believe is a democracy. Like Belarus, it is unlikely to change much anytime soon. But the courage embodied in Alain's seemingly small act can add up to something bigger.

Similarly, I met again with Pravit, the brave Thai journalist who has been repeatedly detained by the ruling junta, for a second time in March of 2016. "I feel 50 per cent less optimistic than when we last spoke," he told me in Bangkok. "The new draft constitution means that the junta is not going anywhere probably for at least five years and America is helping them by acting completely Janus-faced. They say one thing but act a different way because they will not let China steal Thailand away from them." And yet, Pravit himself represents a glimmer of hope. In spite of repeated "attitude adjustment," his attitude is surprisingly resilient and his voice has proved stubbornly difficult to silence. Even though his most recent detention was appalling, as he was tossed into a scorching hot "4 meter by 4 meter cell, with no air conditioning," Pravit has a sense of humor about his continued resistance. "They tried to intimidate me by telling me that there is a soldier who has the full-time job of monitoring my Facebook posts and my tweets," he said with a smirk. "Poor guy! A full-time job, just for me! At least I hope I am teaching him some English!" He paused to laugh. "If they want to waste their time with me and go after other people for posting shitty memes on the Internet, they can go right ahead."

Our conversation was filled with quips like these and laughter throughout, albeit some pretty dark humor, but Pravit's devotion to his principles is serious. "There's a saying in Thai we have, that eventually a pig no longer fears being slaughtered. Well, I'm now that pig, and I'm not going anywhere, and I'm not going to stop speaking up either. But for now, I'm trapped—along with all Thai people—in juntaland." People like Pravit deserve more Western support. "I'm pinning my hopes on the Scandinavian countries, maybe the Germans if we are lucky. But the EU as a bloc just wants to advance its business interests, and the US has too much to lose here in geopolitics to really push for democracy."Thailand's short-term prospects are dim partly because the West is only thinking short-term too. But people like Pravit make me hopeful that Thailand's long-term trajectory can change.

There are also success stories, albeit fewer than in the 1990s. Tunisian torture victims provide an unlikely source of hope, but that's what shone through as they told me about their optimistic vision for a democratic future. I'll never forget Said Ferjani's booming laugh overshadowing the winces from daily bodily pain, the lingering specter of unspeakable suffering at the hands of a Western-supported despot. Ferjani was in exile for decades; now he's part of a new generation of reformers in power, doing everything they can to avoid the mistakes of Tunisia's dark past.

But most of all, perhaps, I remember the joviality of Lieutenant Colonel Mohammed Ahmed, the military officer who was falsely accused of a coup plot, tortured, and stripped of his rank, uniform, and pension. For two decades, Lt Col Ahmed languished, hoping for nothing more than to have his suffering acknowledged, to be granted a formal apology, and to be given the right to wear his uniform again. By 2010, he had long since given up hope. Then, in the span of a few weeks, his torturer was toppled and everything changed. In June 2014, he sent me a jubilant e-mail:

> I am delighted to tell you some great news. We have achieved an exceptional tour de force: the Constituent National Assembly has adopted a law of rehabilitation and recognition of the rights of us victims. Our careers will be reinstated, with three ranks added on to our previous ranks, and we will be given full pensions at that level.

This small victory would have been unthinkable without Tunisia's transition to democracy.

There are thousands of similarly unthinkable victories out there, small and large. They have been forged by democratic change, like Tunisia's, that often seemed laughably improbable—until it happened. Authoritarian stability that seems ironclad is frequently a mirage that leaves the West looking foolish in an unforgiving geopolitical desert. Yet Western policy is all too often based on that shimmering mirage. If you had predicted Tunisia's transition in 2010, or Syria's bloody spiral into tragic civil war at the same time, politicians, scholars, foreign policy analysts, and journalists would have dismissed you as a crackpot.

Political risk maps at the time showed Egypt, Syria, Tunisia, and Bahrain as some of the safest bets out there for stability. Needless to say, the maps the following year looked different.

Alternatively, imagine stepping into Riga's KGB Corner House in 1989 and telling prisoners that they are standing in a soon-to-be museum, a place where tourists would make donations in the same currency that people use on the Champs-Élysées, and that Riga will soon be one of Europe's "culture capitals." Or imagine whispering about the future of democracy under the tyranny of the American-backed Chilean despot Augusto Pinochet in the late 1980s, only to watch genuine democracy take root. Today, in Myanmar, there is a new dawn for democracy. It may not pan out, just as Tunisia's fledgling democracy is no guarantee, but there is, finally, hope—a hope that used to be unthinkable. In global politics, the terrain can shift quickly. That means there should always be hope.

In this struggle for democracy, the victims are usually the people living under despotism, as their leaders have conducted a heist, stealing their voices and depriving them of meaningful choice. But once the West acts as an accomplice to these undemocratic crimes across the globe, we all become victims of the shared costs of authoritarian rule. Global security, prosperity, and justice have suffered. But, as in Chile, Tunisia, Latvia, or perhaps Myanmar, that suffering can be alleviated. Democracy can again be on the march if the West becomes the democrat's accomplice instead.

Voters in the West have been born into a privileged position precisely because they have a say in their governments, which happen to form the most powerful bloc of countries in the world. To democratize the world, whether out of moral duty or self-interest, Western voters may demand a change in their government's interactions with the rest of the world. The decline of democracy or its prolonged stagnation does not have to continue. There is a better way. It may not be easy, it may not always work, and it is fraught with peril. But we have to try.

# NOTES

## INTRODUCTION: ACCESSORY TO AUTHORITARIANISM

1. Freedom House (2015). 'Freedom in the World. Discarding Democracy: Return to the Iron Fist', https://freedomhouse.org/report/freedom-world/freedom-world-2015#.VvziW2R97UQ, last accessed 31 March 2016. See also Diamond, Larry (2015). 'Facing up to the Democratic Recession,' *Journal of Democracy*, 26(1), 141–55; and Diamond, Larry and Marc F. Plattner (2015). *Democracy in Decline?*, Baltimore, MD: Johns Hopkins University Press.
2. Nathan, Andrew (2015). 'Authoritarian Resurgence: China's Challenge,' *Journal of Democracy*, 26(1), 156–70.
3. Scholars have referred to this concept by many names. Fareed Zakaria popularized 'illiberal democracy', which I do not find useful, because these countries are not democracies. Others have used conceptually accurate but political science jargon to describe them, including anocracy, competitive authoritarianism, and electoral authoritarianism.
6. Levitsky, Steven and Lucan Way (2006). 'Linkage versus Leverage. Rethinking the International Dimension of Regime Change', *Comparative Politics*, 38(4), 379–400.
7. Carothers, Thomas (2003). 'Promoting Democracy and Fighting Terror', *Foreign Affairs*, 82(1), 84–97.
8. Diehl, Jackson (2011). 'Can the U.S. Get on the Right Side in Egypt?', *The Washington Post*, 28 January 2011, http://www.washingtonpost.com/wp-dyn/content/article/2011/01/27/AR2011012707456.html, last accessed 4 March 2016.
9. World Bank (2013). 'Madagascar: Measuring the Impact of the Political Crisis', http://www.worldbank.org/en/news/feature/2013/06/05/madagascar-measuring-the-impact-of-the-political-crisis, last accessed 16 December 2015.

10. Holland, Jennifer S. (2014). 'Locusts Eat the Crops Of Madagascar—and Each Other, Too', *National Public Radio*, 3 September 2014, http://www.npr.org/sections/goatsandsoda/2014/09/03/345258382/locusts-eat-the-crops-of-madagascar-and-each-other-too, last accessed 17 March 2016.

11. *Indian Ocean Times* (n.d.). 'Madagascar: 3,572 zebus stolen between May and April 2014 by the dahalo', http://en.indian-ocean-times.com/Madagascar-3-572-zebus-stolen-between-April–and-May–2014-by-the-dahalo_a3763.html, last accessed 7 January 2016. See also Amnesty International (2012). 'Madagascar Must End Mass Killings and Investigate Security Forces', 20 November 2012, https://www.amnesty.org/en/latest/news/2012/11/madagascar-must-end-mass-killings-and-investigate-security-forces/, last accessed 7 January 2016.

12. Ffooks, John (2012). Lawyer and Political Analyst. Personal interview, 14 September 2012, Antananarivo, Madagascar.

13. *BBC News* (2013). 'Madagascar Election is Free and Fair, Observers Say', 27 October 2013, http://www.bbc.com/news/world-africa-24694421, last accessed 8 January 2016.

14. *The New York Times* (2009). 'Text: Obama's Speech in Cairo', 4 June 2009, http://www.nytimes.com/2009/06/04/us/politics/04obama.text.html?_r=0, last accessed 24 March 2016.

15. Center for Strategic and International Studies (2015). 'Military Spending and Arms Sales in the Gulf', Washington, DC: CSIS, 28 April 2015. See also: Blanchard, Christopher (2016). 'Saudi Arabia: Background and U.S. Relations', Congressional Research Service, 22 April 2016, https://www.fas.org/sgp/crs/mideast/RL33533.pdf, last accessed 19 February 2016.

16. Kaphle, Anup (2015). '13 Times U.S. Presidents and Saudi Kings Have Met', *The Washington Post*, 27 January 2015, https://www.washingtonpost.com/news/worldviews/wp/2015/01/27/13-times-u-s-presidents-and-saudi-kings-have-met/, last accessed 7 January 2016.

17. US State Department (2011). 'Saudi Arabia: 2010 Country Reports on Human Rights Practices', p. 4, http://www.state.gov/j/drl/rls/hrrpt/2010/, last accessed 7 January 2016.

18. *The Telegraph* (2010). 'Indonesian Maid has Lips Cut Off by Employer,' 23 November 2010, http://www.telegraph.co.uk/news/worldnews/asia/indonesia/8154287/Indonesian-maid-has-lips-cut-off-by-employer.html, last accessed 7 January 2016.

19. Donaghy, Rori (2015). 'Rare Footage Shows Public Beheadings in Saudi Arabia,' *Middle East Eye*, 7 November 2015, http://www.middleeasteye.net/news/rare-footage-shows-public-beheadings-saudi-arabia-318277846, last accessed 7 January 2016.

20. Blanchard (2016).
21. Shokr, Ahmad (2011). 'The 18 Days of Tahrir', *Middle East Report*, 258, 14–19.
22. Snider, Erin and David Faris (2011). 'The Arab Spring: US Democracy Promotion in Egypt,' *Middle East Policy*, 18(3), 49–62.
23. Dumke, David (2006). 'Congress and the Arab Heavyweights: Questioning the Saudi and Egyptian Alliances,' *Middle East Policy*, 13(3), 88–100.
24. *The Economist* (2013). 'Coup-lio: America's Response to Coups,' 23 July 2013, http://www.economist.com/blogs/democracyinamerica/2013/07/americas-response-coups, last accessed 21 March 2016.
25. Hassan, Oz (2015). 'Undermining the Transatlantic Democracy Agenda? The Arab Spring and Saudi Arabia's Counteracting Democracy Strategy,' *Democratization*, 22(3), 479–95.
26. Blanchard (2016).
27. Burke, Jason (2015). 'Saudi Blogger Raif Badawi May Receive Second Set of Lashes on Friday,' *The Guardian*, 11 June 2015, http://www.theguardian.com/world/2015/jun/11/saudi-blogger-raif-badawi-next-lashes-friday, last accessed 4 February 2016.
28. Valentine, Simon Ross (2015). *Force and Fanaticism: Wahhabism in Saudi Arabia and Beyond*, Oxford: Oxford University Press.
29. Klaas, Brian (2015). 'Why Tunisia Absolutely, Totally Deserves the Nobel Peace Prize', *Foreign Policy*, 9 October 2015, http://foreignpolicy.com/2015/10/09/why-tunisia-absolutely-totally-deserves-the-nobel-peace-prize/, last accessed 7 February 2016.

## 1. A CONCISE BIOGRAPHY OF DEMOCRACY

1. Segal, Charles (1998). *Aglaia: The Poetry of Alcman, Sappho, Pindar, Bacchylides, and Corinna*, Oxford: Rowman & Littlefield.
2. Carter, D. M. (2013). *Sophocles: Ajax*, Cambridge: Cambridge University Press.
3. Plattner, Marc (2010). 'Populism, Pluralism, and Liberal Democracy,' *Journal of Democracy*, 21(1), 81–92.
4. World Bank (n.d.) 'GDP Per Capita (Current US$)', http://data.worldbank.org/indicator/NY.GDP.PCAP.CD, last accessed 13 March 2016.
5. Russia and China are the exceptions. Of course, many of the other eight were not always democracies during their development into industrial powerhouses.
6. These are Qatar, Singapore, Kuwait, Brunei, the United Arab Emirates and Saudi Arabia. However, if countries that are dependent on oil exports are removed from the equation, then only Singapore graces the top twenty-five.

7. Sen, Amartya (2001). *Development as Freedom*, Oxford: Oxford University Press.

8. Tang, Beibei (2014). 'Development and Prospects of Deliberative Democracy in China: The Dimensions of Deliberative Capacity Building,' *Journal of Chinese Political Science*, 19(2), 115–32.

9. Morton, Ella (2014), 'Golden Statues and Mother Bread: The Bizarre Legacy of Turkmenistan's Former Dictator', *Slate*, 6 February 2014, http://www.slate.com/blogs/atlas_obscura/2014/02/06/saparmurat_niyazov_former_president_of_turkmenistan_has_left_quite_the_legacy.html, last accessed 12 January 2016.

10. Dadabaev, Timur (2006). 'Living Conditions, Intra-Societal Trust, and Public Concerns in Post-Socialist Turkmenistan,' *Central Asia and the Caucasus*, 4(40), 122–32.

11. Horák, Slavomír (2005). 'The Ideology of the Turkmenbashy Regime,' *Perspectives on European Politics and Society*, 6(2), 305–19.

12. Bodeen, Christopher (2003). 'Beijing Builds 1,000-bed SARS Hospital in 8 Days', *Associated Press*, 1 May 2003.

13. Gallie, W. B. (1955). 'Essentially Contested Concepts', *Proceedings of the Aristotelian Society*, 56(1), 167–98.

14. See Fukuyama, Francis (2015). 'Why Is Democracy Performing So Poorly?', *Journal of Democracy*, 26(1), 11–20.

15. Forsdyke, Sara (2001). 'Athenian Democratic Ideology and Herodotus' Histories', *American Journal of Philology*, 122(3), 329–58.

16. Keane, John (2009). *The Life and Death of Democracy*, London: Simon and Schuster.

17. Isakhan, Benjamin (2011). 'What is so "Primitive" About "Primitive Democracy"? Comparing the Ancient Middle East and Classical Athens', in *The Secret History of Democracy*, London: Palgrave Macmillan, 19–34.

18. Keane (2009).

19. Historians have enlisted handwriting experts who believe there is evidence that many ballots were written with the same hand, indicating possible evidence for vote rigging, as Ajax claimed in the vote over Achilles' armor.

20. Brickhouse, Thomas and Nicholas Smith (1990). *Socrates on Trial*, Oxford: Oxford University Press.

21. Of course, Socrates probably never would have gained prominence, or would have been killed far sooner, under a tyranny.

22. Price, Melissa (2016). Member of Parliament from Durack District, Western Australia. Telephone interview, 3 March 2016.

23. Nunavut district in Canada, with 31,000 electors spread over 787,000 square miles, is the largest district in the world. It is larger than Mexico, and is nearly nine times the size of the United Kingdom. The

northernmost city, Alert, is just 500 miles from the North Pole, roughly the distance that separates London from Copenhagen.

24. Keane (2009).
25. Henry the Impotent was not impotent when it came to his second wife, Joan of Portugal, who was his first cousin. They had a daughter together. Bermudo the Gouty was more accurately named.
26. See Villadangos, Esther Seijas (2015). 'The Decreta of Leon (Spain) of 1188 as the Birthplace of Parliamentarism: An Historical Review from a Time of Crisis', UCD Working Papers in Law, Criminology & Socio-Legal Studies Research Paper No. 08/2015.
27. Cole, Peter (n.d.). 'King Charls, His Speech, Made Upon the Scaffold at Whitehall-Gate Immediately Before His Execution On Tuesday the 30th of Jan. 1648 With a Relation of the Maner of His Going to Execution,' available from Project Canterbury, http://anglicanhistory.org/charles/charles1.html, last accessed 18 January 2016.
28. Keane (2009).
29. Conniff, James (1980). 'The Enlightenment and American Political Thought: A Study of the Origins of Madison's Federalist Number 10', *Political Theory*, 8(3), 381–402.
30. Elster, Jon and Rune Slagstad (1988). *Constitutionalism and Democracy*, Cambridge: Cambridge University Press. See also Holmes, Stephen (1995). *Passions and Constraint: On the Theory of Liberal Democracy*, Chicago, IL: University of Chicago Press.
31. United States Constitution. Article 1, Section 2, Paragraph 3.
32. Limongi Neto, Fernando et al. (1996). 'What Makes Democracies Endure?', *Journal of Democracy*, 7(1), 39–55.
33. Craske, Nikki (1999). *Women and Politics in Latin America*, New Brunswick, NJ: Rutgers University Press.
34. Lynch, John (2001). *Argentine Caudillo: Juan Manuel de Rosas*, London: Rowman & Littlefield.
35. Ibid.
36. Perlmutter, Amos (1997). *Making the World Safe for Democracy: A Century of Wilsonianism and its Totalitarian Challengers*, Chapel Hill, NC: University of North Carolina Press.
37. Cox, Michael, Timothy Lynch, and Nicolas Bouchet (2013). *US Foreign Policy and Democracy Promotion: From Theodore Roosevelt to Barack Obama*, New York: Routledge.
38. Putnam, Thomas (n.d.). 'The Real Meaning of *Ich Bin ein Berliner*', *The Atlantic*, http://www.theatlantic.com/magazine/archive/2013/08/the-real-meaning-of-ich-bin-ein-berliner/309500/, last accessed 9 December 2015.

## 2. SPOOKING DEMOCRACY

1. Ghasimi, Reza (2011). 'Iran's Oil Nationalization and Mossadegh's Involvement with the World Bank', *The Middle East Journal*, 65(3), 442–56.

2. There has never been firm evidence that, as Washington was led to believe, Mossadegh was forging close ties with Iran's communist-leaning Tudeh Party.

3. For an extremely rich and meticulously researched account of Operation Ajax, see *All the Shah's Men* by Stephen Kinzer.

4. Kinzer, Stephen (2003). *All the Shah's Men: An American Coup and the Roots of Middle East Terror*. Hoboken, NJ: J. Wiley & Sons.

5. Ibid. See also Roberts, Mervyn (2012). 'Analysis of Radio Propaganda in the 1953 Iran Coup', *Iranian Studies*, 45(6), 759–77.

6. Kinzer (2003).

7. Ibid. See also Gasiorowski, Mark and Malcolm Byrne (2004). *Mohammad Mosaddeq and the 1953 Coup in Iran*. Syracuse, NY: Syracuse University Press.

8. Kinzer (2003).

9. Riley, Morris (1999). *Philby: The Hidden Years*. London: Janus.

10. Willame, Jean-Claude (1990). *Patrice Lumumba: La crise congolaise revisitée*. Paris: Karthala, 23.

11. Weissman, Stephen (2014). 'What Really Happened in Congo', *Foreign Affairs*, 93(4), 14–24.

12. Devlin, Larry (2008). *Chief of Station, Congo: Fighting the Cold War in a Hot Zone*. New York: PublicAffairs.

13. Ibid.

14. Martin, Guy (2005). 'Conflict in the Congo: Historical and Regional Perspectives', *African Studies Review*, 48(1), 127–37. See also: Gerard, Emmanuel and Bruce Kuklick (2015). *Death in the Congo: Murdering Patrice Lumumba*, Cambridge, MA: Harvard University Press.

15. Barr, Burlin (2011). 'Raoul Peck's "Lumumba" and "Lumumba: La Mort du Prophète": On Cultural Amnesia and Historical Erasure', *African Studies Review*, 54(1), 85–116.

16. de Witte, Lude (2001). *The Assassination of Lumumba*, London: Verso.

17. Isaacson, Walter (1992). *Kissinger: A Biography*. New York: Simon & Schuster.

18. Kim, Jaechun (2005). 'Democratic Peace and Covert War: A Case Study of the US Covert War in Chile,' *Journal of International and Area Studies*, 12(1), 25–47.

19. Kornbluh, Peter (1999). 'Declassifying US intervention in Chile,' *NACLA Report on the Americas*, 32(6), 36.

20. The White House (1970). 'Kissinger, Memorandum for the President,

"Subject: NSC Meeting, November 6-Chile'", 5 November 1970. Available from the George Washington University National Security Archive, http://nsarchive.gwu.edu/NSAEBB/NSAEBB437/, last accessed 16 February 2016.

21. The White House (1970).

22. Viron Vaky to Kissinger (1970). "Chile—40 Committee Meeting, Monday—September 14", 14 September 1970. Available from the George Washington University National Security Archive, http://nsarchive.gwu.edu/NSAEBB/NSAEBB437/, last accessed 16 February 2016.

23. Jacobson, Matthew (2013). 'Where We Stand: US Empire at Street Level and in the Archive', *American Quarterly*, 65(2), 265–90.

24. Kornbluh, Peter (2003). 'The El Mercurio File', *Columbia Journalism Review*, 42(3), 14.

25. *BBC News* (2013). 'Chile Caravan of Death: Eight Guilty of Murder', 23 December 2013, http://www.bbc.com/news/world-latin-america-25499373, last accessed 4 March 2016.

26. Top of Form Kornbluh, Peter (2003). *The Pinochet File: A Declassified Dossier on Atrocity and Accountability*. New York: New Press.Bottom of Form

27. Harcourt, Bernard (2015). *Exposed: Desire and Disobedience in the Digital Age*. Cambridge, MA: Harvard University Press.

28. Associated Press, 'US Secretly Created "Cuban Twitter" to Stir Unrest and Undermine Government', *The Guardian*, 3 April 2014, http://www.theguardian.com/world/2014/apr/03/us-cuban-twitter-zunzuneo-stir-unrest, last accessed 11 March 2016.

3. TUNNEL VISION

1. Sharif returned to power in 2013; at the time of writing, he is the current prime minister of Pakistan.

2. *BBC News*, 'How the 1999 Pakistan Coup Unfolded', 23 August 2007, http://news.bbc.co.uk/2/hi/south_asia/6960670.stm, last accessed 21 March 2016.

3. Weiner, Tim (1999). 'Countdown to Pakistan's Coup: A Duel of Nerves in the Air', *The New York Times*, 17 October 1999, http://www.nytimes.com/1999/10/17/world/countdown-to-pakistan-s-coup-a-duel-of-nerves-in-the-air.html, last accessed 21 March 2016.

4. Rizvi, Hasan-Askari (2000). 'Pakistan in 1999: Back to Square One', *Asian Survey*, 40(1), 208–18.

5. Human Rights Watch (2000). 'Pakistan Coup Anniversary: Human Rights Abuses Rampant', 9 October 2000, https://www.hrw.org/

news/2000/10/09/pakistan-coup-anniversary-human-rights-abuses-rampant, last accessed 8 January 2016.

6. Carothers, Thomas (2003). 'Promoting Democracy and Fighting Terror', *Foreign Affairs*, 82(1), 84–97.

7. Miller, Greg (2009). 'CIA Pays for Support in Pakistan: It has Spent Millions Funding the ISI Spy Agency, Despite Fears of Corruption. But Some Say it is Worth It', *Los Angeles Times*, 15 November 2009, http://articles.latimes.com/2009/nov/15/world/fg-cia-pakistan15,     last accessed 8 January 2016.

8. Blum, John (2004). 'History Starts Today', *The Yale Review*, 92(4), 128–39.

9. Hersh, Seymour (2015). 'The Killing of Osama Bin Laden', *London Review of Books*, 37(10), 3–12. See also Gall, Carlotta (2015). 'The Detail in Seymour Hersh's Bin Laden Story that Rings True,' *New York Times Magazine*, 12 May 2015, http://www.nytimes.com/2015/05/12/magazine/the-detail-in-seymour-hershs-bin-laden-story-that-rings-true.html, last accessed 8 January 2016.

10. Olson, Mancur (1993). 'Dictatorship, Democracy, and Development', *American Political Science Review*, 87(3), 567–76.

11. Democratic leaders obviously care about their legacies, but the short-term bias can overshadow long-term projects even for those who take posterity's image of them seriously.

12. This imperative partly accounts for why the invasion of Iraq was disingenuously pitched to the public as an attack on both al-Qaeda and tyranny.

13. Akbar Zaidi, S. (2011). 'Who Benefits from U.S. Aid to Pakistan?' Carnegie Endowment for International Peace, 21 September 2011, http://carnegieendowment.org/files/pakistan_aid2011.pdf,     last accessed 11 January 2016.

14. Dutta, Nabamita, Peter T. Leeson, and Claudia R. Williamson (2013). 'The Amplification Effect: Foreign Aid's Impact on Political Institutions', *Kyklos*, 66(2), 208–28.

15. Rothkopf, David (2014). 'Obama's "Don't Do Stupid Shit" Foreign Policy', *Foreign Policy*, 4 June 2014, http://foreignpolicy.com/2014/06/04/obamas-dont-do-stupid-shit-foreign-policy/, last accessed 16 January 2016.

16. Nagaraj, Vijay (2015). '"Beltway Bandits" and "Poverty Barons": For Profit International Development Contracting and the Military Development Assemblage', *Development and Change*, 46(4), 585–617.

17. Bush, Sarah Sunn (2015). *The Taming of Democracy Assistance*, Cambridge: Cambridge University Press.

18. As I make clear in Chapter 5, however, even countries like Madagascar do not face substantial pressure to create meaningful democratic

reforms; they simply have to clear a laughably low bar for the minimum acceptable level of 'democracy'.

19. Ibid.

20. Ibid.

21. *BBC News* (2015). 'Russia's Putin Signs Law Against "Undesirable" NGOs', 24 May 2015, http://www.bbc.com/news/world-europe-32860526, last accessed 24 March 2016.

22. Bennett, Brian (2011). *The Last Dictatorship in Europe: Belarus under Lukashenko*, London: Hurst & Co.

23. Statkevich, Mikolai (2015). Former presidential candidate. Personal interview, 17 December 2015, Minsk, Belarus.

24. Senior Belarusian policy analyst and former diplomat, anonymous here at his request. Personal interview, 18 December 2015, Minsk, Belarus.

25. Council of Europe (2009). 'Manipulation of the Final Outcome of the 2006 Presidential Election in Belarus', Strasbourg: Council of Europe, 14 September 2009.

26. Nyaklyayew, Uladzimir. Former presidential candidate and poet. Personal interview, 16 December 2015, Minsk, Belarus.

27. Stakevich (2015).

28. Woehrel, Steven (2011). 'Belarus: Background and US Policy Concerns', Washington, DC: Congressional Research Service, 1 February 2011.

29. Marples, David (2009). 'Outpost of Tyranny? The Failure of Democratization in Belarus', *Democratization*, 16(4), 756–76.

30. Woehrel (2011).

31. *Belsat* (2015). 'Belarus GDP Falls Almost 4% in Ten Months', 18 November 2015, http://belsat.eu/en/news/za-dzesyats-mesyatsau-vup-belarusi-upau-amal-na-4/, last accessed 17 February 2016.

32. Organization for Security and Co-operation in Europe (2015). 'Presidential Election, 11 October 2015', http://www.osce.org/odihr/elections/belarus/174776, last accessed 18 February 2016.

33. Belarusian Ministry of Foreign Affairs (n.d.). 'Foreign Trade of Belarus', http://mfa.gov.by/en/foreign_trade, last accessed 29 July 2016.

34. Norman, Laurence (2015). 'EU Suspends Most Sanctions on Belarus', *The Wall Street Journal*, 30 October 2015, http://www.wsj.com/articles/eu-suspends-sanctions-on-belarus-1446128237, last accessed 18 February 2016.

35. Ostroukh, Andrey (2015). 'Plan for Russian Air Base Adds Twist to Belarus Election', *Wall Street Journal*, 8 October 2015, http://www.wsj.com/articles/plan-for-russian-air-base-adds-twist-to-belarus-election-1444330107, last accessed 18 February 2016.

36. Rankin, Jennifer (2016). 'EU Lifts Most Sanctions against Belarus Despite Human Rights Concerns,' *The Guardian*, 15 February 2016,

http://www.theguardian.com/world/2016/feb/15/eu-lifts-most-sanctions-against-belarus-despite-human-rights-concerns, last accessed 18 February 2016.

## 4. THE "SAVAGE WARS OF PEACE"

1. *Reuters* (2009). 'U.S. Helicopter Accidentally Dumps Afghan Ballot Boxes', 26 August 2009, http://uk.reuters.com/article/uk-afghanistan-election-helicopter-sb-idUKTRE57P16J20090826, last accessed 24 February 2016.
2. Gall, Carlotta (2009). 'Growing Accounts of Fraud Cloud Afghan Election', *The New York Times*, 30 August 2009, http://www.nytimes.com/2009/08/31/world/asia/31fraud.html, last accessed 24 February 2016.
3. Crilly, Rob (2014). 'Afghan Election Official Stands Aside to Defuse Crisis', *The Telegraph*, 23 June 2014, http://www.telegraph.co.uk/news/worldnews/asia/afghanistan/10920322/Afghan-election-official-stands-aside-to-defuse-crisis.html, last accessed 24 February 2016.
4. Pfiffner, James (2010). 'US Blunders in Iraq: De-Baathification and Disbanding the Army,' *Intelligence and National Security*, 25(1), 76–85.
5. Caryl, Christian (2013). 'The Democracy Boondoggle in Iraq', *Foreign Policy*, 6 March 2013, http://foreignpolicy.com/2013/03/06/the-democracy-boondoggle-in-iraq/, last accessed 19 January 2016.
6. Bowen, Stuart W. (2013). 'Learning from Iraq: Final Report from Special Inspector General for Iraq Reconstruction, March 2013', available from Carnegie Endowment for International Peace, http://www.cfr.org/iraq/learning-iraq-final-report-special-inspector-general-iraq-reconstruction-march-2013/p30167, last accessed 19 January 2016.
7. Withnall, Adam (2015). 'Isis's War on Democracy: Militants Execute 300 Civil Servants from Iraqi Electoral Commission,' *The Independent*, 9 August 2015, http://www.independent.co.uk/news/world/middle-east/isiss-war-on-democracy-militants-execute-300-civil-servants-from-iraqi-electoral-commission-10447519.html, last accessed 21 January 2016.
8. Fukuyama, Francis (2008). *Nation-building: Beyond Afghanistan and Iraq*. Baltimore, MD: Johns Hopkins University Press.
9. Mansfield, Edward and Jack Snyder (1995) 'Democratization and War', *Foreign Affairs*, 74(3), 79–86.
10. The White House (2011). 'Remarks by the President in Address to the Nation on Libya', 28 March 2011, https://www.whitehouse.gov/the-press-office/2011/03/28/remarks-president-address-nation-libya, last accessed 1 March 2016.

11. Muaddi, Nadeem (2011). 'Eccentricities of an enigmatic Gaddafi', *Al-Jazeera*, 7 November 2011, http://www.aljazeera.com/indepth/features/2011/09/20119410422383796.html, last accessed 1 March 2016.

12. Weiner, Juli. 'More Horrendously Creepy Details About Qaddafi's Condoleezza Rice Obsession,' *Vanity Fair*, 21 October 2011, http://www.vanityfair.com/news/2011/10/more-horrendously-creepy-details-about-qaddafis-condoleezza-rice, last accessed 2 April 2016.

13. Rogers, Simon (2011). 'NATO Operations in Libya: Data Journalism Breaks Down which Country Does What,' *The Guardian*, 31 October 2011, http://www.theguardian.com/news/datablog/2011/may/22/nato-libya-data-journalism-operations-country, last accessed 1 March 2016.

14. McCain, John (2011). 'Remarks By Senator John McCain at the Dean Acheson Lecture at U.S. Institute Of Peace', 19 May 2011, http://www.mccain.senate.gov/public/index.cfm/speeches?ID=0a52e626–9bbf-8c1b-af06–9ac2360d7c8c, last accessed 1 March 2016.

15. Zenko, Micah (2011). 'Libya: Justifications for Intervention', New York: Council on Foreign Relations, 24 June 2011, http://blogs.cfr.org/zenko/2011/06/24/libya-justifications-for-intervention/, last accessed 2 March 2016.

16. Klaas, Brian and Jason Pack (2015). 'Talking with the Wrong Libyans', *The New York Times*, 14 June 2015, http://www.nytimes.com/2015/06/15/opinion/talking-with-the-wrong-libyans.html, last accessed 2 March 2016.

17. Freeman, Colin (2016). 'Libya's Central Bank Causing "Civil War" by Paying Rival Militias, Says UK Envoy', *The Telegraph*, 8 February 2016, http://www.telegraph.co.uk/news/worldnews/africaandindianocean/libya/12146453/Libyas-central-bank-causing-civil-war-by-paying-warring-militias-says-UK-envoy.html, last accessed 2 March 2016.

18. Schmitt, Eric (2016). 'U.S. Scrambles to Contain Growing ISIS Threat in Libya', *The New York Times*, 21 February 2016, http://www.nytimes.com/2016/02/22/world/africa/us-scrambles-to-contain-growing-isis-threat-in-libya.html, last accessed 2 March 2016.

5. THE CURSE OF LOW EXPECTATIONS

1. For an example of this argument, see Lindberg, Staffan (2009). *Democratization by Elections: A New Mode of Transition*, Baltimore, MD: Johns Hopkins University Press.

2. Center for Systemic Peace (n.d.). 'Polity IV Data: Polity-Case Format, 1800–2013', http://www.systemicpeace.org/polityproject.html, last accessed 29 July 2016.

3. Higgins, Andrew (2010). 'Pricey Real Estate Deals in Dubai Raise Questions about Azerbaijan's President', *The Washington Post*, 5 March 2010, http://www.washingtonpost.com/wp-dyn/content/article/2010/03/04/AR2010030405390.html, last accessed 2 April 2016.

4. Fisher, Max (2013). 'Oops: Azerbaijan Released Election Results Before Voting Had Even Started', *The Washington Post*, 9 October 2013, https://www.washingtonpost.com/news/worldviews/wp/2013/10/09/oops-azerbaijan-released-election-results-before-voting-had-even-started/, last accessed 18 February 2016.

5. Herszenhorn, David (2013). 'Observers Differ on Fairness of Election in Azerbaijan', *The New York Times*, 10 October 2013, http://www.nytimes.com/2013/10/11/world/asia/observers-say-azerbaijan-election-marred-by-fraud.html, last accessed 18 February 2016.

6. Herszenhorn (2013).

7. There have since been further condemnations of the human rights situation, including a forceful denouncement in August 2015 by PACE, but these are eclipsed by the high-level diplomacy that tends to place such concerns lower on the list of geostrategic priorities.

8. Haring, Melinda (2013). 'Reforming the Democracy Bureaucracy', *Foreign Policy*, 3 June 2013, http://foreignpolicy.com/2013/06/03/reforming-the-democracy-bureaucracy/, last accessed 20 February 2016.

9. Klaas, Brian (2015). 'Bullets over Ballots: How Electoral Exclusion Increases the Risk of Coups d'État and Civil Wars', DPhil Dissertation, University of Oxford.

10. Often, election observation reports avoid these over-simplifications, such as those of the Carter Center, former US president Jimmy Carter's NGO (see below). However, the press conferences that are held in the immediate aftermath of election day nonetheless gravitate toward this simple thumbs up, thumbs down concept.

11. This is a common problem in most elections around the world; the scholars of the Electoral Integrity Project found that more than two-thirds of elections in 2015 failed to meet international standards for campaign financing. Many of these same elections were highly praised and eagerly endorsed by international diplomats.

12. The Carter Center, 'Legislative and Second Round of Presidential Elections in Madagascar: Final Report', December 2013, https://www.cartercenter.org/resources/pdfs/news/peace_publications/election_reports/madagascar-2013-final.pdf, last accessed 26 March 2016.

13. Lough, Richard and Alain Iloniaina (2013). 'European, African Observers Say Madagascar Election Credible', *Reuters*, 27 October 2013, http://www.reuters.com/article/us-madagascar-election-idUSBRE99Q04120131027, last accessed 26 March 2016.

14. World Bank, 'Proportion of Seats Held by Women in National Parliaments', World Development Indicators, original data source from Inter-Parliamentary Union, http://data.worldbank.org/indicator/SG.GEN.PARL.ZS, last accessed 2 April 2016.
15. McGreal, Chris (2010). 'Tony Blair Defends Support for Rwandan Leader Paul Kagame', *The Guardian*, 31 December 2010, http://www.theguardian.com/world/2010/dec/31/tony-blair-rwanda-paul-kagame, last accessed 21 February 2016.
16. Birrell, Ian (2014). 'Darling of the West, Terror to his Opponents: Meet Rwanda's New Scourge—Paul Kagame', *The Independent*, 4 January 2014, http://www.independent.co.uk/news/world/africa/darling-of-the-west-terror-to-his-opponents-meet-rwanda-s-new-scourge-paul-kagame-9037914.html, last accessed 22 February 2016.
17. Gettleman, Jeffrey (2013). 'The Global Elite's Favorite Strongman', *New York Times Magazine*, 4 September 2013, http://www.nytimes.com/2013/09/08/magazine/paul-kagame-rwanda.html, last accessed 24 February 2016.
18. Ibid.
19. Ibid.
20. Rever, Judi and Geoffrey York (2014). 'Assassination in Africa: Inside the Plots to Kill Rwanda's Dissidents', *The Globe and Mail*, 2 May 2014, http://www.theglobeandmail.com/news/world/secret-recording-says-former-rwandan-army-major-proves-government-hires-assassins-to-kill-critics-abroad/article18396349/, last accessed 26 February 2016.
21. Kron, Josh and Jeffrey Gettleman (2011). 'British Police Warn Rwandan Dissident of Threat,' *The New York Times*, 19 May 2011, http://www.nytimes.com/2011/05/20/world/africa/20rwanda.html, last accessed 26 February 2016.
22. Collier, Paul and David Dollar (2004). 'Development Effectiveness: What Have We Learnt?', *The Economic Journal*, 114(496), 244–71.
23. Agence France-Presse, 'Rwanda Votes Yes to Allow Extra Terms for Paul Kagame', *Daily Nation*, 19 December 2015, http://www.nation.co.ke/news/africa/Rwanda-votes-yes-to-extend-Kagame-rule-until-2034/-/1066/3002448/-/6ho5p8z/-/index.html, last accessed 18 February 2016.
24. The White House (2015). 'Remarks by President Obama to the People of Africa', African Union Headquarters, Addis Ababa, Ethiopia, 28 July 2015, https://www.whitehouse.gov/the-press-office/2015/07/28/remarks-president-obama-people-africa, last accessed 18 February 2016.

## 6. BACKING THE WRONG HORSE

1. Mistry, Kaeten (2011). 'Re-thinking American Intervention in the 1948 Italian Election: Beyond a Success–Failure Dichotomy,' *Modern Italy*, 16(2), 179–94.
2. Forsythe, David (1992). 'Democracy, War, and Covert Action', *Journal of Peace Research*, 29(4), 385–95.
3. See, for example, Ojha, Hemant (2015). 'The India-Nepal Crisis', *The Diplomat*, 27 November 2015, http://thediplomat.com/2015/11/the-india-nepal-crisis/, last accessed 2 April 2016.
4. Worth, Robert (2009). 'Foreign Money Seeks to Buy Lebanese Votes', *The New York Times*, 22 April 2009, http://www.nytimes.com/2009/04/23/world/middleeast/23lebanon.html, last accessed 21 February 2016.
5. The White House, 'President Bush Calls for New Palestinian Leadership', 24 June 2002, http://georgewbush-whitehouse.archives.gov/news/releases/2002/06/20020624–3.html, last accessed 24 February 2016.
6. Corstange, Daniel and Nikolay Marinov (2012). 'Taking Sides in Other People's Elections: the Polarizing Effect of Foreign Intervention', *American Journal of Political Science*, 56(3), 655–70.
7. Mark, Clyde (2005). 'United States Aid to the Palestinians', Congressional Research Service, 4 March 2005, https://www.fas.org/sgp/crs/mideast/RS21594.pdf, last accessed 24 February 2016.
8. Weisman, Steven (2006). 'Rice Admits U.S. Underestimated Hamas Strength,' *New York Times*, 30 January 2006, http://www.nytimes.com/2006/01/30/international/middleeast/30diplo.html?pagewanted=print, last accessed 22 February 2016.
9. Sharp, Jeremy and Christopher Blanchard (2006). 'U.S. Foreign Aid to the Palestinians', Congressional Research Service, 27 June 2006, http://fpc.state.gov/documents/organization/68794.pdf, last accessed 22 February 2016.
10. Wilson, Scott and Glenn Kessler (2006). 'U.S. Funds Enter Fray in Palestinian Elections', *The Washington Post*, 22 January 2006, http://www.washingtonpost.com/wp-dyn/content/article/2006/01/21/AR2006012101431.html, last accessed 23 February 2016.
11. Ibid.
12. Ibid.
13. Greenberg, Hanan (2006). 'Baby Hurt in Rocket Attack', *YNet News*, 3 February 2006, http://www.ynetnews.com/articles/0,7340,L-32 10491,00.html, last accessed 24 February 2006.
14. Obviously, the situation in the Gaza Strip was (and is) dire and there are many volumes written about the conflict more broadly. It is not

my place here to weigh in on justifications or lack of justification for rocket fire from Gaza, but rather to highlight that Hamas—which uses rocket fire against civilian targets—won the elections.

15. Weisman (2006).
16. Weisman, Steven (2006). 'In Hamas Victory, U.S. Assumptions Undermined', *The New York Times*, 29 January 2006, http://www.nytimes.com/2006/01/29/world/africa/29iht-diplo.html?pagewanted=all, last accessed 24 February 2016.
17. Oved, Marco Chown (2011). 'In Côte d'Ivoire, a Model of Successful Intervention', *The Atlantic*, 9 June 2011, http://www.theatlantic.com/international/archive/2011/06/in-c-te-divoire-a-model-of-successful-intervention/240164/, last accessed 26 February 2016.
18. Human Rights Watch, 'One Year On, Duékoué Massacre Belies Ouattara Government's Promises of Impartial Justice,' 29 March 2012, https://www.hrw.org/news/2012/03/29/one-year-duekoue-massacre-belies-ouattara-governments-promises-impartial-justice, last accessed 17 February 2016. See also Klaas, Brian and David Landry (2015). 'Votes and Hope in Côte d'Ivoire,' *Foreign Affairs*, 22 October 2015, https://www.foreignaffairs.com/articles/cote-dlvoire/2015–10–22/votes-and-hope-c-te-d-ivoire, last accessed 29 July 2016.
19. Oved (2011).

## 7. GOLDEN HANDCUFFS

1. Stockman, Farah and Milton J. Valencia (2011). 'US Officials Thought a BU Post Might Ease Gbagbo Out', *The Boston Globe*, 13 April 2011, http://archive.boston.com/news/education/higher/articles/2011/04/13/us_officials_thought_a_bu_post_might_ease_gbagbo_out/, last accessed 2 April 2016.
2. Goemans, Henk, Kristian Skrede Gleditsch, and Giacomo Chiozza (2009). 'Introducing Archigos: A Dataset of Political Leaders,' *Journal of Peace Research*, 46(2), 269–83.
3. Holland, Steve and Jonathan Allen (2015). 'Hillary, Bill Clinton report total income of $140 million since 2007', *Reuters*, 31 July 2015, http://www.reuters.com/article/us-usa-election-clinton-taxes-idUSKCN0Q52IH20150801, last accessed 3 April 2016.
4. Goemans, Skrede Gleditsch and Chiozza (2009).
5. Mungai, Christine (2015). 'He's All We've Ever Known! A New Ranking for Long-serving African Leaders, Relative to Age of Country Population', *Mail & Guardian*, 8 September 2015.
6. Goemans, Skrede Gleditsch and Chiozza (2009). See also Geddes, Barbara, Joseph Wright, and Erica Frantz (2014). 'Autocratic Break-

down and Regime Transitions: A New Data Set', *Perspectives on Politics*, 12(2), 313–31.

7. Lentz, Harris (1999). *Encyclopedia of Heads of States and Governments: 1900 through 1945*. McFarland, 219.

8. Girard, Philippe (2005). 'A Glimmer of Hope: Aristide's Rise to Power (1988–1991)'. In *Paradise Lost*, New York: Palgrave Macmillan, 110–27.

9. Girard, Philippe (2002). *The Eagle and the Rooster: The 1994 US Invasion of Haiti*, PhD dissertation, Ohio University, https://etd.ohiolink.edu/rws_etd/document/get/ohiou1035828999/inline, last accessed 21 January 2016.

10. Sprague, Jeb (2012). *Paramilitarism and the Assault on Democracy in Haiti*, New York: NYU Press.

11. Ibid., 67.

12. Girard, Philippe (2004). *Clinton in Haiti: the 1994 US invasion of Haiti*. New York: Palgrave Macmillan, 2.

13. Ibid.

14. Dowd, Maureen (1994). 'Unimpeded, Intruder Crashes Plane Into White House', *The New York Times*, 12 September 1994, http://www.nytimes.com/1994/09/13/us/crash-white-house-overview-unimpeded-intruder-crashes-plane-into-white-house.html?pagewanted=all, last accessed 22 January 2016.

15. Girard (2002).

16. Freed, Kenneth, 'U.S. Gave Cedras $1 Million in Exchange for Resignation', *Los Angeles Times*, 14 October 1994.

17. Ballard, John (1998). *Upholding Democracy: the United States Military Campaign in Haiti, 1994–1997*. Westport, CT: Greenwood Publishing Group, 124.

18. Jehl, Douglas (1994). 'Haiti Generals Regain Access to $79 Million,' *The New York Times*, 14 October 1994, http://www.nytimes.com/1994/10/14/world/haiti-generals-regain-access-to-79-million.html, last accessed 18 January 2016.

19. Freed (1994).

20. This calibration needs to be managed exceptionally carefully so that it does not become an inducement for despots to rapidly militarize, as a means of staving off Western involvement.

21. *BBC News*, 'Gambia's Yahya Jammeh Ready for 'Billion-year' Rule', 12 December 2011, http://www.bbc.co.uk/news/world-africa-16148458, last accessed 26 January 2016.

22. Julien, Maud (2015). 'DR Congo President Unlikely to Give Up Power', *BBC News*, 23 December 2015, http://www.bbc.co.uk/news/world-africa-35072001, last accessed 4 February 2016.

## 8. THE UNTHINKABLE OLIVE BRANCH

1. Lieutenant Colonel Mohammed Ahmed, personal interview, Tunis, Tunisia, 13 November 2013. See also Klaas, Brian (2013). 'The Long Shadow of Ben Ali', *Foreign Policy*, 17 December 2013.
2. Shadid, Anthony (2012). 'Islamists' Ideas on Democracy and Faith Face Test in Tunisia', *The New York Times*, 17 February 2012, http://www.nytimes.com/2012/02/18/world/africa/tunisia-islamists-test-ideas-decades-in-the-making.html, last accessed 22 February 2016.
3. Allani, Alaya (2009). 'The Islamists in Tunisia Between Confrontation and Participation: 1980–2008', *The Journal of North African Studies*, 14(2), 257–72.
4. Shahid (2012).
5. Klaas, Brian and Marcel Dirsus (2014). 'The Tunisia Model,' *Foreign Affairs*, 23 October 2014.
6. *Muftah*, 'Excluding the Old Regime: Political Participation in Tunisia,' 5 May 2014, http://muftah.org/excluding-the-old-regime-political-participation-in-tunisia/#.VwDD5jZ97UQ, last accessed 11 February 2016.
7. Klaas, Brian (2015). 'Bullets over Ballots: How Electoral Exclusion Increases the Risk of Coups d'État and Civil Wars,' DPhil Dissertation, University of Oxford.
8. *BBC News* (2015). 'Tunisia's Secularists and Islamists Form New Government', 5 February 2015, http://www.bbc.co.uk/news/world-africa-31147402, last accessed 18 February 2016.
9. Klaas, Brian (2016). 'Tumult in Tunisia', *Foreign Affairs*, 31 January 2016, https://www.foreignaffairs.com/articles/tunisia/2016–01–31/tumult-tunisia, last accessed 19 February 2016.

## 9. FOOL'S ERRANDS

1. Minter, Adam (2009). 'E-waste: There's an App for That', Foreign Policy, 23 September 2009, http://foreignpolicy.com/2009/09/23/e-waste-theres-an-app-for-that/, last accessed 23 February 2016.
2. See Bush, Sarah Sunn (2015). *The Taming of Democracy Assistance*, Cambridge: Cambridge University Press.
3. Gandhi, Jennifer (2008). *Political Institutions under Dictatorship*, Cambridge: Cambridge University Press.
4. USAID Press Office (2014). 'USAID Awards Afghan Women's Empowerment Program', 16 October 2014, https://www.usaid.gov/afghanistan/news-information/press-releases/usaid-awards-afghan-women%E2%80%99s-empowerment-program, last accessed 3 April 2016.

5. Sopko, John F. (2015). 'Letter from John F. Sopko to Hon. Alfonso Lenhardt', Office of the Special Inspector General for Afghanistan Reconstruction, 27 March 2015, https://www.sigar.mil/pdf/special%20projects/SIGAR-15–44-SP.pdf, last accessed 2 March 2016.
6. Women's Rights and Empowerment in Afghanistan Conference (2014). 'Keynote Address by H.E. Rula Ghani, First Lady of the Islamic Republic of Afghanistan,', 23 November 2014, http://www.afghanwomenoslosymposium.org/pop.cfm?FuseAction=Doc&pAction=View&pDocumentId=60158, last accessed 29 July 2016.
7. World Bank (n.d.). 'GDP Per Capita, Current US$', http://data.worldbank.org/indicator/NY.GDP.PCAP.CD, last accessed 2 March 2016.
8. Sopko (2015).
9. Human Rights Watch (2016). 'Uzbekistan: Events in 2015', https://www.hrw.org/world-report/2016/country-chapters/uzbekistan, last accessed 4 April 2016.
10. Lillis, Joanna (2014). 'Uzbekistan Students Stage Rare Protest Against Forced Labour in Cotton Fields,' The Guardian, 13 November 2014, http://www.theguardian.com/world/2014/nov/13/uzbekistan-students-rare-protest-forced-labour-cotton-picking, last accessed 6 March 2016.
11. Bloom, John (2008). 'Terrifying Ally Against Terror', The Globe & Mail, 26 July 2008, http://www.theglobeandmail.com/opinion/terrifying-ally-against-terror/article20385731/, last accessed 3 April 2016.
12. 'Uzbekistan "Unspeakable Abuse" of Political Prisoners', BBC News, 26 September 2014, http://www.bbc.co.uk/news/world-asia-2936 5617, last accessed 15 March 2016.
13. Freedom House (2012). 'Uzbekistan: 2012 Country Overview', https://freedomhouse.org/report/nations-transit/2012/uzbekistan, last accessed 15 March 2016.
14. Liljas, Per (2014). 'The Uzbek Leader's Daughter Seems to Have a Thing for Nationally Owned Artwork', TIME, 6 January 2014, http://world.time.com/2014/01/06/gulnara-karimova-accused-of-taking-uzbek-national-treasuresf-stealing-national-treasures/, last accessed 3 April 2016. See also Kutcher, Felix (2015). 'Uzbekistan Bans Teaching of Political Science', Eurasia Times, 7 September 2015, http://www.eurasiatimes.org/en/uzbekistan-bans-teaching-of-political-science/, last accessed 3 April 2016.
15. Patrucic, Miranda (2015). 'Uzbekistan: How The President's Daughter Controlled The Telecom Industry', Organized Crime and Corruption Reporting Project, 21 March 2015, https://www.occrp.org/corruptistan/uzbekistan/gulnara_karimova/the-prodigal-daughter/how-the-

presents-daughter-controlled-the-telecom-industry.php, last accessed 3 April 2016.

16. Noack, Rick (2014). 'The Strange Story of Uzbekistan's "Jailed Princess"', *The Washington Post*, 29 August 2014, https://www.washingtonpost.com/news/worldviews/wp/2014/08/29/the-strange-story-of-uzbekistans-jailed-princess/, last accessed 3 April 2016.

17. USAID (n.d.). 'Uzbekistan: Democracy, Human Rights, and Governance', https://www.usaid.gov/uzbekistan/democracy-human-rights-and-governance, last accessed 3 April 2016.

18. This includes a major sale of 300 mine-resistant ambush protected (MRAP) vehicles to Uzbekistan in January 2015.

19. Country director for major international democracy promotion organization based in the Middle East, anonymous by request. Telephone interview, 13 January 2016.

20. Carothers, Thomas (2015). Vice President for Studies, Carnegie Endowment for International Peace. Telephone interview, 11 November 2015.

21. USAID (n.d.).

22. Todorovic, Djordje, International Republican Institute, and Nicole Rowsell, National Democratic Institute. Personal interviews, October 2013, Tunis, Tunisia.

23. Finkel, Steven, Aníbal Pérez-Liñán, and Mitchell A. Seligson (2007). 'The Effects of US Foreign Assistance on Democracy Building, 1990–2003', *World Politics*, 59(3), 404–39.

24. Gyimah-Boadi, Emmanuel (2010). 'Assessing Democracy Assistance: Ghana', *Ghana Center for Democratic Development* and *FRIDE*, May 2010, http://fride.org/download/IP_WMD_Ghana_ENG_jul10.pdf, last accessed 12 February 2016.

25. World Bank, 'GDP Growth (Annual %)', World Development Indicators, http://data.worldbank.org/indicator/NY.GDP.MKTP.KD.ZG, last accessed 21 February 2016.

26. This strategy can backfire, however. More on this in Chapter 13.

27. Carothers (2015).

## 10. THE CARROT

1. *City Paper* (2015). 'The House on the Corner: Riga's KGB Past', 31 May 2015, http://www.citypaper.lv/the_house_on_the_corner__riga___s_kgb_past/, last accessed 3 April 2016.

2. Eglitis, Daina (2010). *Imagining the Nation: History, Modernity, and Revolution in Latvia*, State College, PA: Penn State Press.

3. Presser, Brandon (2014). 'Secret KGB Torture House Opens Its Doors

in Riga', *The Daily Beast*, 4 June 2014, http://www.thedailybeast. com/articles/2014/06/04/secret-kgb-torture-house-opens-its-doors-in-riga.html, last accessed 1 February 2016.

4. Agence France-Presse (2014). 'Latvia's Former KGB Headquarters Gives Up Its Dark Secrets', *Inquirer.net*, 8 August 2014, http://newsinfo.inquirer.net/627468/latvias-former-kgb-headquarters-gives-up-its-dark-secrets, last accessed 1 February 2016.

5. McGuinness, Damian (2015). 'Latvians Refuse to Lift Lid on KGB Past', *BBC News*, 20 May 2015, http://www.bbc.co.uk/news/world-europe-32788317, last accessed 1 February 2016.

6. All GDP per capita figures from World Bank (n.d.). 'GDP Per Capita, Current US$', World Development Indicators, http://data.worldbank.org/indicator/NY.GDP.PCAP.CD, last accessed 3 April 2016.

7. *Reuters* (2015). '"Hello, Dictator!"': Juncker Tries Humor to Defuse Hungary Row', 22 May 2015, http://www.reuters.com/article/us-hungary-eu-dictator-idUSKBN0O71RP20150522, last accessed 14 March 2016.

8. World Bank (n.d.).

9. Simon, Zoltan (2011). 'Hungary First to Write a Constitution on iPad, Lawmaker Says', *Bloomberg News*, 4 March 2011, http://www.bloomberg.com/news/articles/2011-03-04/hungary-first-to-write-a-constitution-on-ipad-lawmaker-says, last accessed 14 March 2016.

10. Kounalakis, Eleni (2015). *Madam Ambassador*, New York: New Press.

11. Gleditsch, Kristian Skrede, and Michael D. Ward (2008). 'Diffusion and the Spread of Democratic Institutions', In Simmons, Beth A., Frank Dobbin and Geoffrey Garrett, eds (2008). *The Global Diffusion of Markets and Democracy*, Cambridge: Cambridge University Press, 261–302.

12. Kagan, Robert (2008). 'The Case for a League of Democracies', *Financial Times*, 13 May 2008; Sidoti, Liz (2007). 'McCain Favors a "League of Democracies"', *The Washington Post*, 30 April 2007.

13. European Commission (n.d.). 'Trade Agreements', http://ec.europa.eu/trade/policy/countries-and-regions/agreements/index_en.htm#_customs-unions, last accessed 3 April 2016.

14. Lenway, Stefanie Ann (1988). 'Between War and Commerce: Economic Sanctions as a Tool of Statecraft', *International Organization*, 42(2), 397–426.

15. Allen, Susan Hannah, and David J. Lektzian (2013). 'Economic Sanctions: A Blunt Instrument?,' *Journal of Peace Research*, 50(1), 121–35.

16. Levy, Phillip (1999). 'Sanctions on South Africa: What Did They Do?', *The American Economic Review*, 89(2), 415–20.

17. Cortright, David and George Lopez (2002). *Smart Sanctions: Targeting Economic Statecraft*, New York: Rowman & Littlefield.

18. As with Belarus, the EU suddenly lifted most of its sanctions on Zimbabwe in February 2016.

19. Grebe, Jan (2010). 'And They Are Still Targeting: Assessing the Effectiveness of Targeted Sanctions against Zimbabwe', *Africa Spectrum*, 45(1), 3–29.

20. Afrobarometer (n.d.)., 'Data, Round 5, Merged Data', http://www. afrobarometer.org/data, last accessed 3 April 2016.

## 11. THE NEW BATTLEGROUND

1. Kaplan, Sarah (2015). 'A Turkish Court Appointed Five "Lord of the Rings" Experts to Figure Out Whether this Gollum Meme is Offensive', *The Washington Post*, 2 December 2015, https://www.washingtonpost. com/news/morning-mix/wp/2015/12/02/a-turkish-court-appointed-five-lord-of-the-rings-experts-to-figure-out-whether-this-gollum-meme-is-offensive/, last accessed 3 April 2016.

2. Twitter (n.d.). 'Removal Requests: Turkey', *Twitter Transparency Report*, https://transparency.twitter.com/country/tr, last accessed 3 April 2016. See also Human Rights Watch (2015). 'Turkey: End Prosecutions for Insulting the President,' 29 April 2015, https://www.hrw.org/news/2015/04/29/turkey-end-prosecutions-insulting-president, last accessed 29 July 2016.

3. Molloy, Mark and Raziye Akkoc (2015). 'Director Peter Jackson Wades into Turkish Debate over "Evil" Gollum', *The Telegraph*, 3 December 2015, http://www.telegraph.co.uk/news/worldnews/europe/turkey/12030987/Lord-of-the-Rigns-director-Peter-Jackson-wades-into-Recep-Tayyip-Erdogan-Gollum-debate.html, last accessed 3 April 2016.

4. Fukuyama, Francis (1992). *The End of History and the Last Man*, New York: Free Press.

5. Khan, Urmee (2009). 'Twitter Should Win Nobel Peace Prize, Says Former US Security Adviser,' *The Telegraph*, 7 July 2009, http://www. telegraph.co.uk/technology/twitter/5768159/Twitter-should-win-Nobel-Peace-Prize-says-former-US-security-adviser.html, last accessed 3 April 2016.

6. Dobson, William J. (2012). *The Dictator's Learning Curve: Inside the Global Battle for Democracy*, New York: Random House.

7. Ibid., Chapter 3.

8. Interestingly, Afifi was funded directly by the United States government, through the National Endowment for Democracy. His organization (of which he was the only employee) received well over $100,000 in funding between 2008, when he became a fellow of the organization, and 2012, when he advocated violent means to help overthrow Egypt's democratically elected, but not pro-American, president.

9. Mekay, Emad (2013). 'US Bankrolled Anti-Morsi Activists', *Al-Jazeera*, 10 July 2013, http://www.aljazeera.com/indepth/features/2013/07/2013710113522489801.html, last accessed 3 April 2016.

10. Fernquest, Jon (2014). 'Line Stickers: $7 million Baht Too Much?', *The Bangkok Post*, 17 December 2014.

11. *Sky News* (2014). 'Thai Propaganda Video Slammed For Hitler Image', 15 December 2014, http://news.sky.com/story/1389483/thai-propaganda-video-slammed-for-hitler-image, last accessed 3 April 2016.

12. Pongsudhirak, Thitinan (2014). 'The Roots of Thailand's Political Polarization in Comparative Perspective', 2014 Annual Conference on Taiwan Democracy, 17–18 October 2014, http://fsi.stanford.edu/sites/default/files/pongsudhirak.thaipolpolarization-cddrl-17oct2014.pdf.

13. Fuller, Thomas (2015). 'Thai Man May Go to Prison for Insulting King's Dog', *The New York Times*, 14 December 2015, http://www.nytimes.com/2015/12/15/world/asia/thailand-lese-majeste-tongdaeng.html, last accessed 24 February 2016.

14. Turkson, Nshira (2016). 'A Social-Media Shutdown in Uganda's Presidential Election', *The Atlantic*, 18 February 2016.

15. *The Washington Times* (2009). 'Editorial: Iran's Twitter Revolution', 16 June 2009, http://www.washingtontimes.com/news/2009/jun/16/irans-twitter-revolution/, last accessed 2 April 2016.

16. Keller, Jared (2010). 'Evaluating Iran's Twitter Revolution', *The Atlantic*, 18 June 2010, http://www.theatlantic.com/technology/archive/2010/06/evaluating-irans-twitter-revolution/58337/, last accessed 19 February 2016.

17. Weaver, Matthew (2010). 'Oxfordgirl vs Ahmadinejad: the Twitter User Taking on the Iranian Regime', *The Guardian*, 10 February 2010, http://www.theguardian.com/world/2010/feb/10/oxfordgirl-ahmadinejad-twitter-iran, last accessed 21 February 2016.

18. Howard, Phillip and Muzammil Hussain (2013). *Democracy's Fourth Wave? Digital Media and the Arab Spring*, Oxford: Oxford University Press.

19. Morozov, Evgeny (2011). *The Net Delusion: How Not to Liberate the World*, London: Penguin, 11.

20. Ibid., 11.

21. Ibid., 17.

22. Tsui, Lokman (2015). 'The Coming Colonization of Hong Kong Cyberspace: Government Responses to the Use of New Technologies by the Umbrella Movement', *Chinese Journal of Communication*, 8(4), 1–9.

23. Olson, Parmy (2014). 'The Largest Cyber Attack In History Has Been Hitting Hong Kong Sites,' *Forbes*, 20 November 2014, http://www.

forbes.com/sites/parmyolson/2014/11/20/the-largest-cyber-attack-in-history-has-been-hitting-hong-kong-sites/#54353e8a3fc4, last accessed 5 March 2016.

24. Han, Rongpin (2015). 'Manufacturing Consent in Cyberspace: China's Fifty-cent Army', *Journal of Current Chinese Affairs*, 44(2), 105–34.

25. Kwok, Donny and Yimou Lee (2015). 'Hong Kong Vetoes China-backed Electoral Reform Proposal,' *Reuters*, 18 June 2015, http://www.reuters.com/article/us-hongkong-politics-idUSKBN0OY063 20150618, last accessed 5 March 2016.

26. *South China Morning Post* (2016). 'Shots Fired and Bricks Thrown: Hong Kong Tense After Mong Kok Mob Violence on First Day of Lunar New Year', 9 February 2016, http://www.scmp.com/news/hong-kong/law-crime/article/1910845/shots-fired-and-bricks-thrown-hong-kong-tense-after-mong, last accessed 6 March 2016.

27. *South China Morning Post* (2016). 'Pro-democracy Candidate Alvin Yeung Wins Hotly Contested Hong Kong By-election, While Localist Edward Leung Has Credible Showing with 15pc of Vote', 29 February 2016, http://www.scmp.com/news/hong-kong/politics/article/1918450/pro-democracy-candidate-alvin-yeung-wins-hotly-contested, last accessed 5 March 2016.

28. Strom, Stephanie (2012). 'Web Sites Shine Light on Petty Bribery Worldwide', *The New York Times*, 6 March 2012, http://www.nytimes.com/2012/03/07/business/web-sites-shine-light-on-petty-bribery-worldwide.html?_r=0, last accessed 8 March 2016.

29. Campion, Mukti Jain (2011). 'Bribery in India: A Website for Whistleblowers', *BBC News*, 6 June 2011, http://www.bbc.co.uk/news/world-south-asia-13616123, last accessed 4 April 2016.

30. Bharadwaj, K.V. Aditya (2015). 'Karnataka Lokayukta Quits to Avoid Removal', *The Hindu*, 9 December 2015, http://www.thehindu.com/news/national/karnataka/y-bhaskar-rao-resigns-as-lokayukta/article7961608.ece, last accessed 4 April 2016.

31. Diamond, Larry (2014). 'Chasing Away the Democracy Blues', *Foreign Policy*, 24 October 2014, http://foreignpolicy.com/2014/10/24/chasing-away-the-democracy-blues/, last accessed 7 March 2016.

32. Onigbinde, Oluseun (2014). 'The Nigerian Budget: Using Creative Technology to Intersect Civic Engagement and Institutional Reform', *Field Actions Science Reports, The Journal of Field Actions*, Special Issue 11.

33. Young, Andrew and Stefaan Verhulst (2016). 'Mexico's Mejora Tu Escuela: Empowering Citizens to Make Data-Driven Decisions About Education', *GovLab*, January 2016, http://odimpact.org/case-mexicos-mejora-tu-escuela.html, last accessed 4 April 2016.

34. Guy, Gillian (2016). 'When Feedback is Easier, Services are Better',

*Public Finance*, 14 March 2016, http://www.publicfinance.co.uk/opin-ion/2016/03/when-feedback-easier-services-are-better, last accessed 4 April 2016.

35. House, Karen E. (2012). *On Saudi Arabia: Its People, Past, Religion, Fault Lines, and Future*, New York: Alfred A. Knopf.
36. Beber, Bernd and Alexandra Scacco (2012). 'What the Numbers Say: A Digit-Based Test for Election Fraud', *Political Analysis*, 20(2), 211–34.
37. See Keeter, Scott (2006). 'The Impact of Cell Phone Noncoverage Bias on Polling in the 2004 Presidential Election', *Public Opinion Quarterly*, 70(1), 88–98.
38. Named after the African-American politician and former Los Angeles mayor Tom Bradley, who was widely tipped in polls to win the California governor's race easily, but then lost because voters had overstated their intention to back him, to avoid being seen as racist.
39. Stout, Christopher and Reuben Kline (2008). 'Ashamed Not to Vote for an African-American; Ashamed to Vote for a Woman: An Analysis of the Bradley Effect from 1982–2006', Center for the Study of Democracy, Working Paper Series.

## 12. CITY ON A SWAMP

1. Reagan, Ronald (1989). 'Farewell Address to the Nation', *The American Presidency Project*, 11 January 1989, http://www.presidency.ucsb.edu/ws/?pid=29650, last accessed 17 March 2016.
2. Ibid.
3. Rohrschneider, Robert (2002). 'The Democracy Deficit and Mass Support for an EU-wide Government', *American Journal of Political Science*, 46(2), 463–75.
4. Mulvey, Stephen (2003). 'The EU's Democratic Challenge', *BBC News*, 21 November 2003, http://news.bbc.co.uk/2/hi/europe/3224666.stm, last accessed 4 April 2016.
5. *The New York Times*, 'The Worst Voter Turnout in 72 Years', 11 November 2014, http://www.nytimes.com/2014/11/12/opinion/the-worst-voter-turnout-in-72-years.html, last accessed 4 April 2016.
6. *Ballotpedia* (n.d.). 'Margin of Victory Analysis for the 2014 Congress-ional Elections', https://ballotpedia.org/Margin_of_victory_analysis_for_the_2014_congressional_elections, last accessed 18 March 2016.
7. Pearson, Rick (2011). 'Federal Court Upholds Illinois Congressional Map', *Chicago Tribune*, 16 December 2011, http://articles.chicagotri-bune.com/2011–12–16/news/ct-met-congress-map-court-20111216_1_congressional-map-earmuff-shaped-new-map, last accessed 1 April 2016.

8. Stacking involves diluting a rival demographic group by stacking the district with more of your supporters; cracking means breaking up a rival demographic group so that they are a minority in several districts rather than a majority in any district; packing involves cutting losses by jamming a rival demographic group into a single district in the hopes that they will not influence any surrounding districts.

9. McGhee, Eric (2014). 'Measuring Partisan Bias in Single-Member District Electoral Systems', *Legislative Studies Quarterly*, 39(1), 55–85.

10. Wang, Sam (2013). 'The Great Gerrymander of 2012', *The New York Times*, 2 February 2013, http://www.nytimes.com/2013/02/03/opinion/sunday/the-great-gerrymander-of-2012.html?pagewanted=all, last accessed 13 January 2016.

11. Dube, Brian and Peter Makaye (2013). 'How ZANU-PF "Won" the 2013 Harmonized Elections in Zimbabwe', *International Journal of Humanities and Social Science Invention*, 2(10), 33–9.

12. *Ballotpedia* (n.d.).

13. Peckham, Matt (2013). 'Congress Now Less Popular than Head Lice, Cockroaches and the Donald', *TIME*, 8 January 2013, http://newsfeed.time.com/2013/01/08/congress-now-less-popular-than-head-lice-cockroaches-and-the-donald/, last accessed 21 January 2016.

14. Blake, Aaron (2013). 'Majority Say Shutdown Did "Serious Damage" to U.S. Image in World', *The Washington Post*, 22 October 2013, https://www.washingtonpost.com/news/post-politics/wp/2013/10/22/majority-say-shutdown-did-serious-damage-to-u-s-image/, last accessed 21 January 2016.

15. Parti, Tarini (2013). 'FEC: $7B Spent on 2012 Campaign', *POLITICO*, 31 January 2013, http://www.politico.com/story/2013/01/7-billion-spent-on-2012-campaign-fec-says-087051, last accessed 1 February 2016.

16. 'The Families Funding the 2016 Presidential Election', *The New York Times*, 10 October 2015, http://www.nytimes.com/interactive/2015/10/11/us/politics/2016-presidential-election-super-pac-donors.html, last accessed 21 March 2016.

17. From 2009 to 2014, the 200 most politically active companies spent a combined $5.8 billion in lobbying efforts.

18. Gilens, Martin and Benjamin Page (2014). 'Testing Theories of American Politics: Elites, Interest Groups, and Average Citizens', *Perspectives on Politics*, 12(3), 564–81.

19. Saad, Lydia (2012). 'Americans Want Stricter Gun Laws, Still Oppose Bans', *Gallup*, 27 December 2012, http://www.gallup.com/poll/159569/americans-stricter-gun-laws-oppose-bans.aspx, last accessed 27 March 2016.

20. Radil, Amy (2000). 'Dayton's Gun Control Position Questioned', *Minnesota Public Radio*, 3 November 2000, http://news.minnesota.publicradio.org/features/200011/03_radila_daytonguns/, last accessed 4 April 2016.

21. See Marois, Michael (2013). 'California's Redistricting Shake-Up Shakes Out Politicians', 23 March 2013, http://www.bloomberg.com/news/articles/2013-03-21/californias-redistricting-shake-up-shakes-out-politicians, last accessed 27 March 2016.

22. Chasmar, Jessica (2016). 'Donald Trump: I Consult Myself on Foreign Policy, "Because I have a Very Good Brain"', *The Washington Times*, 17 March 2016, http://www.washingtontimes.com/news/2016/mar/17/donald-trump-i-consult-myself-on-foreign-policy-be/, last accessed 29 July 2016.

23. Carothers, Thomas (2016). 'Look Homeward, Democracy Promoter', 27 January 2016, *Foreign Policy*, http://foreignpolicy.com/2016/01/27/look-homeward-democracy-promoter/, last accessed 18 March 2016.

24. Ibid.

25. See The Electoral Integrity Project, http://www.electoralintegrityproject.com, last accessed 29 July 2016.

26. Van de Walle, Nicolas (2002). 'Africa's Range of Regimes', *Journal of Democracy*, 13(2), 66–80.

27. At the time of my visit in 2012, Hillary Clinton was secretary of state and it was not yet known whether she would stand for the presidency again.

## 13. THE BEAR AND THE DRAGON

1. World Bank (n.d.). 'GDP at Market Prices (Current US$)', World Development Indicators, http://data.worldbank.org/indicator/NY.GDP.MKTP.CD?order=wbapi_data_value_2014+wbapi_data_value+wbapi_data_value-last&sort=desc, last accessed 4 April 2016.

2. Kramer, Andrew (2012). 'Peeking Through Years, and the Wall, at Oswald', *The New York Times*, 2 November 2012, http://www.nytimes.com/2012/11/03/world/europe/intimate-glimpses-of-lee-harvey-oswalds-time-in-minsk.html, last accessed 27 March 2016.

3. See: Bennett, Brian (2012). *The Last Dictatorship in Europe: Belarus Under Lukashenko*, London: Hurst & Co.

4. Ibid.

5. Beichelt, Timm (2004). 'Autocracy and Democracy in Belarus, Russia and Ukraine, *Democratization*, 11(5), 113–32.

6. See ibid. and Bennett (2012).

7.  Anishchanka, Mikalai (2015). 'Is Belarus and Russia's "Brotherly Love" Coming to an End?', *The Guardian*, 29 May 2015, http://www.theguardian.com/world/2015/may/28/belarus-russia-brotherly-love-ukraine-crisis, last accessed 24 February 2016.

8.  Ambrosio, Thomas (2006). 'The Political Success of Russia-Belarus Relations: Insulating Minsk from a Color Revolution,' *Demokratizatsiya*, 14(3), 407.

9.  Verbegt, Matthew (2016). 'EU Lifts Most Sanctions on Belarus', *Wall Street Journal*, 15 February 2016, http://www.wsj.com/articles/eu-lifts-most-sanctions-on-belarus-1455552756, last accessed 18 February 2016.

10. Of course, Western governments are more likely to impose sanctions on a country seen as a lost cause firmly in the orbit of a geopolitical enemy than on countries that could plausibly cozy back up to the West. Generally speaking, sanctions are most easily applied to countries that are geopolitically irrelevant or that directly antagonize the geopolitical goals of Western governments.

11. Way, Lucan (2016). 'Weaknesses of Autocracy Promotion', *Journal of Democracy*, 27(1), 64–75.

12. See McCargo, Duncan (2015). 'Thailand in 2014: The Trouble with Magic Swords', *Southeast Asian Affairs*, 2015(1), 335–58 and Chachavalpongpun, Pavin (2014). *Good Coup Gone Bad: Thailand's Political Development Since Thaksin's Downfall*, Singapore: Institute of Southeast Asian Studies.

13. The 2008 change of power is sometimes called a 'judicial coup'. See Chen, Pei-Hsiu (2014). 'The Vulnerability of Thai Democracy: Coups d'état and Political Changes in Modern Thailand'. In Liamputtong, Pranee, ed. (2014). *Contemporary Socio-Cultural and Political Perspectives in Thailand*, 185–207. Amsterdam: Springer.

14. See Pongsudhirak, Thitinan (2016). 'An Unaligned Alliance: Thailand/US Relations in the Early 21st Century', *Asian Politics & Policy*, 8(1), 63–74.

15. Rappa, A. L. (2015). 'Autochthonous Politics and Capitalist Development in Thailand.' *Journal of Political Sciences and Public Affairs*, 3(176), 232–61.

16. Bunbongkarn, Suchit (2015). 'What Went Wrong with the Thai Democracy?', *Southeast Asian Affairs*, 2015(1), 359–68.

17. See McCargo, Duncan (2015). 'Peopling Thailand's 2015 Draft Constitution,' *Contemporary Southeast Asia*, 37(3), 329–54.

18. *BBC News* (2010). 'Verdict on Thaksin Billions Unlikely to Heal Divide', 26 February 2010, http://news.bbc.co.uk/2/hi/asia-pacific/8539305.stm, last accessed 4 April 2016.

19. Pongsudhirak (2016).
20. Joehnk, Tom Felix and Ilya Garger (2016). 'How America Can Put Thailand Back on Track,' *The New York Times*, 22 March 2016, http://www.nytimes.com/2016/03/23/opinion/how-america-can-put-thailand-back-on-track.html, last accessed 24 March 2016.
21. Chambers, Paul (2004). 'US-Thai Relations After 9/11: a New Era in Cooperation?' *Contemporary Southeast Asia: A Journal of International and Strategic Affairs*, 26(3), 460–79.
22. McCargo, Duncan (2006). 'Thaksin and the Resurgence of Violence in the Thai South: Network Monarchy Strikes Back?' *Critical Asian Studies*, 38(1), 39–71.
23. Hodal, Kate (2014). 'Thailand Denies it Ran Secret Prison for CIA or Allowed Torture on its Territory', *The Guardian*, 12 December 2014, http://www.theguardian.com/us-news/2014/dec/12/thailand-denies-secret-prison-torture-senate-cia, last accessed 19 March 2016.
24. *BBC News* (2003). 'Foreign Troops in Iraq', 29 November 2003, http://news.bbc.co.uk/2/hi/middle_east/3267451.stm, last accessed 2 April 2016.
25. Henderson, Barney (2010). 'Thai Court Seizes £1bn of Thaksin Shinawatra's Assets', *The Telegraph*, 26 February 2010, http://www.telegraph.co.uk/news/worldnews/asia/thailand/7326177/Thai-court-seizes-1bn-of-Thaksin-Shinawatras-assets.html, last accessed 24 March 2016.
26. Human Rights Watch (2011). 'Descent into Chaos: Thailand's 2010 Red Shirt Protests and the Government Crackdown', 3 May 2011, https://www.hrw.org/report/2011/05/03/descent-chaos/thailands-2010-red-shirt-protests-and-government-crackdown, last accessed 29 March 2016.
27. US Department of State (2010). 'Statement: Situation in Thailand', Daily Press Briefing, 19 May 2010, http://bangkok.usembassy.gov/051910statement_thailand.html, last accessed 2 April 2016.
28. Crispin, Shawn (2016). 'China-Thailand Rail Project Gets Untracked', *The Diplomat*, 1 April 2016, http://thediplomat.com/2016/04/china-thailand-railway-project-gets-untracked/, last accessed 2 April 2016.
29. Tull, Dennis (2006). 'China's Engagement in Africa: Scope, Significance and Consequences', *The Journal of Modern African Studies*, 44(3), 459–79.
30. World Bank (n.d.). 'GDP Growth (Annual %)', World Development Indicators, http://data.worldbank.org/indicator/NY.GDP.MKTP.KD.ZG?page=1, last accessed 2 April 2016.
31. Kurlantzick, Joshua (2013). 'Why the "China Model" Isn't Going Away', *The Atlantic*, 21 March 2013, http://www.theatlantic.com/

china/archive/2013/03/why-the-china-model-isnt-going-away/274 237/, last accessed 19 March 2016.

32. Zavadski, Katie (2015). 'Putin's Propaganda TV Lies About Its Popularity', *The Daily Beast*, 17 September 2015, http://www.thedailybeast. com/articles/2015/09/17/putin-s-propaganda-tv-lies-about-ratings. html, last accessed 26 March 2016.

33. Ibid.

34. *RT America* (2014). 'Accused: The US Manufactured Ebola', broadcast on 25 September 2014, video available from: https://www.youtube. com/watch?v=9VCu04-FM8s, last accessed 29 July 2016.

35. The Blueberry Hill video had just under six million views in April 2016; see https://www.youtube.com/watch?v=IV4IjHz2yIo, last accessed 29 July 2016.

36. Porter, Tom (2016). 'Russia: Putin's State TV Incited Racial Hatred After 'Fake' Report of Girl's Rape by Refugees,' *International Business Times*, 20 January 2016, http://www.ibtimes.co.uk/russia-putins-state-tv-incited-racial-hatred-after-fake-report-girls-rape-by-refugees-15390 27, last accessed 17 March 2016.

37. Gitter, David (2016). 'The 2016 Chinese New Year Gala: a Propaganda Disaster', *The Diplomat*, 9 February 2016, http://thediplomat.com/ 2016/02/the-2016-chinese-new-year-gala-a-propaganda-disaster/, last accessed 18 March 2016.

38. Walker, Christopher (2016). 'The Hijacking of Soft Power', *Journal of Democracy* 27(1), 49–63.

39. Confucius Institute Headquarters (Hanban) (n.d.). 'Confucius Institutes Around the World', http://english.hanban.org/, last accessed 27 March 2016.

40. Brady, Anne-Marie (2015). 'China's Foreign Propaganda Machine', *Journal of Democracy*, 26(4), 51–9.

41. Ibid., 52.

42. See Dobson, William (2012). *The Dictator's Learning Curve: Inside the Global Battle for Democracy*, New York: Random House.

43. Pomerantsev, Peter and Michael Weiss (2014). 'The Menace of Unreality: How the Kremlin Weaponizes Information, Culture, and Money', *The Interpreter*, http://www.interpretermag.com/wp-content/ uploads/2014/11/The_Menace_of_Unreality_Final.pdf, last accessed 20 March 2016.

44. For those who claim politics is boring, this is the second mention of zombies in the book, something I would have found unlikely when I started writing about democracy.

45. Cooley, Alexander (2015). 'Countering Democratic Norms', *Journal of Democracy*, 26(3), 49–63.

CONCLUSION: THE RESURGENCE OF DEMOCRACY

1. Zakaria, Fareed (2007). *The Future of Freedom: Illiberal Democracy at Home and Abroad* (Revised Edition), New York: WW Norton & company.
2. See Przeworski, Adam and Fernando Limongi (1997). 'Modernization: Theories and Facts', *World Politics*, 49(2), 155–83.
3. Kagan, Robert (2003). 'The Ungreat Washed', *New Republic*, 7 July 2003, https://newrepublic.com/article/90784/fareed-zakaria-democracy, last accessed 25 March 2016.
4. Center for Systemic Peace (n.d.). 'The Polity Project: About Polity', http://www.systemicpeace.org/polityproject.html, last accessed 29 July 2016.

# INDEX

# INDEX

# INDEX